UNCOMMON WOMEN

UNCOMMON WOMEN

Gender and Representation in
Nineteenth-Century U.S. Women's Writing

LAURA LAFFRADO

 THE OHIO STATE UNIVERSITY PRESS • COLUMBUS

Copyright © 2009 by The Ohio State University.
All rights reserved.

Library of Congress Cataloging-in-Publication Data
Laffrado, Laura.
Uncommon women : gender and representation in nineteenth-century U.S. women's writing / Laura Laffrado.
   p. cm.
Includes bibliographical references and index.
ISBN 978-0-8142-0618-8 (cloth : alk. paper)—ISBN 978-0-8142-9186-3 (CD-ROM) 1. American literature—Women authors—History and criticism. 2. American literature—19th century—History and criticism. 3. Women in literature. 4. Women, White, in literature. 5. Sex role in literature. 6. Women and literature—United States—History—19th century 7. Feminism and literature—United States—History—19th century I. Title.
PS152.L34 2009
810.9'9287—dc22
              2008045776

This book is available in the following editions:
Cloth (ISBN 978-0-8142-0618-8)
CD-ROM (ISBN 978-0-8142-9186-3)

Cover design by James Baumann
Text design by Juliet Williams
Type set in ITC Veljovic

∞ The paper used in this publication meets the minimum requirements of the American National Standard for Information Sciences—Permanence of Paper for Printed Library Materials. ANSI Z39.48-1992.
9 8 7 6 5 4 3 2 1

CONTENTS

Acknowledgments   vii

INTRODUCTION	"Without Any Resort to Amazonian Conventions": Women, Writing, Representation	1
CHAPTER 1	"A More Masculine Courage": Women's Voice and the Nineteenth-Century Publication of Sarah Kemble Knight's *Journal*	23
CHAPTER 2	"Everything by Turns and Nothing Long": Configurations of Female Selfhood in Fanny Fern's Early Periodical Writing	54
CHAPTER 3	"How Could You Leave Me Alone When the Room Was Full of Men!": Gender and Self-Representation in Louisa May Alcott's *Hospital Sketches*	79
CHAPTER 4	"I Am Other than My Appearance Indicates": Sex-Gender Representation in Women's Nineteenth-Century Civil War Reminiscences	106
CONCLUSION	"I Found It Hard to Preserve My Self-Control": Race, Women, Representation	134

Notes   157
Works Cited   171
Index   181

ACKNOWLEDGMENTS

I AM HAPPY to acknowledge the people and institutions whose help has been so valuable during the writing of this book.

Western Washington University awarded me generous and timely funding in the form of research grants and professional leave. Both Dean Ronald Kleinknecht and Dean Peter Elich provided important support of my work. I am also grateful for the helpful assistance I received from English Department chairs Kathleen Lundeen and Marc Geisler.

Frank Haulgren and his staff at Western Washington University's Wilson Library tirelessly and patiently located long lists of obscure sources for me, particularly during my research on women's Civil War narratives.

I spent many enjoyable days reading the Fanny Fern papers as well as nineteenth-century U.S. literary papers in the Sophia Smith Collection at Smith College.

It has been such a pleasure to work with both Sandy Crooms and Maggie Diehl at The Ohio State University Press. The anonymous readers arranged for by the press provided meticulous commentary at different stages of this project. This book is much better for their insightful and generous readings.

Papers and drafts of articles that have become part of this book have benefited from valuable readings by Jana Argersinger, Beverly Lyon Clark, Sherry Lee Linkon, Jane Schultz, and Kathryn Zabelle Stodola.

Colleagues and staff in the English Department at Western Washington University assisted me in countless ways, especially Linda C. Flanagan, Aline Franklin, Tina Nelson, and Pam Race. I owe special thanks to Allison Giffen, who generously put aside her own work to read my chapter on Sarah Kemble Knight. I am indebted to Bill Lyne and John Purdy for their support as well as for the scholarly model they provide in their own work. Bill Smith supplied steady friendship as well as a companionable presence as we kept workaholic hours in our offices.

Graduate and undergraduate students in my American literature courses brought enthusiasm and ready engagement to these readings. In particular, Gabe Galanda, Brooke Hoffard, Lynda Jensen, Ann Keefer, David Robinson, Hannah Root, Lindsey St. Hilaire, Shurla Thibou, and Jessica Van Horn raised the intellectual temperature of our classrooms.

My dear friend Sara Balogh has long been an example of intelligence and joie de vivre to me. Debbi Hansen's friendship has given me such pleasure during the years I have worked on this book. Doug Iannelli has repeatedly been a friend in my times of need. Erik Papritz's kindness and encouragement meant a great deal to me during the last stages of this project. And Sharlane Shaffer provided a model of feminist courage and grace that continues to inspire me.

I am most deeply indebted to my family. My sister has unstintingly given me encouragement and assistance well above and beyond the call of duty. I am humbly and eternally grateful to her. My brothers have been loyal and loving supporters of my choices. Their children, Jenny, Julie, Anthony, and Andrew, grew along with this book. It gives me great pleasure to witness their ever-increasing literacies. My parents have always taken pride in my scholarly work. Though my father did not live to see this book completed, up until his death he made weekly inquiries regarding its progress. My mother, among her innumerable selfless acts, allowed me to instruct her in nineteenth-century U.S. women's writing. This book is dedicated to her and to the memory of my father.

Several passages in chapter 2 appeared in an essay in *In Her Own Voice: Nineteenth-Century American Women Essayists*, ed. Sherry Lee Linkon (New York: Garland, 1997). An earlier version of chapter 3 appeared in *ESQ* 48, nos. 1 and 2 (2002), copyright 2003 by the Board of Regents of Washington State University. An earlier version of chapter 4 appeared in *Over Here: A European Journal of American Culture* 17, no. 2 (1997).

INTRODUCTION

"Without Any Resort to Amazonian Conventions"

Women, Writing, Representation

IN A BRIEF periodical piece, "Independence," published in the *New York Ledger* on July 30, 1859, Sara Willis Parton, writing as Fanny Fern, viewed the nation's July Fourth celebration through a gendered lens. Using rhetorical questions, Fern sketched restrictions governing public behavior of nineteenth-century U.S. middle-class women:

> Can I go out of an evening without a hat at my side? Can I go out with one on my head without danger of a station-house? Can I clap my hands at some public speaker when I am nearly bursting with delight? Can I signify the contrary when my hair stands on end with vexation? Can I stand up in the cars "like a gentleman" without being immediately invited "to sit down"? Can I get into an omnibus without having my sixpence taken from my hand and given to the driver? Can I cross Broadway without having a policeman tackled to my helpless elbow? Can I go see anything *pleasant,* like an execution or a dissection? (Warren, *Ruth Hall* 314–15)

Ending her list of questions with whether she could be nominated for governor, senator, or president, Fern concluded, "Bah—you know I can't. 'Free!' Humph!" Fern's "Independence" simultaneously protests and consents to the entrenched nature of public behavioral restrictions for white middle-class women. The periodical piece's apparent subject—that Independence Day in the United States disregards the absence of female independence—enables Fern to disparage gendered cultural restrictions, implicitly invoking images of herself booing public lecturers, avidly observing dissections, and freely walking out alone at night. However, by offering no possibilities of Fern's actually performing these imagined disruptive acts, the piece suggests Fern's dependable compliance with current social arrangements. By 1859, the year this piece was written, Willis had scandalously and repeatedly transgressed normative middle-class gender assumptions through divorce and a sensationalistic career, and she had elicited public excoriation for unwomanly behavior as the author of the novel *Ruth Hall*.[1] Despite or perhaps because of those events, in "Independence" Fern constructs herself as a woman who at times may internally resist public constraints but who will always behave appropriately. The provocative American women under examination in *Uncommon Women: Gender and Representation in Nineteenth-Century U.S. Women's Writing* enact central features of Fern's text. All violate a presumptive normativity in their lives, writings, and self-representations while correspondingly and contradictorily aligning themselves with prevailing gendered assumptions.

Uncommon Women considers challenging female representations in diverse, highly readable, U.S. women's texts first published in the nineteenth century. Throughout this study, I consider women's autobiographical concealments in forms ranging from cross-dressing to pseudonymity to posturing. My discussion centers on texts of six white women—Sarah Kemble Knight, Sara Willis Parton ("Fanny Fern"), Louisa May Alcott, and S. Emma E. Edmonds, with lesser though still significant critical attention to Mary Livermore and Annie Turner Wittenmyer—and one Black woman, Harriet Jacobs.

I first examine the nineteenth-century publication of the eighteenth-century travel journal written by white middle-class Sarah Kemble Knight. Knight, a part-time scrivener and estate settler, chronicled her unconventional journey from Boston to New Haven and New York in the period 1704–5 to help settle a relative's estate. I next investigate the popular and controversial early periodical writing of Fanny Fern (the adopted persona of Sara Willis Parton). Willis, a white middle-class woman, began writing for literary papers in financial desperation after the sudden death of her husband and subsequent economic abandonment by her relatives. I then turn to Louisa May Alcott's *Hospital Sketches* (1863), a text partially derived from the journal that thirty-year-old Alcott kept during the six weeks she nursed wounded male soldiers in a Washington, DC, Civil War hospital. Next I consider *Nurse and Spy in the Union Army* (1865), a sometimes fictive account of war service by S. Emma E. Edmonds, a white woman who successfully cross-dressed as a Union soldier. Edmonds's narrative is read against two later Civil War reminiscences by former women's war effort organizers—Mary Livermore's *My Story of the War* (1889) and Annie Turner Wittenmyer's *Under the Guns: A Woman's Reminiscences of the Civil War* (1895). My concluding chapter views these texts through the lens of *Incidents in the Life of a Slave Girl* (1861), African American Harriet Jacobs's account of her life in and after slavery.

All these texts complicate notions of self-writing and female agency. I consider generic forms, language, illustrations, and other textual apparatuses of these often daring life-writing texts and situate them in specific U.S. cultural/historical moments. For example, in their navigation of and commentary on female representations, the writers under discussion at times employ topics of androgyny, asexuality, and lesbianism. These issues appear in various forms in the texts, sometimes muted, sometimes plainly apparent. In all cases, individually and collectively, these uses form a commentary on the rigidity and inadequacy of heterosexual female constructions. I follow Sidonie Smith and Julia Watson's understanding of "the autobiographical" as "autobiographical acts of narration, situated in historical time and cultural places, deploy[ing] discourses of identity to organize acts of remembering that are directed to multiple addresses or readers" (*Interfaces* 11). These autobiographical texts indicate heightened attention to cultural pressures for women to organize their lives in accordance with dominant cultural scripts such as apolitical passivity, domesticity, heterosexuality, marriage, and motherhood. I make critically visible the ways in which these texts dispute restrictive constructions of the female, test boundaries of race and class, and anticipate conventional reaction to their disruptive discourses. At the same time, I maintain my awareness of these texts as autobiographical, historical, and literary documents reflective of American beliefs, practices, and values.

This study makes no claim to an overview of women's autobiographical writing in the nineteenth-century United States. Rather, I have carefully selected the white middle-class women writers and texts in this project in order to focus on women whose race and class markers located them conventionally in the normative ordering system. These women were, in effect, members of the same cultural subset, trained to adhere to conformist gendered models. This study discusses their texts separately and in relation to each other. At various moments in their texts, these women clearly signal their awareness of conventional behaviors expected of them by the larger culture. In their rhetoric and appearance, these are women who would be identified as less disruptive. With class and race identities generally correspondent with prevailing assumptions, significant difficulties of female autobiographical writing emerge that are linked directly to white/male defined discourses of gender. These women who could be (under)read as compliant struggled to attempt narratives of female selfhood and autonomy. Their struggles mark the even more extensive obstacles to autobiographical writing confronted by women whose race, class, or sexuality marked them as more transgressive. The concluding fifth chapter of this study discusses one such female author and text—African American Harriet Jacobs and her autobiographical *Incidents in the Life of a Slave Girl*. I move from white women's autobiographical writing to Jacobs's foundational text in order to ensure that generalizations in previous chapters work across ethnic/racial lines. This conclusion also significantly extends the discussion in the rest of the book.

Taken together, these texts trace a trajectory of general improvement in representations by/of women from the Federalist period to the post–Civil War era. However, as my discussion will reveal, it would be an oversimplification to claim that this progress was necessarily linear. In order to illustrate various obstacles in this movement, I have selected a diversity of texts for consideration, and I also perform fresh readings or significant rereadings of these texts. For instance, I discuss once-well-known but now nearly forgotten women and texts, such as S. Emma E. Edmonds and her popular Civil War narrative concerning her life as a cross-dressing spy in the Union Army. Other women and their texts are considered in particular ways for the first time, such as Sarah Kemble Knight, whose eighteenth-century travel journal I read through the lens of the text's rarely examined nineteenth-century publication. While all chapters examine intersections of women and culture, two chapters specifically consider female gender construction and the Civil War. The variety of texts under discussion as well as the combination of my approaches to them underscores the mixed nature of women's developing cultural enfranchisement in the United States in the nineteenth century.

Though this book takes as its focus texts by women, my discussion includes men who edited, published, rejected, or reviewed these texts, such as Robert Bonner, Theodore Dwight, William Dean Howells, and Nathaniel Parker Willis. Additionally, my concentration on autobiographical prose incorporates a multiplicity of genres, such as the hospital sketch, journal, periodical writing, slave narrative, travel narrative, and war memoir. I also examine related correspondence, editions, illustrations, introductions, and reviews. The cultural period under discussion includes the rise of interest in women's education and literacy, the beginning of the collapse of the slavocracy, the Civil War, and the post–Civil War era, among other historical/cultural moments.

While my discussion is very much informed by feminist criticism, my methodology supplements and extends feminist criticism's responses to these texts. The vital passion to uncover American women's writing of earlier periods has resulted in the welcome retrieval of a number of texts. However, many of these works, although recovered, have remained on the margins of literary considerations. I fill such gaps with an insistence on the primary nature of the texts in this study. I argue that these texts are compelling in their own right and are valuable for what they reveal and for the way they augment our knowledge of women and representation in the nineteenth-century United States. My collective discussions of autobiographical women's writing in this study, as well as my use of neglected texts and contexts, generate valuable attention for these works. These very readable American women's texts will engage the general reader as well as scholars and teachers.

The larger part of *Uncommon Women* considers conflicted attempts of white middle-class women to narrate female selfhood. These texts present women whom the culture initially classifies as known and safe as they behave against conventional expectations and narrate their deviations from normative assumptions, while simultaneously proclaiming their propriety. On the road on at night with a male guide, Sarah Kemble Knight nonetheless critically scrutinizes and condemns the behavior of other women as "rude [and] unmannerly" (Knight 91). Financially independent and professionally successful, Fanny Fern catalogs her conformity: "I like a man's arm to lean on. I like a man's counsel and advice. . . . I love babies too, and flowers, and all pretty and sweet things" ("One Sort of Woman" 1870). Traveling alone by steamboat and train on her way to nurse soldiers in a Civil War hospital, Louisa May Alcott describes herself as a "bashful individual," "quite ready to be a 'timid trembler,' if necessary" (Showalter 6, 9). Having lived, traveled, spied, and fought in battle disguised as a man, S. Emma E. Edmonds still names herself a "poor, cowardly, nervous, whining woman" (Edmonds 359). The contradictory female self-representations in these works illuminate vexed contours of nineteenth-century U.S. women's autobiographical texts. Such contours signal the compulsory nature of prevailing cultural assumptions, suggesting what Rachel Adams in another context has termed the "tyranny of the normal" (553).[2]

THE TYRANNY OF THE NORMAL

Since its initial publication in 1966, Barbara Welter's groundbreaking work on nineteenth-century U.S. white women's culture and the ideology of "true womanhood" has been rightly complicated and nuanced by scholars.[3] As Mary Kelley has written in a recent retrospective, "In revisiting Barbara Welter's influential paradigm thirty years after its publication, we learn that True Womanhood's impact, which was presumed to have been uniform and transparent, was instead as diverse and complicated as the lives of those for whom the ideology had been designed." Indeed, as Kelley argues, "instead of limiting impulses of self-determination, white women revised its tenets to serve expansive purposes" (Commentary 70). My project extends such scholarly revisions of the True Womanhood paradigm in order to further uncover and situate ways in which women diverged from conventional gender scripts and also wrote of their divergences, implicitly offering subversive alternative female models.

Nineteenth-century U.S. middle-class female scripts of behavior were more various than public representations would lead us to believe. To realize this, we need only think of white middle-class women whose biographical outlines survive. For example, Annie Fields, widow of James T. Fields, owner of the publishing house Ticknor and Fields, led an influential group of women writers and found happiness with partner Sarah Orne Jewett.[4] Delia Bacon, public lecturer on historical subjects, moved to England to attempt to prove her controversial conviction that William Shakespeare did not write works attributed to him.[5] Maria Mitchell, first female astronomer in the United States and discoverer of the comet of 1847, was awarded the first advanced degree given to a woman, was the first woman appointed to the Academy of Arts and Sciences, and was elected president of the American Association for the Advancement of Women. In violation of public female constructions, these women and many others were childless, intellectual, professional, radical, and unmarried.

However, in constructions relayed by the means of nineteenth-century U.S. representation—advertisements, illustrations, magazines, newspapers, novels, poetry, sermons, songs, stories—gender scripts were starkly limited and typically unyieldingly rigid.[6] For example, the article "British Philanthropy and American Slavery" in the March 1853 issue of *DeBow's Review,* the South's most widely circulated journal, praised an anonymous female contributor ("The author, though known to fame, prefers the discharge of domestic duties to the noisy applause of the world" ["British Philanthropy" 258]) whose work "asserted and maintained the dignity, the elevation, the beauty of female character in its relation to that of the male, in the present constitution of society, and without any resort to Amazonian conventions" [258]). The short story "The Nest at Home," written by Mrs. Joseph C. Neal and published in the February 1850 issue of *Godey's Lady's Book,* a popular Northern journal, featured an illustration of a seated white woman, her hair in curls, her cap and dress trimmed with lace, and her arms (and, by implication, her worthy life) full of two sleeping infants (88).[7] In his book *Rational Religion and Morals* (1852), Thomas Vaiden praised "woman's conduct" as "her best jewel" (916). Susan Jewett's story "How I Came to Be Spontaneous" (1858) praised a "most dutiful and loving daughter" as

> a generous girl, full of disinterested notions about providing for the declining years of her parents, and the increasing demands of her young brothers and sisters, [who] resolved to consecrate her life to them, and after dismissing her lover, determined not to marry at all. [She] devoted herself most assiduously to the care of the household, and nobody knew how much she suffered, for she tried to be cheerful and to make others so. (271)

In these realms, women were compliant by cultural standards. The nature of their lives varied depending on the role in which they were cast. Sisters, daughters, loving mothers, or devoted wives, they were virtually interchangeable.

When behavior or appearance of women in fictive locations deviated from normative standards, aberrations were intentional. For instance, the manifest example of Zenobia, the childless, intellectual, unmarried woman in Nathaniel Hawthorne's *The Blithedale Romance,* is constructed as vain, proud, and unsuccessfully competitive for male attention with the demure, submissive Priscilla. Zenobia's behavior leads to her suicide and to debasement of her corpse. Why would a woman in the United States wish to resemble her? In a sensationalized illustration of Maria Bickford's real-life prostitution and murder, the circumstances of her death are fictionalized. Though in reality Bickford's throat was slit so severely that she was almost decapitated, the illustration instead depicts her as stabbed with her own bedpost. Bickford's gruesome murder could have been portrayed so as to invoke sympathetic audience horror for the tragic circumstances of her death. Instead, the illustration encourages censure of Bickford's putative violations of female purity by imagining the post of her (sexualized, unclean) bed as the murder weapon.[8] What woman wouldn't recoil at her fate? In his 1853 *Life Scenes,* writer and playwright Francis Durivage mocks the "withered face, bearded lip, and sharp nose of the ancient spinster" who forces a young man to kiss her (235). In Durivage's construction, unmarried women exist on the margins of nature ("withered," "ancient"), gender ("bearded," "sharp"), and desire (the kiss "forced" from a young man). Who would wish to resemble this caricature? In an anonymous 1855 narrative, a woman who is "victim of society's mummeries, of society's frivolities, and of society's skeleton religion" dies damned to hell, leaving her orphaned child behind ("Which: the right, or the left?" 214). What woman wouldn't fear this end? These aberrations are creations of patriarchy. They serve as cautionary tales, as negative reinforcement of women constructed as normative.

In nineteenth-century U.S. culture, the dominant appearance and behavioral scripts promoted for women were narrow, limited, and nearly impossible to avoid. The women who best met these standards were fictions of the patriarchal gaze: fantasy illustrations or living women significantly modified by indoctrination, dependence, and repression. For women, cultural approbation of one's behavior was constructed as crucial. In private life, women who entered the historical record and women who did not were various and varied. In public models created by the machines of representation, little variety existed.

In his collection *The Farm and the Fireside* (1852), Episcopalian minister and editor John Lauris Blake reinforced constraints of women's social and cultural position:

> Knowing what we do of the warm susceptibilities of the female heart, an irreligious woman seems to us almost a paradox—sometimes we have thought her a monster! Knowing also the high mission assigned to her by the Author of her being, we shudder at the very idea of her ever becoming recreant to the faith or the practice of the Christian. (221)

Nineteenth-century U.S. middle-class women were perpetually and precariously close to classification as perversions of the natural order. Any deviation from compulsory restrictive scripts could result in revulsion and denunciation.

Public women who violated behavioral strictures even in small ways received swift, gendered censure. Mary (Todd) Lincoln, widow of Abraham Lincoln, attempted to sell her fashionable clothes to raise money and was publicly labeled "an intensely vulgar woman," "dreadful," "avaricious," and "wanting in all the true instincts and delicacy which belong to worthy women" (Fleischner 310). Boston publisher and editor Joseph T. Buckingham excoriated women's public behavior in his collection *Specimens of Newspaper Literature* (1852): "Ladies in assemblies and public places, of the most exquisite forms, render themselves, by affectation and visible conceit, too odious to be looked at without disgust" (302). "A creature, who spends its whole time in dressing, prating, gaming, and gadding, is . . . nearly on a level with the monkey species" (302). An anonymous article ("from the pen of a distinguished citizen of South Carolina" [584]), "American Institutions," described Harriet Beecher Stowe (infamous in the South as the author of *Uncle Tom's Cabin*) as "that vulgar, ill-bred woman" ("American Institutions" 1853, 586). Reverend J. T. Barr, writing in *The Ladies' Repository* in June 1854, quoted the cautionary verse on the tombstone of Mary Ashford, "a farmer's daughter—beautiful in person, and possessing . . . an accomplished mind":

> As a warning to female virtue
> And a humble monument to female chastity,
> This stone marks the grave of
> MARY ASHFORD,
> Who, in the 20th year of her age, having incautiously
> Repaired to a scene of amusement, without proper protection,
> Was shamefully violated and murdered. (260)

The night after she attended a ball, "the corpse of poor Mary, bearing marks of brutal violence, was discovered in a field" (260). Barr reduces Mary Ashford's rape and murder to "a warning to young females against frequenting places of public amusement" (260). All these women had been perceived as behaving disruptively in the public eye. In response, cultural agents condemned them in commentary employing gendered discourses of class ("intensely vulgar," "ill-bred"), appearance ("odious," "dressing, prating, gaming, and gadding"), and sexual purity ("female virtue," "female chastity").

Far too many egregious examples exist that demonstrate harsh response to women's public deviations from the norm. With such reactions to small violations, surely the women under consideration in this book—whose partial refusals to comply were so much more extensive—should be unpublished and unheard of. Why did these American women and their nineteenth-century texts receive any attention at all? (Or, as one of my students asked thoughtfully and hesitantly, "But . . . shouldn't, like, they have been killed?").

WHY WEREN'T THESE WOMEN SILENCED?

The absence of extensive public condemnation of these women and their texts may be understood in several ways. Because gendered assumptions authorized a very restrictive range of female types, a woman's salient identity markers served to cast her in a reductive, recognizable female model. Thus, the texts and motivations of women under consideration here would have been reduced to stereotypical creations of patriarchy. In this crude view, Sarah Kemble Knight would be regarded as a devoted cousin traveling to aid a relative, her charitable motive serving to diminish the very unusual autonomy of her journey. Fanny Fern would be seen as the desperate widowed mother forced to write for paid publication after she had exhausted socially respectable ways to feed her fatherless children. Louisa May Alcott would be read as the energetic Yankee daughter, a recognizable product of her parents' abolitionist beliefs and New England's well-known antislavery politics and activism. S. Emma E. Edmonds would be reduced to the imprudent patriot, a woman so motivated by love of her country that she dressed as a man in order to defend the Union. Harriet Jacobs would be the mother so selflessly devoted to her children that she preferred hardships of a seven-year Southern concealment near them rather than Northern freedom away from them. As a result of underreadings that classify them in less threatening roles, these women and their works would have been read as less disruptive. Further, irregularities of their lives and texts were novelties and so were more entertaining than alarming in their singularity.

This is not to suggest that these women were ever far from an oppressive silencing as a result of their behaviors and the texts that publicized such behaviors. The most evident sign of their hazardous status is the uncommon nature of their texts: while other women may have traveled on dangerous, solitary journeys, cross-dressed as men, or remained concealed in a garret for seven years, few women at the time recorded such experiences. Additionally, each of these women was confronted with the fear or reality of physical assault and/or strong public censure. Cultural toleration of these women and their work was not fixed; a slight shift in appearance, behaviors, or writing could provoke hostility and violence. The texts under discussion in this study reflect awareness of such penalties and corresponding strategies to circumvent them.

Knight's female autonomy and assertive voice disrupted passive, domestic notions of the female. As she traveled in the woods at night with a hired male guide, Knight risked her chastity, reputation, and personal safety. When she wrote about these experiences and then circulated her text among family and friends, she extended her jeopardy further by publicizing such events. However, though the text's private circulation—with its limited, selected readership—could have authorized Knight to construct herself more disruptively, Knight aligned herself fervently with white middle-class mainstream discourse. Though the text provoked in its independent, woman-centered focus, its larger context was that of the recognizable, white middle-class woman behaving well. In salient, formulaic ways, Knight's journal resembled acceptable female middle-class discourse, consequently locating Knight herself within conventional parameters. As I discuss later in this introduction and then more closely in the first chapter, the 1825 publication of and response to Knight's eighteenth-century *Journal* reveals contours of a larger cultural discourse concerning gender and representation that informs publication of nineteenth-century U.S. women's texts.

Employing the persona "Fanny Fern" enabled Sara Willis Parton to adopt a range of roles in her early periodical writing—children, mothers, observers, and wives, among other personae. In these assumed identities, Fern sought reader understanding, working to persuade readers to view Fern through the lens of their own fears and desires. In other periodical pieces, Fern drew on topics and used tones that activated conjecture regarding her sex-gender identity. For example, Fern's writing about men, combined with her use of an authoritative manner that evoked male agency, prompted readers to assume that the author must also be male. In her early periodical writing, Fern is able to diversely portray individual female selves and to present an ambiguous sex-gender identity. Notwithstanding such stimulating gendered variety in her writing, Fern's general alignment with customary notions of women protected her. My focus on Fern's critically neglected early periodical writing provides a fresh opportunity for consideration of the intersection of anonymity and women's autobiographical writing.

Before her fame as the author of *Little Women* and other books, Louisa May Alcott was a nurse in a Washington, DC, Civil War hospital. She subsequently wrote about the experience in *Hospital Sketches*, a narrative that uncovered autobiographic anxieties of her identity, sexuality, and gender. Some chapters of what later became *Hospital Sketches* were initially serialized in the Boston *Commonwealth*. Because of the *Commonwealth*'s antislavery focus, the text's abolitionism worked to mute Alcott's sex-gender investigations. The success of these serialized sections resulted in arrangements to publish the sketches as a book—that is, to a larger and less self-selected audience. As a result, Alcott pragmatically added two new chapters to the text, which reordered her material and further diminished the text's sex-gender explorations. Indeed, over the years, Alcott continued to modify *Hospital Sketches* for increased conventionality and book sales: she allowed it to be bound with more overtly fictional stories which undercut the autobiographical nature of *Hospital Sketches;* and she censored various sections ("by taking out all Biblical allusions [regarding her criticism of a chaplain] . . . the book may be made 'quite perfect,' I am told. Anything to suit customers" [Myerson et al. 164]). Throughout her successful writing career, Alcott displayed anxious, heightened awareness of public expectations and scrutiny of her writing/self. In successive stages of her early work *Hospital Sketches,* Alcott decreased her rhetorical focus on sex-gender conflicts, resulting in a text—and an author— that could be read as more aligned with normative assumptions.

In S. Emma E. Edmonds's popular *Nurse and Spy in the Union Army* (1865), readers were told that Edmonds had volunteered for the war effort and was hired to disguise herself as a male soldier and spy for the Union Army. In reality, Edmonds had disguised herself as a man, enlisted, and served as a soldier perceived as male until she was wounded. She fled the hospital in the middle of the night rather than be uncovered as female. Soon afterwards she wrote and published her successful narrative. Twenty years after the publication of *Nurse and Spy in the Union Army,* Edmonds publicly revealed her past identity, exposing the narrative deception that her wartime employment had been based on the perception that she was a man and not, as her text had maintained, a woman. Edmonds's declaring the truth of her wartime cross-dressing was prompted by her desire to receive a military pension and to have her desertion charge dismissed. Two decades earlier, sex-gender assumptions had led Edmonds to flee the Army and to excise her passing as a male from her narrative rather than have it exposed. Twenty years later, when she revealed her former male identity, the resulting publicity marked such cross-gender impersonation as unusual, but, by the 1880s, it was titillating and newsworthy rather than sharply disturbing. Edmonds's delaying announcement of her autobiographical truths until such a disclosure was, to some degree, culturally allowable protected her from a public response that in her words would have been "'far worse than death'" (Fladeland 455).

In *Incidents in the Life of a Slave Girl* (1861), Harriet Jacobs related the decision of her autobiographic persona, "Linda Brent," to have sex with Mr. Sands, a white man whose protection would then secure her from the persistent, aggressive sexual demands of another white man. These sections of Jacobs's narrative disquietingly signaled female sexual knowledge and agency ("I knew what I did, and I did it with deliberate calculation" [46]), subjects prohibited by cultural scripts of female chastity and passivity. Furthermore, Jacobs's naming of Black female/white male sexual intercourse disrupted multiple taboos regarding sexual desire, interracial sex, and rape. However, in other salient parts of the text, Jacobs repeatedly foregrounded the nineteenth-century construction of devoted motherhood, aligning herself with white female readers. Additionally, well-known white abolitionist Lydia Maria Child's agreement to serve as editor of and write an introduction to Jacobs's *Incidents* authorized a reading of Jacobs as upright, submissive, and remorseful.

Notwithstanding these suppressions, editings, misreadings, and silencings, Knight, Fern, Alcott, Edmonds, and Jacobs enacted the autobiographic in their texts through a mix of generic and rhetorical strategies such as the use of conventional discourse, alignment with female scripts, textual revisions, and adoption of fictive personae, among other methods. Such strategies enabled them to negotiate entrenched normative restrictions in their writing, eliding extensive censure.

AUTOBIOGRAPHICS

Particular generic spaces adapted by Knight, Fern, Alcott, Edmonds, and Jacobs for purposes of self-representation reveal and contest confining female roles. Knight's generic locations of self-invention include the journal, travel narrative, and humor writing. Fern employs periodical writing to address topical subjects as well as self-construction. Alcott mixes the hospital sketch, journal, and travel narrative. Edmonds moves from the autobiography to the war narrative to the fictive. Jacobs combines the slave narrative and elements of the fallen woman narrative. As with all women engaged in autobiographical practices, Knight, Fern, Alcott, Edmonds, and Jacobs negotiate a complex web of gender and genre constructions in their attempts to locate a momentary coherence of self. Chapters in this book discuss each female writer's choice of a particular genre or genres, as well as what was gained or lost through adopting such forms.

Leigh Gilmore has suggested that at times women write autobiographically in other genres; that is, women may write autobiographically when not writing autobiography. Gilmore names this generic space "autobiographics," using the term to

> describe those elements of self-representation which are not bound by a philosophical definition of the self derived from Augustine or the literary history or concept of the book which defines autobiography as a genre; instead, autobiographics marks a location in a text where self-invention, self-discovery, and self-representation emerge within the technologies of autobiography, namely those legalistic, literary, cultural, and ecclesiastical discourses of truth and identity through which the subject of autobiography is produced. (185)

For Gilmore, engaging autobiographical strategies when working in forms that do not fundamentally require "a stable *I* anchored within a relatively stable genre" (185) provides space for women's autobiographical practices while evading more trenchant obstacles and narrower possibilities for self-representation of female autobiography. I extend Gilmore's arguments by demonstrating U.S. women's continuing multiple generic adaptations and female narratives of identity. These women expanded Gilmore's claims by adapting forms such as essay collection, historical account, hospital sketch, journal, periodical writing, slave narrative, and travel narrative for their autobiographical practices.

This is, of course, not to suggest that these women and their texts share what Sidonie Smith and Julia Watson have termed a comprehensive "relationality" (*Women, Autobiography, Theory* 37)—that is, one common female identity or experience that transcends form. As

Felicity Nussbaum has cautioned, "thinking about . . . the spoken and unspoken commonplaces [women] share must be grounded, I think, in particular and local instances of history if we are to avoid the generalizations that contribute to oppression based on gender" (148). The representational projects I examine are separated by differences of the women's subject positions and experiences. Their self-narratives emerge from varied backgrounds of scrivener, daughter, mother, and wife (Knight); middle-class widow and mother (Fern); abolitionist daughter (Alcott); patriot (Edmonds); and slave, daughter, and mother (Jacobs). Additionally, these women and their texts were not equally well-known. Large segments of the culture remained (un)aware of some of these women and their texts.

These texts are also separated by differences of the women writers' regional affiliations and professions, among other divergences. Their geographic locations are as various as eighteenth-century Boston; nineteenth-century New York and Boston; the Washington, DC, Civil War hospital; Northern and Southern Civil War battlefields; and the slave state of North Carolina. The women writers' sometimes temporary professions (estate settler, literary-paper columnist, war nurse, soldier, nursemaid), however diverse, determine their generic choices (hospital sketch, periodical writing, slave narrative, travel journal, and war narrative, among others).

However, these differences are not absolute. For all these women and their texts, the middle-class white United States and public representations of women served as dominant cultural centers. Notwithstanding their variations, each woman writer's autobiographical practices confronted and navigated the larger ordering system. These unconventional women shared the historically difficult position of women writing in cultures that to significant degrees resisted female autonomy and agency. The act of subject formation necessarily created conflicted female discourses of identity and independence. The resulting texts were complicated by gendered issues of representation and voice. In this way, as Felicity Nussbaum valuably puts it, "cultural constructions of self and gender intermingle with the individual subject's interest and engagement in taking up the particular discourses available at given historical moments" (149).

The texts under discussion all made initial print appearances in the broader nineteenth-century United States. During the latter part of this period, the national discourse concerning the U.S. Civil War contained issues also seen in women's texts studied here—that is, vexed conflicts of identity, representation, and boundaries. The central cultural debates in political disputes regarding the war, and the publication and popularity of women's autobiographic texts all indicate fractures within the evolving normative ordering system. This study is not limited to the period of the U.S. Civil War, nor is the Civil War the organizing principle. However, as a necessary part of my desire to locate this project in the period of the broader nineteenth-century United States, a significant portion of its discussion occurs in the context of the Civil War era.

In the early 1860s, autobiographical texts by Knight, Fern, Alcott, Edmonds, and Jacobs shared the same cultural moment. Knight's *Journal*, which had emerged as a public text in the nineteenth-century United States, was reprinted in 1865; Fern's periodical writings were appearing regularly in the *New York Ledger* in 1865; Alcott's *Hospital Sketches* was published in 1863; Edmonds's *Nurse and Spy* was published in 1865; and Jacobs's *Incidents* was published in 1861. The historical period that Knight had documented in her journal was the focus of new interest. Fern's essays continued to draw a wide readership. Edmonds's account of her war experiences was sold and read by Northerners devoted to the Union cause. Jacobs's narrative attracted a white Northern female reading audience. As the Civil War fragmented and threatened to destroy the nation, these uncommon women's life narrations which challenged restrictive female representations, put pressure on race and class boundaries, and considered conformist responses to their disruptive autobiographical practices, were—tellingly, as I will argue most specifically in chapters 3 and 4—part of the nation's common literary discourse.

In general, anxieties of identity and autonomy seen in these texts—anxieties emerging from a range of cultural locations—tested constraints of social and political arrangements. The women's works under consideration here exposed oppressions that complicated women's life writing as their representations signaled restrictive gender conventions of the dominant culture. In temporarily coherent moments of selfhood, these texts reflected complexities of female positioning. As they attempted to declare the "I" in their various writings, Knight, Fern, Alcott, Edmonds, and Jacobs expanded female possibilities for U.S. women and positioned readers to consider other forms of repressive social insistence.

Uncommon Women begins with Knight's eighteenth-century *Journal* principally because of the work's provocative position as an autobiographical text written by a woman in the early eighteenth century and then published for the first time in the nineteenth century. In chapter 1, "'A More Masculine Courage': Women's Voice and the Nineteenth-Century Publication of Sarah Kemble Knight's *Journal*," I consider why the text—unconventional as it is—would be published and then multiply republished in the nineteenth century. I then examine how publications of Knight's text intersect with publication of other women's writing at the time. The *Journal*, though privately circulated by Knight, remained unpublished until 1825, nearly a full century after her death. The 1825 publication of the *Journal*—its original public issuing—has been almost entirely neglected in the critical record, as have the *Journal*'s subsequent republications later in the nineteenth century. I perform a fresh reading of Knight's text, situating it in the context of its nineteenth-century print appearances. I argue that the publication context of the *Journal* is a sign of a nascent receptivity to women's writing, a receptivity also seen in publication of women's texts that, unlike Knight's *Journal*, were both written and published in the nineteenth century.

Though Knight's text may have influenced other authors whom I discuss here, I have no evidence of that. I make no claim that Fern, Alcott, Edmonds, Livermore, Wittenmyer or Jacobs read Knight's *Journal*. However, the 1825 publication of the journal signals its participation in an emergent national debate concerning gender and representation. That is, the nineteenth-century revival of Knight's *Journal* informs publication of women's texts that, unlike Knight's, were both written and published in the nineteenth century. That this book begins with Knight's *Journal* invites speculation about the testing of this unstable gendered ground. An examination of Knight's text suggests a context for the discourse of this moment and informs the nineteenth-century U.S. women's texts later discussed in this book.

Knight, a woman visibly disrupting gender assumptions by traveling alone, paradoxically represents herself as promoting culturally sanctioned female scripts. Her choice of the journal enables her to record her autonomous travels and, despite the unorthodox nature of her journey, to construct a conventionally gendered self. In spaces between the independence of her journey and that constructed self, discourses of truth and identity emerge. For instance, left behind in the woods by her guide at night, Knight rejects conventional reliance on piety and instead voices and genders her fears: "Now Returned my distressed aprehensions of the place where I was . . . encompased with Terrifying darkness enough to startle a more Masculine courage" (93). Emerging from her frightening hilly climb, she locates gendered images of reassurance:

> But being got to the Top, was there amply recompenced with the friendly Appearance of the Kind Conductress of the night. . . . The Raptures which the Sight of that fair Planett produced in mee, caus'd mee, for the Moment, to forgett my present wearyness and past toils; and Inspir'd me for most of the remaining way with very divirting tho'ts, some of which, with the other Occurances of the day, I reserved to note down when I should come to my Stage. (93)

Ahead of her time in embarking on and recording such a journey, Knight afterward circulated her journal privately. The journal remained in manuscript form until 1825, when Theodore Dwight, Jr., anonymously edited and published it. The publication of Knight's unconventional *Journal* in the nineteenth century compels our notice as it points new attention to representations of and texts by women.

Reading against the first chapter's concern with a somewhat private woman-centered genre and voice, chapter 2, "'Everything by Turns and Nothing Long': Configurations of Female Selfhood in Fanny Fern's Early Periodical Writing," explores popular form and gender flexibility. I examine texts from Fern's periodical writing beginning in 1851, when her work was first published, until 1854. During this time, as she wrote anonymously as Fanny Fern, Sara Willis Parton's identity was a well-kept secret. In 1854, Willis interrupted her periodical writing to compose her first novel, *Ruth Hall;* its publication led to the revealing of her identity. Thus, once she resumed periodical writing, her use of fictive female personae was necessarily transparent. For Willis, writing as Fanny Fern, a columnist whose "true" identity is the subject of heightened public conjecture, gender and public voice intersect in her early periodical writing, encouraging her to adopt multiple self-representations. I am interested in Willis's early periodical pieces—written before her public exposure as "Fanny Fern"—which employ strategies of female representation. My study conducts a significant reading of Fern's critically neglected early periodical writing and considers a mix of these early writings to uncover links between the weekly appearance of an author's work—its anticipated, recognizable form and voice—and her self-redefinitions. The chapter extends examination of autobiography's limited possibilities for self-interpretation. Autobiography's generic confines appear even more restrictive when compared to the periodical piece's extension of the process of self-representation, which emerges rhetorically from Fern's engagement with fictive stories of selfhood.

Chapter 3, "'How Could You Leave Me Alone When the Room Was Full of Men!': Gender and Self-Representation in Louisa May Alcott's *Hospital Sketches*," focuses on ways in which generic choice freed Alcott in *Hospital Sketches* (1863) to write about male/female physical contact without invoking male and female sexuality for herself or her nineteenth-century U.S. readership. The chapter explores how Alcott's use of the hospital sketch and her construction of herself as Civil War nurse Tribulation Periwinkle evades issues of sexuality, allowing her, within the permeable fictive/autobiographical boundaries of her text, to invent an alternative sex-gender identity for a white middle-class woman in the nineteenth-century United States. For example, discussing her loss of hair due to illness, Trib partially scripts female hair loss as wartime sacrifice, not unlike a wound incurred as a result of her service for her country: "I take some satisfaction in the thought that, if I could not lay my head on the altar of my country, I have my hair" (61). Such moments also allow for Alcott's use of subversive humor. Within the divided national space, elements of the professionalization of nursing and the transformation of the sex-gender system met in the temporary wartime hospital. These cultural changes combined with Alcott's nurse/soldier/mother self-definitions to invite reconfiguration of possibilities of her gendered identity. Readers of *Hospital Sketches* were thus able temporarily to imagine thoughts and behaviors beyond customary gender constraints. Alcott's experiential and literary journey outside her white middle-class location led to the Civil War hospital, as well as to nineteenth-century U.S. boundaries of gender, race, and nation.

Chapter 4, "'I Am Other than My Appearance Indicates': Sex-Gender Representation in Women's Nineteenth-Century Civil War Reminiscences," extends the discussion of Alcott's invention of an alternative sex/gender identity, begun in chapter 3, by turning to Civil War reminiscences by S. Emma E. Edmonds, Mary Livermore, and Annie Turner Wittenmyer; these works record the experiences of women who disguised themselves as male soldiers. The chapter begins with a discussion of cross-dressing, gender construction, and authenticity in nineteenth-century U.S. Civil War narratives. I then historicize these works in the context of nineteenth-century sexology's attempts to order, contain, and stabilize ambiguous and contradictory sex-gender constructions. The "Publisher's Notice" which introduces readers to *Nurse and Spy in the Union Army* foregrounds Edmonds's agency: "In the 'Secret Service' as a 'Spy,' which is one of the most hazardous positions in the army—she penetrated the enemy's lines . . . no less than eleven times; always with complete success and without detection" (5). At the same time, the notice responds to the disruption of a woman passing as a man: "Should any of her readers object to some of her disguises, it may be sufficient to remind them it was from the purest motives and most praiseworthy patriotism, that she laid aside, for a time, her own costume, and assumed that of the opposite sex" (6).

Such narratives were written by women on both sides of the Mason-Dixon Line during and after the war. These texts have subsequently provoked gendered questions of realism and historical accuracy. By selecting the Civil War narrative, women writers privilege a nationalistic, subjective accounting of U.S. history. In the larger context of chronicling women's war efforts, Edmonds details wartime self-representations that cross boundaries of gender and race. These cross-gender impersonations, for the most part assumed during her employment as a Union spy, would be read as shockingly wrong were they situated outside the narrative of wartime patriotism. In their recordings of Civil War history, Livermore and Wittenmyer, self-defined conventional women, discover desire and ambivalence in their conflicted responses to encounters with wartime women who had tested gendered confines.

The conclusion, "'I Found It Hard to Preserve My Self-Control': Race, Women, Representation," discusses Harriet Jacobs's *Incidents in the Life of a Slave Girl* (1861). Jacobs's *Incidents* offers compelling documentation that autobiographic writing is even more difficult for women whose race, class, or sexuality marks them as multiply transgressive. This final chapter extends the discussion of previous chapters and examines how generalizations developed in those chapters are maintained across ethnic/racial lines. I conclude with Jacobs's text primarily because of its position as "the most sophisticated, sustained narrative dissection of the conventions of true womanhood by a black author before emancipation" (Carby 47). Jacobs's *Incidents* has certainly garnered more critical response than any of the other texts discussed in this book. In my evaluation of the main Black female autobiographical text of the nineteenth-century United States beside other, lesser-known white women's autobiographical texts, previously less visible privileges of whiteness emerge. Such analysis is valuable to this book as it exposes possibilities of access and authority granted to and unnoticed by nineteenth-century middle-class white women in the United States. Viewed through the lens of Jacobs's text, whiteness is foregrounded as the default race in Knight's, Fern's, Alcott's, Edmonds's,

Livermore's, and Wittenmyer's texts. A consideration of Jacobs's *Incidents* with these texts clearly uncovers unexamined assumptions of those perceived as white, as we recognize Jacobs's awareness that she is at all times identified as Black.

Gendered representations in American women's autobiographical work considered in *Uncommon Women* mark recognition of cultural pressures for women whose actions resulted in increased female visibility to identify themselves as conventional women. They also reflect the women writers' own conflicted struggles to declare a momentary coherence of self within genres that do not fundamentally require "a stable *I* anchored within a relatively stable genre" (Gilmore 185). In these (partially) successful displays of self-presence, these women, through their endeavors, articulated the complexity of female positioning. By engaging in these attempts at self-definition, Knight, Fern, Alcott, Edmonds, and Jacobs extended available female representations for all women. Sidonie Smith and Julia Watson argue that women's "narratives of self-discovery" authorize readers to "claim kinship in a literature of possibility. Most centrally, women reading other women's autobiographical writings have experienced them as 'mirrors' of their own unvoiced aspirations" (Introduction, *Women, Autobiography, Theory* 5). The multiple forms of difference engendered in these texts make their individual and collective participation in female self-representation particularly worthy of study and valuable for other women. The critical recovery of and attention to these women's autobiographical texts adds them to our increasingly nuanced understandings of autobiographical practices of white women writers and their negotiations of nineteenth-century U.S. middle-class culture. Overall, in *Uncommon Women*, women's autobiographical texts are presented as central and vital participants in evolving representations of women in the nineteenth-century United States.

CHAPTER 1

"A More Masculine Courage"

Women's Voice and the Nineteenth-Century Publication of Sarah Kemble Knight's *Journal*

> *The Journal of Madam Knight has been remembered with much interest, since we read the original edition, given to the world by our honored friend . . . Theodore Dwight, of New York. [We] hav[e] been for years desirous of reprinting it, as a unique specimen of the voyages and travels, life and manners of that early time. . . . The whole work, of seventy pages in the original, is contained in this number.*
>
> —The Living Age *(26 June 1858)*

THE 1825 PUBLICATION of Sarah Kemble Knight's early-eighteenth-century travel journal places it on the scene of a developing cultural discourse concerning gender and representation. I begin *Uncommon Women* with Knight's *Journal* in order to overtly put pressure on that ambivalent moment. As this chapter demonstrates, a reading and analysis of Knight's work provides a context for that discourse and inflects the nineteenth-century U.S. women's texts subsequently discussed here.

My locating Knight's text with other texts written by women and published in the nineteenth-century United States emerges from the initial publishing and subsequent republishings of and various print references to Knight's *Journal*.[1] Knight's *Journal* was first published in 1825, nearly a full century after Knight's death. Thus its original public issuing locates it in nineteenth-century U.S. culture. This context for Knight's *Journal* has been almost entirely overlooked in the critical record, as have the text's republications later in the nineteenth century.[2] Regardless of that neglect, Knight's *Journal* shares its public beginnings with nineteenth-century U.S. women's writing.

In this chapter, I perform a fresh reading of Knight's *Journal* by locating it explicitly in the nineteenth-century U.S. context in which

23

it was published and in which it achieved public literary recognition. In order to do so, I conduct the most in-depth consideration to date of Theodore Dwight's 1825 edition of Knight's *Journal,* the first public edition of Knight's text.[3] I closely examine Dwight's introduction to the text, as well as his reasons and motives for recovering and publishing it. I also look at the mixed nineteenth-century print reception of Dwight's edition of Knight's journal, and I break new ground by charting nineteenth-century reissuings as well as print references to the text and to Knight in nineteenth-century U.S. books and periodicals.[4] My critical examinations include a reading of the earliest published reference to Knight in Hannah Mather Crocker's *Observations on the Real Rights of Women, with Their Appropriate Duties, Agreeable to Scripture, Reason, and Common Sense* (1818), as well as a review of Knight's *Journal* by William Dean Howells which I bring to the attention of Knight scholars for the first time. My recovery of nineteenth-century print references to Knight's *Journal* makes evident this eighteenth-century text's place and significance in nineteenth-century U.S. literary discourse.

Some information used in this chapter regarding publication and reception of Knight's *Journal* appeared in critical articles published across the twentieth century. For instance, Alan Margolies's 1964 foundational essay on the publication history of Knight's text provides essential data. The writing of Sargent Bush, Jr. offers crucial scope and detail. And Mary McAleer Balkun supplies important discussion of the 1825 publication of the journal. However, this chapter is the first text to gather all information regarding nineteenth-century U.S. publication and reception of, as well as print references to, Knight's *Journal.* I have taken pains to establish this context in order to provide material for a reading of the nineteenth-century publication of the *Journal* as provocative commentary on an emerging cultural permission that also allowed publication of women's texts that, unlike Knight's, were both written and published in the nineteenth century.

To commence plainly, Sarah Kemble Knight's *Journal* is an autobiographical text written by a thirty-eight-year-old white woman in early-eighteenth-century New England. In it, Knight chronicles her 1704–5 trip to New Haven and New York to help settle a relative's estate. Written in the early eighteenth century, the journal was published for the first time in the nineteenth century. As Bush writes, Knight "participated in two key moments in American cultural history—that in which she wrote and that in which her writing received a wider audience through publication" (Introduction 80). This chapter discusses Knight's *Journal* in six parts: first, Knight's biographical contexts and particulars of the

1825 publication and reception of her text; second, a detailing and discussion of subsequent nineteenth-century reissuings and print references to her journal; third, an examination of generic conventions of the travel narrative and Knight's adaptations of that form; fourth, a consideration of Knight's dis/alignments with early American women; fifth, a reading of the intersection of orality, literacy, and female status in the text; and finally, a concluding section regarding Knight and the (im)possibilities of an eighteenth-century American female community.

I.

Sarah Kemble was born in Boston on April 19, 1666, to Captain Thomas Kemble, a merchant and landowner, and Elizabeth Trerice Kemble. In 1688 or 1689, she married Richard Knight, possibly a shipmaster, who was probably much older than she. Sarah Kemble may have been his second wife. Their only child, Elizabeth, was born in Boston on May 8, 1689. Knight acquired business and legal skills, perhaps from running the family business after her father's death in 1689. She used her expertise to help settle estates, and she kept a shop and a house on Moon Street in Boston. She also ran a school in which she taught handwriting to children (putatively attended by a young Ben Franklin). Even before Richard Knight died (probably in 1706), his wife may have assumed his business responsibilities. From then on, she was known as Widow Knight or Madam Knight, which was, as Bush explains, in keeping with "the early eighteenth-century manner of address for a middle-aged matron" (Introduction 69).[5]

When Knight learned about the estate settlement of a New Haven cousin, Caleb Trowbridge (whose young widow may have been her sister), she departed on an unchaperoned journey from Boston to New York and New Haven on October 2, 1704. She left behind her fifteen-year-old daughter and elderly mother; her husband was on business abroad. She returned from this five-month business trip in March, having kept a detailed travel journal. After her daughter married John Livingston of New London, Connecticut, in 1714, Knight, now widowed, moved to live near her. She continued to work successfully as a shopkeeper and property owner. When she died in 1727, she left a substantial £1800 estate.

Knight's journal remained unpublished in her lifetime. Michaelsen speculates that the *Journal* "was not published in its day because it was too secular a work . . . to come off the Massachusetts presses" (44n21). Bush maintains that it was not intended for publication and instead circulated privately (Introduction 74). He writes that Knight "surely wrote for an audience other than herself," arguing that her

> treatment of self [in the journal] would have appealed to an intimate circle of friends who already knew the bumptious good humor and superior physical stamina as well as mental readiness for the unforeseen which Madam Knight clearly possessed. It seems very likely that her anticipation of such an appreciative audience of listeners or readers prompted her to write her lively narrative. (Introduction 74, 75)

David S. Shields states that Knight "composed [her journal] for and read [it] to her circle in Boston" ("Eighteenth-Century" 460).[6] Susan Clair Imbarrato, noting that "circulation figures for early America are . . . difficult to determine," posits that "a general comparison to the letter suggests that twenty to thirty people, or the size of an extended family, may have either read a traveler's journal or heard about its contents" (27). Though the text was probably read by/to Knight's family and friends, it was not prepared for commercial publication, published or read widely in her lifetime. After Knight's death, it remained in manuscript for almost a full century.

In 1825, Knight's journal was anonymously edited and published by Theodore Dwight, Jr. (1796–1866), teacher and author of biographies, histories, and travel narratives. Dwight's short introduction regarding Knight and her text was published with his edition. His introduction presents Knight's text to the nineteenth-century U.S. reading public and foregrounds his interest in the American past. He assures readers that the journal is historically authentic, "not a work of fiction, as the scarcity of old American manuscripts may induce some to imagine; but it is a faithful copy from a diary in the author's own handwriting, compiled soon after her return home, as it appears, from notes recorded daily, while on the road" (85). He declares that he preserved the text's antiquarian value by not updating Knight's language "for fear of introducing any unwarrantable modernism" (85). Dwight's motives in publishing the journal emerge from his promotion of the value of documenting the American past:

> The object proposed in printing this little work is not only to please those who have particularly studied the progressive history of our country, but to direct the attention of others to subjects of that description,

unfashionable as they still are; and also to remind the public that documents, even as unpretending as the following, may possess a real value, if they contain facts which will be hereafter sought for to illustrate interesting periods in our history. (78, 79)[7]

Dwight's classification of Knight's text as an "unpretending document" makes clear that he claims no intellectual value for it. Indeed, his assumption—perhaps suggested most plainly by his use of a phrase within which to classify Knight's text—is that readers will similarly view the text as an "unpretending document." Instead, what Dwight does argue for is the *Journal*'s historical value. However, even that value is somewhat incidental to the narrative of the text. That is, it is the details which Knight uses when relating her experiences—particulars of travel, landscape, lodging—that are "facts which will be hereafter sought to illustrate interesting periods in our history" (85).

Returning to what he perceives as neglect of the American past, Dwight chastises readers for being "so ready to open our minds to the most minute details of foreign governments, and the modes and men of distant countries, with which we can have only a collateral connection" instead of focusing on "subjects so closely connected with ourselves [that they] ought to excite a degree of curiosity and interest" (85). Dwight encourages readers to appreciate what he sees as advances of the nineteenth-century United States by reading Knight's text: "The reader will find frequent occasion to compare the state of things in the time of our author with that of the present period, particularly with regard to the number of inhabitants, and the facilities and accommodations prepared for the travelers" (86). Dwight also recognizes the hardships of Knight's eighteenth-century journey when contrasted with similar nineteenth-century travel:

> Over that tract of country where she traveled about a fortnight, on horseback, under the direction of a hired guide, with frequent risks of life and limb, and sometimes without food or shelter for many miles, we proceed at our ease, without exposure and almost without fatigue, in a day and a half, through a well peopled land, supplied with good stagecoaches and public houses, or the still greater luxuries of the elegant steam boats which daily traverse our waters. (86)

In comparison to what he views as primitive eighteenth-century New England, Dwight identifies nineteenth-century New England as populated, modern, and equipped for easy and expedient travel.[8] With publication of Knight's *Journal*, Dwight seeks to develop a nationalistic strategy to discover and publish earlier American works, parts of which—parts seemingly as slight as a clause or even a single word—can then be used to document a rapidly disappearing and too infrequently recorded American past. It is in this potential for textual extraction that Dwight locates the primary worth of Knight's *Journal*.

Though Dwight's interest is primarily antiquarian, this interest does not lead him to dismiss Knight herself. Rather, he praises her as "a lady of uncommon literary attainments, as well as of great taste and strength of mind" (85). He recognizes and appreciates Knight's lively wit:

> It is to be regretted that the brevity of the work should have allowed the author so little room for the display of the cultivated mind and the brilliant fancy which frequently betray themselves in the course of the narrative; and no one can rise from the perusal without wishing some happy chance might yet discover more full delineations of life and character from the same practiced hand. (85)

His striking praise reveals his high opinion of Knight's writing skill—"uncommon literary attainments," "great taste and strength of mind," "cultivated mind," "brilliant fancy." His assertion that readers will finish the *Journal* hoping for more writing by Knight, along with his characterizing of her "practiced hand," indicates respect for her literary talent.

Dwight's selection of Knight's *Journal*—given its female authorship, unconventional tone, and "unpretending" nature—for publication in 1825 marks a receptivity to female representation, especially in texts written by and about women. This is not to suggest, however, that his choice to publish the journal be read as protofeminist. I do not imagine Dwight as a man ahead of his time, envisioning and promoting women's writing. Rather, Dwight, an author and educator interested in documenting New England history, wanted to make public Knight's detailed description of her eighteenth-century progress through that region. However, a close reading of his introduction makes clear he has sufficient intellectual resources to appreciate Knight's unconventional women's writing. Indeed, Dwight published his edition at a moment when readers were becoming receptive to historical and fictive accounts of "women's experiences in the wilderness" (Balkun 22).[9] As Balkun writes, "A number of [such] popular texts . . . were published within a year or two of Knight's: [Lydia Maria] Child's *Hobomok*

(1824), [James E.] Seaver's *Narrative of the Life of Mrs. Mary Jemison* (1826), and [Catharine Maria] Sedgwick's *Hope Leslie* (1827)" (22). Further, as Michael Davitt Bell observes, "many of the new American novels published in the 1820s were . . . works of historical fiction" (38). For instance, Lydia Maria Child "published three historical novels in the 1820s and 1830s" (38). Child's *Hobomok* (1824) is set in seventeenth-century Massachusetts, while *The Rebels* (1825) takes place in pre-Revolutionary era Boston. Sarah Josepha Hale's *Northwood* (1827) is "a New England local-color novel" (Bell 39). Catharine Maria Sedgwick, "one of the most influential American fiction writers of her generation," "turned to historical fiction in 1827 with *Hope Leslie,* set in seventeenth-century Massachusetts" (Bell 42). *Hope Leslie*'s popularity "made its author the most celebrated American woman writer before Harriet Beecher Stowe" (Bell 42). Works such as these by nineteenth-century U.S. writers concerning women in early American history, and American history in general, provided readers with context for reading Knight's account of her travel a century earlier through the New England wild. Further, the publication, reviews, and sometimes popularity of such texts suggest market forces which Dwight may or may not have been fully aware of at the time. Whatever Dwight's degree of awareness, a potential receptivity to such works was in the air when he chose to edit and publish Knight's journal.

Dwight's postpublication recognition of both market forces and their vagaries is later seen in an 1846 letter he wrote in response to a query about Knight's authorship. As Margolies notes, this letter and the introduction to Knight's text "are Dwight's only published accounts of his editing of the journal" (25). In the letter, Dwight laments the tepid response two decades earlier to publication of the journal: "The indifference with which that little book was regarded discouraged me from bringing out any more, though I had two or three old manuscripts which I should have liked to bring out at some future time" ("December Meeting" 387). He adds that he has "been earnestly solicited of late to prepare and publish another edition, with notes, embracing the above and other particulars, and have taken some steps; but apprehending a second failure, I have not pursued the plan" (387). In this 1846 letter, Dwight assigns a primacy to market forces—and book sales deriving from them—that determines his resistance to publishing a second edition of Knight's journal. By implication, his inaccurate assessment of market forces in 1825 ("the indifference with which that little book was regarded") resulted in his editing the journal for publication at that time.

Though sales of Knight's *Journal* disappointed Dwight, in 1825 he would have had moderate evidence to assume that it might successfully attract readers. In addition to the writing and publication of works regarding historical or fictive treatment of women, publication of Knight's journal occurred at a time of "increasing interest in travel literature in a variety of forms" (Balkun 21).[10] As Imbarrato has detailed, written accounts of travel in journals, letters, and narratives circulated through publication as well as through private exchange. Additionally, travel guidebooks written for tourists attracted readers (33).[11] Dwight himself had written and published a travel narrative, *A Journal of a Tour in Italy,* in 1824, a year before his edition of Knight's *Journal*. After publication of Knight's journal, he wrote three more travel books, all concerning travels within the United States.

Imbarrato notes that there are "approximately fifty extant women's travel narratives ... published and in manuscript" from the period 1700 to 1830 (2), enough to contribute to Dwight's sense that readers would welcome an edition of Knight's journal.[12] Further, like Knight's *Journal,* other women's accounts of travel were published and reprinted throughout the nineteenth century. Elizabeth Ashbridge's *Some Account of the Fore Part of the Life of Elizabeth Ashbridge,* a conversion narrative "framed by travel" (Imbarrato 148), was first published in 1774 and again in 1807, 1831, and 1886. Anne Grant MacVicar's *Memoirs of an American Lady,* published in 1808, was reprinted in 1809, 1836, 1846, and 1876. Annette Kolodny cites two popular texts—James Seaver's *Narrative of the Life of Mrs. Mary Jemison* (1826) and Timothy Flint's *Biographical Memoir of Daniel Boone* (1833)—as together providing U.S. readers "published access to two real-life white women [Mary Jemison and Rebecca Boone, wife of Daniel] who had learned to survive in the wilderness" (89). As Balkun writes:

> [Knight's] *Journal* has much in common with other travel books of the period: detailed descriptions that enabled the reader to experience vicariously the journey, an underlying no-place-like-home sentiment which measured all things—to their detriment—against the point of origin of the traveler, and an affirmation of American accomplishment and exceptionalism. (22)

I agree with Balkun that "with its factual and cultural information, the *Journal* satisfied the nineteenth-century desire for texts that documented American social history and provided a base for the emergent

American culture" (21). Despite this alignment, Dwight's edition failed to achieve the popularity he seems to have imagined for it. Though sales disappointed Dwight, he had nonetheless been correct in his opinion that central features of Knight's text, such as its narrative of travel, were of interest to readers of the time.

Such literary contexts valuably add to our understandings of the nineteenth-century publication and readership of Knight's journal. I do not claim that publication of Knight's *Journal* in 1825 indicates a transformation in the ways in which women are represented by themselves and others or that only by an alchemy of social and cultural arrangements the journal could only be published for the first time in 1825. However, Knight's *Journal* was published at a point in the early republic when, as Mary Kelley has argued, "newly independent Americans began to consider the subject of female intellect, a topic that had elicited little concern earlier" ("Vindicating" 6). Nearly four hundred "private academies and seminaries . . . were founded exclusively for women between 1790 and 1830." Additionally, public schools began to enroll girls as well as boys in rural and urban locales (1). As Balkun writes, "the publication of [Knight's] *Journal* coincided with the start of the American women's movement, offering readers an intelligent, independent, and capable 'mother of the republic'" (22).

In Mary Suzanne Schriber's observation, the nineteenth-century United States had reached a "historical moment when the meaning and boundaries of woman's sphere were contested and increasingly indefinite; and when the definition of the domestic sphere was being stretched to encompass ever more public terrain, to the expressed consternation of many Victorians" (50). The reception of the 1825 edition of Knight's *Journal* signals the mixed nature of this consideration of female intellect. Margolies details public reaction to Knight's text in the two decades following publication.[13] These responses consist of male-authored articles that in various ways disputed authenticity of Knight's text. For example, Joseph Barlow Felt (1789–1869), well-known pastor, historian, and author, wrote in 1839, "Though the female traveler, Madam Knight, is a fictitious author, yet the representation, quoted from the book, bearing such a name appears to be true" (250).[14] A Boston newspaper labeled the *Journal* a "spurious production" ("December Meeting" 387). William R. Deane (1809–71), historian and genealogist who would later write an introduction to the text, initially classified the *Journal* as fiction written by a man (963n). And the notes of an 1877 meeting of the Massachusetts Historical Society record a discussion of Dwight's 1846 letter concerning the authenticity of Knight's text, stating that "it was confidently believed by many that Madam Knight's Journal proceeded from the fertile fancy of the late Samuel L. Knapp, who had the reputation of writing some clever fictions of a like character" ("December Meeting" 388).[15]

These responses contested authenticity of Knight's text and Knight herself. I read such reactions as indicating that while the cultural moment permitted publication of the journal, it also, at least initially, mandated a degree of resistance to the text's and the author's legitimacy. Indeed, when Dwight wrote to Charles Deane on December 26, 1846 (as noted earlier, the letter and Dwight's introduction to the 1825 edition are his only extant remarks concerning his editing of Knight's text), it was to affirm authenticity of Knight's authorship:[16]

> My dear Sir,—The work to which you refer is well known to me. It is genuine and authentic. I had heard of the manuscript for several years . . . and succeeded in procuring it for publication. I copied it with my own hand, retaining the orthography, and omitting only a few words and phrases which were not very appropriate to a book. A Boston paper, on the appearance of the work, pronounced it a spurious production. ("December Meeting" 386–87)

Having established the text's authenticity, Dwight reiterates views expressed in his introduction twenty-one years earlier: "It gratifies me to find that you and your friends in Boston feel any interest in the Journal of your townswoman, Madam Knight, as I think it highly creditable to her character and education, and valuable for the picture it gives of the state of the country and people at that early period" (387). Thus, though Knight's voice had initially emerged publicly through publication in the nineteenth-century United States, that voice continued to be circumscribed and diminished in subsequent public commentaries over the decades.

II.

Knight's *Journal* soon became part of nineteenth-century U.S. literary discourse. It was recurrently published, as well as mentioned and quoted in print, with the assumption that readers would recognize the reference. I detail below the trajectory of this progression from eighteenth-century white woman's privately circulated text to nineteenth-century white woman's public text, outlining various publications, references, and dates. As stated earlier, I move into new critical ground regarding Knight's text through my detailing and consideration of these references.

Knight's *Journal*, first published in 1825, was reprinted in its entirety in 1847, 1858, and 1865.[17] An excerpt from it was published in 1826. Further, a range of books and articles published in the nineteenth-century United States contained passing references to and quotations from Knight's *Journal*. Though Theodore Dwight was first to print Knight's *Journal* in its entirety, the earliest published reference to Knight herself appeared in Hannah Mather Crocker's (1752–1829) *Observations on the Real Rights of Women, with Their Appropriate Duties, Agreeable to Scripture, Reason, and Common Sense* (1818). Crocker, a married mother of ten who began writing after her children had grown, was the great-great-granddaughter of Richard Mather, great-granddaughter of Increase Mather, and granddaughter of Cotton Mather. She was the daughter of Samuel Mather, Cotton Mather's only surviving son, and Hannah Hutchinson Mather, sister to Massachusetts governor Thomas Hutchinson (Post 85; Westbrook and Westbrook 62).[18] As Constance Post writes in her important work recovering Crocker, *Observations on the Real Rights of Women* was "one of the first books on women's rights written by an American to be published in America" (86). In her *Observations,* Crocker argues that "the wise Author of nature has endowed the female with equal powers and faculties . . . as he gave to the male sex" (5).

Though she did not refer to Knight's *Journal* in her text and may or may not have known of its existence at this point, Crocker had reason to be familiar with Knight. Crocker grew up in the same house in which Knight had grown up and in which Knight's daughter, Elizabeth, had been married by Increase Mather, Crocker's great-grandfather (Titus 101–2; 106). In *Observations,* Crocker employs references to a diverse range of women, including American, biblical, British, classical, French, and modern women. Among them, Crocker identifies Knight as "famous in her day for teaching to write"; as the author of "letters on business, and notes of hand, and letters on friendship"; and as "a smart, witty, sensible woman . . . [who] had considerable influence at that period" (66). Crocker foregrounds Knight's professional status as a paid teacher and writer. Her description of Knight as "smart, witty, [and] sensible" evokes the voice of Knight's journal, suggesting that Crocker may have known of it or perhaps had had it described to her. Had Crocker read Knight's journal or had it read to her at this point, or had she been certain of its existence, she likely would have mentioned it given its correspondence with her argument.[19]

Crocker's assembly of praiseworthy American women such as Martha Dandridge Washington (in her role as wife of George Washington), Revolutionary War–era writer Mercy Otis Warren, and Rachel Donelson Jackson (in her role as wife of Andrew Jackson) establishes a female context within patriarchy. It also indicates a degree of receptivity to representations of American women. Eighteenth-century Knight's initial public appearance in Crocker's early-nineteenth-century book—again, one of the first American books on women's rights written by an American woman—suggests cultural readiness for Dwight's publication of the journal seven years later. The year after Dwight's publication, excerpts were published under the title "Travelling in America" in Eliakim Littell's monthly magazine, *The Museum of Foreign Literature and Science* (Margolies 29).[20] Littell would go on to edit *The Living Age*, which thirty-two years later, as detailed below, would publish Knight's journal in its entirety.

The entire *Journal* was next republished in 1847 in Boston's weekly *Protestant Telegraph* by the Reverend Mortimer Blake (1813–84). Here it appeared serially. In 1858 the literary weekly *The Living Age*, an offshoot of the *Atlantic Monthly*, reprinted Knight's entire journal in a June issue. William R. Deane, who had initially maintained that the journal was written by a man, wrote the introduction to this issue. Deane's introduction describes the *Journal*, provides a biography of Knight (including lengthy descriptions of the lives of her father and her husband), and lists the two previous printings of the text. Deane notes earlier questions of the journal's authorship but takes pains to confirm Knight's existence and authorship.

Deane recognized the unique nature of Knight's travels, writing that "Madam Knight was probably almost the only woman who, at so early a date, made such a journey" (963). He devotes a significant amount of his introduction to Knight's real-estate transactions. His discussion of Knight as a businesswoman suggests prevailing acceptance or tolerance of women's property dealings. Also, as Dwight did thirty-three years earlier, Deane focuses on Knight's descriptions of eighteenth-century New England, marveling at what he views as progress achieved in intervening decades. In doing so, Deane partakes of the white Northern middle-class narrative of improvements accomplished by industrial capitalism.

In 1865 Northern lawyer and judge William Law Learned (1821–1904) prepared an edition of the *Journal* for publication (Margolies 28). Learned reprinted Dwight's 1825 edition, adding a preface and explanatory footnotes. His preface, which draws heavily on Deane's 1858 introduction, provides details of Knight's life, family, and business activities, as well as a brief description of her journey. Learned describes Knight as "energetic and observing," with "some imagination and a good perception of the ludicrous" (xi). He comments that her more irreverent jokes "only a few years earlier, might have convicted her of witchcraft, if they had come to the ears of Cotton Mather" (xi). Learned implicitly classifies female energy, observation, imagination, and humor as positive qualities. He assumes that readers will, as he did, view penalties for such women (e.g., for practicing witchcraft) as part of a remote American past.

The publication of Learned's 1865 edition of Knight's journal coincided with the end of the Civil War. Two suggestive notes written by Learned reflect this historical moment. Both are unusual: the majority of notes in Learned's edition are quotations from other texts/authors, factual explanations, and translations of vernacular or archaic usages.[21] However, the two notes overtly inflected by the war are both Learned's cultural commentary. First, Learned cites Knight's relation of a dispute between a slave and a master which results in the master's admitting fault.[22] Responding to this scene, Learned writes, "From this little incident it may be seen that, even at this early time, slavery, in Connecticut, was a very different thing from the system which has existed in the southern part of our country" (54n1). Learned reads Knight's story through a lens of nineteenth-century Northern views of the Southern slavocracy. His implicitly judgmental language emphasizes the perception of a closed system of white dominance ("a very different thing") in his own time. Within that system, whites were always already in the right. For Learned, in the nineteenth-century United States, the white master would never admit fault, even when or perhaps especially when wrong.

Next, following an observation of Knight's regarding quick marital divorce, Learned, in his longest note, comments, "This facility for obtaining divorce may have arisen from the degradation of marriage to a mere civil contract entered into before a magistrate. . . . Unfortunately the same facility has continued to the present time" (55n1). Learned's extensive commentary is provoked by the ease with which a marital union could be dissolved. I suggest that in his response we also read larger national issues of unions and civil contracts. Learned's dismay at the ease of disuniting two previously joined parties evokes his cultural moment. His note reveals a vital recognition of the fearsome simplicity of disbanding a marriage or disbanding a country.

In addition to these complete and partial reprintings of Knight's *Journal*, references to it appeared regularly and in diverse contexts. For instance, in the July 1854 essay "Holidays" in the *United States Democratic Review*, the anonymous author, discussing New England celebrations, writes, "The preceding remarks are much strengthened by some observations made by Madame Knight in her *Journal of a Tour from Boston to New-York,* in the year 1704, then a most serious and arduous undertaking" (59). This reference is followed by a quotation from the journal, establishing that the writer is aware of Knight's text and also owns or has access to a copy of it. Four years later a brief note in the July 1858 issue of *The Living Age* reports, "A correspondent informs us that Madame Knight taught little Benjamin Franklin to write" (242).[23] Then in October 1858 a letter printed in *Notes & Queries* requests information about a passage in Knight's journal (310). In a November 1860 *Atlantic Monthly* review of Frederick Law Olmsted's *A Journey in the Back-Country,* Knight's name appears in a list of authors who wrote about early New England (636). And in the 1864 book *Huguenots of Westchester and Parish of Fordham,* the author, William Watson Waldron, writes of "Madame Knight, who published a journal of her trip from New-York to Boston, a hundred and sixty years ago, A.D. 1704" (72). Waldron quotes directly from Knight's text, indicating that he too owns or has access to a copy of it.

In July 1871, the *North American Review,* then edited by James Russell Lowell and Charles Eliot Norton, reviewed the book *History of Rye, West Chester County New York 1660–1870* (1871) by Charles W. Baird. Discussing "public-houses" of the time, the reviewer writes that "even the best [public-houses] were not very neat or well-provided. At least Strang's was not, where Madam Knight passed her wretched night in 1704" (226). This notably informed reference both indicates familiarity with the narrative of Knight's trip and accurately cites the year she began her travel; as with earlier references, familiarity with Knight's text is assumed. Further, Moses Coit Tyler, known for his "pioneering work in the scholarly study of colonial and revolutionary literature," included Knight in his "great and enduring stud[y]," *A History of American Literature, 1607–1765,* published in 1878 (Saar 243, 246).[24] Tyler's choice of Knight corresponds with what Saar describes as his view of "literature as a source of social information: he open[ed] the canon to include journals, diaries, and travel literature as proper objects of literary study.... [F]or Tyler, and for the Victorians, the literature of New England exemplified the literature of the nascent nation" (247). Knight's New England focus and detailed observations appealed to Tyler. He was aware of but less fettered by insistent notions of literary aesthetics and so did not automatically exclude Knight because of her position as a woman who had written in what was perceived by many to be a lesser genre.[25]

In 1888 in the *Harper's* feature "Editor's Study," William Dean Howells reviewed the book series *Library of American Literature* edited by Edmund Clarence Stedman (1833-1908) and Ellen Mackay Hutchinson (?-1933).[26,27] Discussing American Puritan writing, Howells writes, "Even with the masters of it, English prose was still in the hippopotamic; the newspaper humorist had not yet arisen to give it the gazelle-like movement in which it now disports itself" (479). Howells admiringly singled out Knight's journal:

> The editors quote from the journals of Madam Sarah Kemble Knight the account of her journey from Boston to New York in 1704, which is both lively and good. It shows touch; and that such easy, vigorous writing should be in a private diary suggests at least a growing literary temperament among the Bostonians of the time. (479)

Howells's 1888 praise—"lively," "good," "easy," "vigorous"—of Knight's 1704-5 writing indicates a change over time in reception of unconventional women's writing. That Knight's text "shows touch" is a marker for Howells "of a growing literary temperament among Bostonians of the time"; that is, by 1888 such women's writing is viewed (at least by Howells and other cultural agents like him) as engaging and acceptable, unlike the more mixed reception Knight's writing had received by some reviewers and readers in earlier decades.

In his 1896 biography *The Life of Thomas Hutchinson*, James Kendall Hosmer (1824-1927) cites "Madame Knight, who made a journey through New England early in the eighteenth century, of which an account remains, sometimes graphic and racy, describes the trading of the time" (18). Hosmer quotes at length from Knight's *Journal*, indicating that he owns or has access to a copy of it. Hosmer's classification of the text as "sometimes graphic and racy" is admiring rather than pejorative, inviting readers to share his response.

Finally, an 1897 essay, "Travel in Early New England," by Amelia Leavitt Hill (?-1962) in *The New England Magazine*, begins with a lengthy section on Knight and her travels. Hill, clearly familiar with Knight's *Journal,* assumes that readers will be, too. Hill's admiration for Knight and her journal are evident throughout the section. Knight's text is a "most interesting journal," and Knight herself is "regarded as little short of a heroine," with qualities of "courage," "quick insight," and a "keen sense of humor and a gift of description" (82). Hill quotes directly from the journal several times, establishing that she, too, owns or has access to a copy of it.

To summarize the trajectory sketched here of nineteenth-century U.S. print appearances of Knight and her journal, the first extant reference to Knight herself is, appropriately, in Hannah Mather Crocker's 1718 treatise on women's rights. Knight's *Journal* was then first published in 1825 and subsequently republished in its entirety three times (1847, 1858, and 1865). An excerpt from the journal was published in 1826, and a variety of references to Knight and her text appeared in print throughout the nineteenth-century United States, particularly in the latter half of the century.[28]

These multiple reprintings of and references to Knight's *Journal* across the nineteenth century stand in contrast to its private, local circulation in the eighteenth century. Further, the various ways in which the text was edited (in single volumes, in periodicals, with commentary by male editors) and received (negatively, positively, as fiction) indicate the shifting cultural status of Knight's text in particular and women's writing in general. Taken together, laudatory references to Knight's journal in the last decades of the nineteenth century by Tyler, Howells, Hosmer, and Hill make plain that by that time, the journal was valued more positively than it had been in earlier decades.

My claim is not that Knight's *Journal* was necessarily read by nineteenth-century U.S. women writers subsequently discussed in this study. That may or may not have been the case. However, in outlining nineteenth-century appearances of the journal, I seek to position Knight's text in a developing cultural discourse regarding gender and representation, one in which women's texts examined in this study are situated.

III.

While Knight's generic choice of the journal or travel narrative corresponds with early American women's writing, her adaptations of form and her unconventional writing are unlike those of other early

American women writers. Rather, Knight's text anticipates and projects generic choices and constructions of female behavior that nineteenth-century U.S. women writers later adopted and developed, consciously or unconsciously.

Similar to narratives by early American women, Knight's text participates in the "amateur" choice of the journal or travel narrative. As mentioned earlier, as far as is known, Knight did not anticipate or prepare her text for publication. Indeed, in adopting the amateur form of the journal, Knight simultaneously adopted the status of an amateur writer. Such status suggests an expectation of later sharing the private journal with a private (not public or commercial) audience of family and friends. The genre of the journal is, as Schriber notes, typically seen as "one of those 'lesser forms' in the autobiographical tradition" (59). Generic conventions of the travel narrative allow for a range of content, including the journey itself, the traveler's observations, and details of the writer's life and experiences. Generic conventions also prompt a prearranged structure of the text that adheres to the journey's itinerary and route. As Schriber observes, "the warrant in the travel genre for culturally authorized and conventionally female forms such as the letter, the diary, and the journal" invites participation of women writers "because these are forms in which women are historically practiced and believe themselves to be competent" (58). The journal requires an experience (travel) to some degree allowable within conventional female scripts. Though women's travel was much more constrained than men's travel, some limited situations allowed women both to travel and to remain viewed as genteel. As Shari Benstock classically writes, the mix of lower-status accessibility and travel experience enables women's self-writing, "serv[ing] as . . . a way by which to find a 'voice'—whether private or public—through which to express that which cannot be expressed in other forms" ("Authorizing the Autobiographical" 5–6).

At the same time, women's travel writing invokes gender issues of authority and autonomy, marking complexity of female positioning and the woman writer's potential disruption of dominant gender constructions. For instance, New England examples of excoriated Puritans Anne Hutchinson and Mary Dyer, as well as the 1692 witchcraft delusion, spanned the seventeenth century, providing cautionary tales for white women who acted with autonomy and spoke in less constrained voices.[29,30] As Schriber writes, travel narrative conventions and travel itself are complicated for women by "prohibitions against female travel for travel's sake [that] have been linked historically to ideas of the feminine, connected in turn with women's sexual vulnerability" (23). Such concerns would have contributed to a convergence of gender and class for the white middle-class woman on a solitary journey and for those who encountered her. Because "women of the genteel classes are assumed to be virtuous women," women who traveled alone would be viewed as lower class—that is, "sexual, dangerous, and barely women at all" (Schriber 87). Schriber concludes that "the public took the measure of women's travel, its value and its meaning, as it took the measure of women, their value and their meaning" (45). Indeed, Knight consistently notes behaviors of women encountered on her journey. Her observations, discussed below, function to reinforce her own class status. The women whom Knight observes serve as "a useful polarity to the woman traveler," crucially enabling her to identify herself as genteel (Schriber 89).

Knight deploys travel narrative conventions by using her journey's structure as the text's structure. Her text follows her trip from Boston to New Haven and New York and back, signaling its principal agenda of recording the journey. However, Knight defies travel narrative conventions with a mix of independence, capitalistic motivation, and witty observations. These disruptions of generic conventions separate Knight and her journal from other early American female travel writers and their texts. Early American women narrators such as Hannah Dustan, Mary Rowlandson, and Hannah Swarton traveled, but were forced to do so as captives; they were commodities, not buyers or sellers, in economic exchange. Their postcaptivity narratives, primarily chronicling physical and spiritual redemption, were promoted as documents of orthodox Puritan piety.

Other early American women travelers such as Elizabeth Ashbridge and Elizabeth House Trist, did, like Knight, journey independently. However, Ashbridge's narrative records her search for spiritual, not monetary, gain. Trist details her conventional reasons for travel (to reunite with her husband and children) within prevailing gender assumptions.[31] Knight's distinctive tone, observations, and motive may help explain why her text remained unpublished in the eighteenth century. In salient ways such as these, I read Knight's text as less typical of eighteenth-century American women's writing and see it corresponding more closely with nineteenth-century U.S. women's writing.

Knight's journey mirrors cultural ambivalence toward female autonomy located in the women's travel narrative. The independence of her unconventional travels alone or with a guide is confined to her reliance on eighteenth-century New England white women's domain.

She is lodged, served, and entertained by women at inns, taverns, and eating places. She turns not to a patriarchal god but to the female moon for guidance on rough roads. And when she completes her return trip, she is greeted not by men but by women—her mother and daughter. These interactions on her travels adhere to gendered cultural contours. Her text privileges observation of women encountered on her journey. As Shields observes, Knight's text is "alert[ing] us to the development of a women's domain in the public sphere" (*Civil* 105). Her text also chronicles her critical scrutiny of women's voices and her perception of their disruptions of conventional gender scripts.

Knight's unusual autonomous travels determine that she will be situated in female locations. Ironically, her travel autonomy limits her writing domain. In fundamental ways, her journal is more gender-specific in its observations than other early American women's travel narratives because the places she travels through on her solitary journey—regardless of her destination—must always be in women's domain. Knight's gendered adaptation of the travel narrative partakes of, yet subordinates, generic conventions of texts "by early explorers, by Puritan historians, and by diarists and travelers" that, as Lawrence Buell has observed, map "the New England landscape and ethos" (283). Within these conventions Knight's *Journal* maps previously uncharted regions of her gendered travels. Her territory is a female, oral New England landscape and ethos of white American eighteenth-century women and women's domain.

Knight's adoption of a nonfictional, almost realist form within which to narrate her journey prefigures autobiographic choices in texts of nineteenth-century U.S. women discussed later in this study. As I demonstrate in subsequent chapters, though Fanny Fern, Louisa May Alcott, S. Emma E. Edmonds, Mary Livermore, Annie Turner Wittenmyer, and Harriet Jacobs sometimes employ degrees of the fictive in their writing, they primarily use the autobiographical in order to "speak" publicly. I argue that Knight's adaptations of a genre perceived as acceptable for women incorporates strategies that nineteenth-century U.S. women writers, with varying degrees of awareness, later take up and expand.

IV.

Knight traveled fairly autonomously—she was mobile, literate, and largely uninfluenced by religious motives. Though she did, when reunited with her mother and daughter, "desire sincearly to adore [her] Great Benefactor for thus graciously carying forth and returning in safety his unworthy handmaid" (116), few religious references appear, and even this last one is wryly phrased. Knight is separated from women she encounters on her travels by their social and spatial confinement as well as by questions of their literacy.[32] As Julia Stern observes, in the journal only Knight "is represented in the act of writing" ("To Relish" 3).[33] Voices of other women may have been limited by illiteracy to the spoken word. Whether or not they were limited thusly, Knight restricts their voices to the spoken word in her journal.[34] Variance between Knight and other white eighteenth-century New England women reveals nuanced gender issues of access and authority in the women's domain situated within the larger patriarchy.[35] Throughout her text, Knight has greater access and authority than the eighteenth-century women she writes of encountering.

However, the degrees of cultural distance separating Knight from other white early American women need not be overstated. Differences among women, no matter how significant, are subsumed by larger forms of social insistence regarding gender. Knight and other white early American women were vulnerable to dangers and gendered anxieties directed toward women whose actions, beliefs, or status resulted in heightened cultural notice. Early American history provided salient representations of risks that accompanied female visibility. For Knight, the most recent and notorious gendered cultural disruption would have been the 1692 Boston/Salem witchcraft delusion, when she was twenty-six years old: four years after her marriage, one year after the birth of her child, and twelve years before her journey. By the time Knight embarked on her early-eighteenth-century trip, the state no longer executed New England women on witchcraft charges. The perception of women's power, autonomy, and visibility as a threatening cultural disruption and the need to control them had become concealed in more "rational" and systemic ways. Despite these (dis)appearances, such formal rules of law served as bloodless, more culturally acceptable forms of containing women's autonomy and power than the hanging of women.

Knight's occupations as scrivener and estate settler invite speculation concerning her access to and considerations of such legal information. Anson Titus detailed Knight's extensive copyist work: "She appears as a witness to a hundred or more deeds of the leading firms and families of Boston" (105). Copying a variety of public documents would have allowed Knight regularly to acquire legal particulars. Official documents involved in settling estates would have also furnished her with such information. In these and other ways, Knight would have been familiar with property laws and legal changes. Such information may have led her to recognize alterations in women's legal status and larger implications of such changes. That awareness, if it existed, had the potential to increase her understandings of codified penalties that often awaited disruptive women.

Up to a point, Knight's activities might seem to depend on, rather than to challenge, Laurel Thatcher Ulrich's classic concept of the "deputy husband," the woman who without cultural disruption serves as her husband's agent in business and other responsibilities. But it would be inaccurate to claim that in Knight's business activities she functioned as her husband's surrogate. Rather, her work seems to have been largely separate from her husband's. Still, any conclusions Knight may have drawn as a result of her autonomous work as scrivener and estate settler would have mixed with views she held as a rational, eighteenth-century, middle-class white merchant. The latter subject position suggests that she may not have necessarily recognized or fully accepted the systemic gendered oppression of such changes. She could have dismissed Hutchinson and Dyer as female religious fanatics who had deliberately courted controversy, and women accused of witchcraft as crazy or hapless victims of an overzealous past. Knight's employment as a copyist, in addition to income it provided, may have served only as a means by which to glean useful knowledge that would help her capitalize further on her business skills. Similarly, knowledge that enabled Knight to help settle estates may have remained conventionally understood by her within immediate limits and applications of the law. Her increasing familiarity with the legal system may not have led her to understand the law in any larger representational sense. Knight's behavior, controlled by bloodless cultural constraints, may have prevented her from more complete recognition of her place on a continuum with these penalized women. Yet her knowledge of such women may have allowed her to intuitively and unconsciously sense gender boundaries.

However Knight and other eighteenth-century New England white women viewed their cultural location and its systemic controls, when Knight began her travels and journal, dangers and social fears of female autonomy and voice remained culturally entrenched. I agree with Julia Stern that Knight's gendered constructions in her journal of herself as conventional and other women as disruptive show her "refocus[ing] the anxiety she feels for having transgressed eighteenth-century gender codes by projecting hostility back onto the female bodies of unknown others" ("To Relish" 6). Her choice of the journal—with its marginal status—to record her voice and the journal's commercial publication over a century after her death implicitly recognizes gendered perils for independent women. At no point does Knight allow herself to feel sympathetic alignment with her historical antecedents or with women she encounters on her journey.

These punitive commonalities help determine that female mutual acceptance and protection could not fully emerge from and be enacted in eighteenth-century white women's domain. Rather, such gendered hazards resulted in Knight's investment in criticizing women she encountered on her travels as speaking and acting inappropriately, yet insisting—despite her unusual, autonomous journey—on her own conventionality. Taken as a whole, Knight's gendered criticisms and class building point to a Federalist America as yet unready for a democratic union of females. Women's texts subsequently discussed in this study (texts both written and published in the nineteenth century) will at times at least partially construct unified female communities. For instance, as later chapters show, Alcott's community of female nurses in the Civil War hospital as seen in *Hospital Sketches,* as well as Edmonds's constructions of cross-dressing women soldiers in *Nurse and Spy in the Union Army,* represents women linked by shared concerns and interests, a grouping only marginally viable in Knight's time and perception.

V.

Near the beginning of her journal, we hear Knight's indignant voice in her transaction to hire a guide, marking that, as Julia Stern aptly phrases it, "things oral . . . constitute the central narrative matter of the *Journal*" ("To Relish" 1). A portion of the manuscript is missing; we enter the bargaining when Knight records this dialogue:

> Peices of eight, I told her no, I would not be acessary to such extortion. Then John shan't go, sais shee. No, indeed, shan't hee; And held forth at that rate a long time, that I began to fear I was got among the Quaking tribe, beleeving not a Limbertong'd sister among them could out do Madm. Hostes. (87)

Knight wishes to hire a male guide but must negotiate with his mother, his female agent, who sets his price and speaks for him so extensively that she invokes for Knight religious oratory and a community of articulate women—the image of professional speaking. When indentured servant Elizabeth Ashbridge (later a Quaker preacher herself) first hears a Quaker woman preaching in the early 1730s she writes, "I looked on her with Pity for her Ignorance (as I thought) & Contempt of her Practise, saying to my self, 'I am sure you are a fool, for if ever I should turn Quaker, which will never be, I would not be a preacher'" (155). Ashbridge's precritical contempt differs from Knight's experienced, ironic response to "Madm. Hostes." Knight views the woman's tirade as performance, using "Quaking tribe" to recall disparagement of Quakers and their commonly mocked fervor, "quaking" in enthusiastic prayer. Though Knight ironizes the lengthy discourse, she also recasts it as woman's professional discourse. Knight locates her disparagement in the woman's prolonged articulation—her voice—not in the occasion for her discourse. For Knight, a woman who speaks at such length—professionally or not—conducts herself inappropriately. Her critical, extended discourse on the extended discourse of another woman leaves unexamined, as Julia Stern observes, "the ways in which her own narrative implicates her in the role of outspoken female" ("To Relish" 2). Knight's presentation of herself as always speaking appropriately even when she is not marks a contradictory self-representation within prevailing gender assumptions that will be consistent throughout the journal.

Judgment of female voice is further promoted when, at the end of the tirade, Knight writes:

> Upon this, to my no small surprise, son John arrose, and gravely demanded what I would give him to go with me? Give you, sais I, are you John? Yes, says he, for want of a Better; And behold! This John look't as old as my Host, and perhaps had bin a man in the last Century. (87)

That a woman spoke on behalf of an adult male extends Knight's reading of the woman's voice as disruptive. Not only did a woman speak at length; she also spoke on behalf of another, a male, and a grown male at that.

When John concludes the bargain for "half a pss. of eight and a dram," "my hostess catechis'd John for going so cheep, saying his poor wife would break her heart" (87). According to Knight, John's bargaining for himself is appropriate culturally and (for her) economically. Yet John's silent presence while his mother bargained suggests his implicit acquiescence to her appropriation of his voice. Only when her bargaining is ineffective does he speak and bargain for himself. The scene centers on articulation and inarticulation, eliding issues of money, family, and travel. The mother speaks at length for the adult son; the son speaks briefly for himself; and then his mother speaks for his wife. Knight's disapproval of the woman is twofold: the length at which the woman preaches and her son's allowing her to speak for him. For Knight—in unexamined contradiction of her own speech as she records it and of her journal entries—any woman who exceeds brief speech on her own behalf violates gender and class codes.

Intersections of class and gender identity appear regularly in the journal. Knight's observations regarding women encountered as she travels emerge from her attention to class difference as well as to gender conventions. Throughout her text, she is preoccupied with classification and criticism of women. As Michaelsen has observed, Knight's investment in rendering distinctions of class suggests "the manner in which women's empowerment is linked in Knight's text to the domination of others" (35). Knight's class status is, for instance, imbricated in her frequent observations of inadequacies of her lodging accommodations. As "a member of an emerging merchant class in Massachusetts" (Michaelsen 41), she partakes of what Lang has described as "a complex of economic circumstances and cultural convictions delimited enough to produce among its members a self-awareness sufficient to reinforce class boundaries, not erase them" (10).

Knight's next recorded female encounter again suggests her conflicted disruption and defense of customary female scripts as well as her attention to class status, as she arrives at an inn unconventionally late for a woman traveling alone:

> [I] had not gone many steps into the Room, ere I was Interogated by a young Lady I understood afterwards was the Eldest daughter of the family, with these, or words to this purpose, (viz.) Law for mee—what in the world brings You here at this time a night?—I never see a woman on the Rode so Dreadfull late, in all the days of my versall life. Who are You? Where are You going? I'me scar'd out of my witts—with much now of the same Kind. (91)

Knight, the woman most overtly violating gender conventions, immediately condemns the woman's startled reaction as inappropriate, telling her "shee treated me very Rudely, and I did not think it my duty to answer her unmannerly Questions" (91).[36] As in her observation of the guide's mother, Knight records the uninterrupted length and breathless nature of the woman's speech. In both cases, despite her "projecting [her] female presence in public places," as Shields aptly phrased it (*Civil* 118), her conspicuous and unusual female autonomy, and the potential for negative cultural responses to her, Knight represents herself as the conventional woman in the room, assaulted and offended by inappropriate female speech. When a woman speaks, according to Knight, rigid, unspoken rules apply. She should not speak for others, or speak at length, or ask questions. Knight represents women's speech as violating a gendered social code, though it is less clear whether the women lack awareness of that code or deliberately break it. Women's speech and Knight's reaction to it reveal voice as a strategy of gendered social classification.[37] In listening to women as she does, Knight, according to Shields, displays her "acute ear for conversations . . . [showing that] talk was a social marker, revealing one's true standing on the index of gentility" (*Civil* 117). Knight's censuring responses to woman's voice correspond with what she perceives as woman's lower status. At the same time, her responses promote Knight herself as a woman who behaves appropriately, suggesting her own higher status. Knight criticizes women's speech (and so determines their lower status) for qualities she herself uses to condemn that speech and, paradoxically, to imply her own higher status in comparison. Her regular attention to women who, in her view, speak excessively offers possibilities of such women as diminished versions of Knight herself. Further, to depict herself as superior to other women in class status, Knight must necessarily portray such women. In doing so, she unconsciously provides glimpses of elements of a prenascent female democratic union.

At the next stage, a woman silently serves Knight a meal inflected with nonverbal suggestions of articulation:

> The woman bro't in a Twisted thing like a cable, but something whiter; and laying it on the bord, tugg'd for life to bring it into a capacity to spread; wch having with great pains accomplished, shee serv'd in a dish of Pork and Cabbage . . . and every thing on the Table service Agreeable to these. I, being hungry, gott a little down; but my stomach was soon cloy'd, and what cabbage I swallowed serv'd me for a Cudd the whole day after. (91-92)

Direct and implied components of speaking occupy this scene. The table service "agrees" with the meal. Knight's stomach is soon cloyed, sickened with excess as from too much sweet speech. The cabbage serves as a cud, regurgitated to be repeatedly chewed again. And the meal mutely served is unpalatable. It can barely be swallowed. Though the woman is silent, the meal she serves suggests gender-specific expression located in food and domestic service, both of which are characteristically associated with women and women's work. The meal is described in terms of generic elements of speech (agreement, sweet words, chewing, mouth), not this particular woman's speech or substitute for her voice. These images, with the silent woman in attendance, are inscribed as disapprovingly as the speech of voluble women. Indeed, in the play between orality and literacy in which Knight engages throughout her text (i.e., she writes while women she encounters talk), Knight's written literacy is superior, and the dialogue of other women inferior. For Knight, excessive talking marks lower class status. Both too much speaking and vulgar eating provoke similar censure from Knight. However, though she is repelled by the food in the scene just discussed, the meal she eats does alleviate her hunger. Similarly, Knight's interactions with women in her text, however dissociating, do gesture toward latent possibilities of a women's community.

The *Journal* repeatedly features images of gendered articulation when no one is speaking. The next day when traveling in a canoe she fears will capsize, Knight is "very circumspect, sitting with my hands fast on each side, my eyes stedy, not daring so much as to lodg my tongue a hair's breadth more on one side of my mouth then tother, nor so much as think on Lott's wife, for a wry thought would have oversett our wherey" (92). Knight recalls another woman's perilous (indeed, tragic) journey to inform her own experiences. She again invokes speech images—tongue, mouth—in a scene where no actual speech occurs. It is revealing of Knight's sensibility—her quick turn to the "wry thought"—that she invokes Lot's wife, hardly a figure of fun, with humor. As Breitwieser correctly observes, Lot's wife "does not speak," "nor are her thoughts and feelings recorded," and she "is explicitly condemned in Genesis" (96, 95).[38] But Knight's concern here and elsewhere in the constructions of gender and articulation that recur in her text is not with particulars of specific women she mentions but with incorporation of voice (spoken or unspoken, hers or other women's) into female scripts.

Left behind by her guide in "the dolesome woods" (93), Knight does not rely on piety in times of difficulty, as typically seen in early American women's captivity narratives. Instead, she first genders her fears ("Now Returned my distressed aprehensions of the place where I was . . . encompased with Terrifying darkness enough to startle a more Masculine courage" [93]) in order to articulate and understand them (she is frightened, but even a brave man would fear this "Terrifying darkness"). She next locates gendered images of reassurance:

> But being got to the Top, was there amply recompenced with the friendly Appearance of the Kind Conductress of the night. . . . The Raptures which the Sight of that fair Planett produced in mee, caus'd mee, for the Moment, to forgett my present wearyness and past toils; and Inspir'd me for most of the remaining way with very divirting tho'ts, some of which, with the other Occurances of the day, I reserved to note down when I should come to my Stage. My tho'ts on the sight of the moon were to this purpose:
>
> Fair Cynthia, all the Homage that I may
> Unto a Creature, unto thee I pay;
> In Lonesome woods to meet so kind a guide,
> To Mee's more worth than all the world
> beside . . . (93)[39]

In circumstances requiring "a more Masculine courage" (generally unavailable to women, but by implication rarely required in the civilized world—that is, Boston—outside the woods), Knight invokes a gendered source, the female moon, for guidance ("Kind Conductress"), encouragement ("Inspir'd me for most of the remaining way"), and motivation to record her voice, her own "very divirting tho'ts." Even in dangerous circumstances, she cannot resist ironic construction of her situation. In the absence of her male human guide, she relies not on a male god but on a female moon, not on reflection on her sins but on "divirting tho'ts," and not on the voice of prayer but on the voice of poetry. Her moon-inspired courage displaces images of piety, submission, and containment seen in early American women's narratives. On a path "very narrow, and on each side [where] the Trees and bushes gave us very unpleasent welcomes with their Branches and bow's" (93), Knight travels uphill and her spirits rise as the moon rises. She progresses from "distressed aprehensions" to gender-specific inspiration to female articulation, all without conventional submission to masculine religion.

When Knight fears that she may drown during a river crossing, her fictive stories of selfhood include "sometimes seing my self drowning, otherwhiles drowned, and at the best like a holy Sister Just come out of a Spiritual Bath in dripping Garments" (92).[40] As in the reference to her guide's mother as a female Quaker preacher, she ironizes comparisons between a woman in secular life (here, Knight herself) and a devout woman ("a holy Sister") practicing religious duties. Indeed, her repeated use of representations of religious women—a female Quaker preacher, Lot's wife, a holy sister—critiques gendered conventions of organized religions. Religious women invoked by Knight in her text are disruptively visible: They speak to men with authority (a female Quaker preacher); they break rules and then transform into a pillar of salt; they enter and exit bodies of water, fully clothed and dripping; and they all participate in sharply constrained roles allowed to some women in some organized religions. At the same time, Knight elides religious doctrine and scriptural implications to provide herself with female points of comparison, while also marking her studied attention to women's public representation. These largely ironic gendered references signal her perception of distances between herself and other women (white American eighteenth-century women she meets on her travels, religious women, and historical women). Whether women speak or remain silent in the journal, they risk behaving inappropriately, particularly "working women" with whom, as Julia Stern observes, Knight is "unwilling to identify" ("To Relish" 1). I agree with Stern's reading, though I argue that as Knight insists on her distance from other women, she also—in preliminary and not fully recognized ways—outlines a potential community of vigorous women in a nascent republic.

At one point Knight meets two silent daughters, "look[ing] as old as the Divel himselfe, and quite as ugly," noting, "We desired entertainm't, but could hardly get a word out of 'um" (98). At the next eating place, "our Hostes, being a pretty full-mouth'd old creature, entertain'd our fellow travailer, the french Doctor, with Inumirable complaints of her bodily infirmities; and whisperd to him so lou'd, that all the House had as full a hearing as hee" (98). Finally, on her return journey, Knight is "invited to Lodg at Mrs. ——, a very kind and civill Gentlewoman, by whom I was handsomely and kindly entertained" (112). Working women talk too little ("could hardly get a word out of 'um"), too much ("full-mouth'd old creature"), or too loudly. Only a "Gentlewoman's" speech is kind, civil, and handsome.

In Knight's journal, white American eighteenth-century woman's voice confirms her class status. Knight uses perceived distances between herself and other women to imply a conventional self-representation: a woman speaking and behaving according to female cultural scripts traveling among women who do not. Yet her disapproval of women she perceives as speaking or behaving inappropriately is subordinated to the independent voice of her journal and the autonomous nature of and occasion for her journey. Knight successfully resists recognition of her own speech and behavior as violating rigid gender codes which she establishes for other women. Though she uses examples of women's disruptive voices to portray herself as conventional, her standards for female behavior result in few women speaking or acting conventionally in the *Journal,* least of all Knight herself.

VI.

In scenes where Knight criticizes outspoken women, she represents herself adhering to culturally sanctioned female codes. In other scenes—for instance, when she travels at night, a woman unaccompanied except by a male guide—her behavior violates those codes. The "private writing of the diary and journal" helps account for what Felicity A. Nussbaum has described as the "contradictions that both produce and reflect historicized concepts of self and gender while sometimes threatening to disrupt or transform them" (149). In her journal Knight records women's voices that similarly satisfy and violate cultural concepts of appropriate gender behavior. She also reacts critically to women she perceives as speaking or behaving inappropriately—that is, threatening to disrupt or transform cultural conceptions of appropriate female behavior. Her observations occur in women's domain, where women speak publicly (e.g., the rude young woman questions Knight at Billings's Inn at Old Dorchester, a public place) yet privately (e.g., the young woman lives at the inn and is alone with Knight when she questions her). The privacy of a gendered sphere—inns and boardinghouses run by women, for example—enables women to speak more freely, just as the privacy of Knight's journal allows her to voice, if not to recognize, her own contradictions.

Through readings of women's voice, Knight discovers, though she does not examine, her own voice in the wider gender-specific sphere to which her culture restricts her. Whatever the distances between Knight and other women she meets on her travels, she responds to their voices with as much personal and cultural investment as her counterparts responded to the New World wilderness and spiritual redemption. By her journal's end, she has invoked biblical women, contemporary women, historical women, professional women, religious women, imaginary, loud, mythical, old, silent, talkative, ugly, young women.

In her disapproval of ways women express themselves, Knight aligns herself with men and women of authority who support gendered social codes restricting women's speech. In her study of early American women's travel narratives, Imbarrato argues that "contrary to gender stereotypes, in their writing women often perpetuate hegemonic sensibilities rather than express a more inclusive attitude" (90). Knight's disapproval of women's voices legitimizes her own ready articulation, as though her criticism of other women's voices renders her own voice more acceptable. Ironically, in her desire to illustrate women's inappropriate speech, she permanently records female voices she wishes to edit or suppress. As she speaks against women who speak too much, too little, or too loudly, Knight unintentionally speaks *for* them. Invoking and criticizing other women's voices in her journal, Knight's own voice ultimately represents a range of female voices.

Knight's multiple female narrations populate her text with women. These women would have been invisible or merely footnotes in the historical record were it not for her invocation of them. It is ironic that the nineteenth-century publication of Knight's journal provokes issues of female authenticity. Knight's voice in the text, containing as it does voices of multiple women, was in the nineteenth century sometimes assumed to be fictive and sometimes assumed to be a fictive voice scripted by a man. Over a century after her critical readings of women's voices, Knight's own voice was criticized and subjected to suppression and revision, labeled, among other things, as a "spurious production" ("December Meeting" 387).

The independence of and motivation for Knight's journey—not forced, not religious or domestic in its purposes—distances her narrative from other female narratives of the period. Woman's voice, whether modified or not by religious or domestic rhetoric, was far too infrequently the voice of the literate, and so other voices that may have resembled Knight's no doubt went unrecorded. Contradictions in Knight's *Journal* and in Knight herself mark the vexed roles of women in the conventional ordering system; their fears of being perceived as defying such arrangements; and, despite these highly restrictive constraints, their desire nonetheless to attempt an articulation of self and voice. It is little surprise, then, that Knight's *Journal* was published long after she wrote it. Theodore Dwight's publication of it in 1825 occurred 121 years after Knight set forth on and recorded her travels. The *Journal*'s public appearance at this point in the United States coincided with an emergent cultural discourse concerning women, writing, and representation. The 1825 publication of Knight's journal was followed by further publications of the text in the form of reissuings, excerpts, and multiple print references throughout the nineteenth century. These public print appearances mark this eighteenth-century text's membership in shifting social and cultural arrangements that informed nineteenth-century U.S. women writers and their texts.

In the next chapter, I turn to the work of one such author, Sara Payson Willis Eldredge Parton. Writing as "Fanny Fern," she crafted frank, appealing periodical pieces that focused on subjects ranging from the sentimental to the controversial. Like Knight, Willis brought an uncommon and compelling mix of independence, wit, and lived experience to her writing. From the start of what would become an immensely successful literary career, Willis's work participated in and expanded accepted representations of women. Willis's popular and influential writings provided diverse models for women readers to negotiate and adopt in order to loosen restrictive cultural norms.

CHAPTER 2

"Everything by Turns and Nothing Long"

Configurations of Female Selfhood in Fanny Fern's Early Periodical Writing

> *I'm a regular "Will o' the Wisp"; everything by turns, and nothing long. Sometimes I'm an old maid, sometimes a wife, then a widow, now a Jack, then a Gill [sic], at present a "Fanny." If there's anything I abominate it's sameness.*
>
> —Fanny Fern, Olive Branch, 3 Mar. 1852

PUBLIC CONSTRUCTION of Fanny Fern, the feminine, mocking pen name adopted by Sara Payson Willis, began September 6, 1851, when "The Little Sunbeam" was published in the Boston *Olive Branch*, "the weekly paper that launched Fanny Fern's career as a national mass-cultural phenomenon" (Homestead 154). Until Willis's identity was maliciously disclosed by a disgruntled editor over four years later, readers repeatedly wondered aloud and in print whether "Fanny Fern" was a man writing under a woman's name or an unruly woman. Even after Willis's identity became public, false photographs of "Fanny Fern" were sold, other women continued to be identified as Fanny Fern, impostors toured the lecture circuit under the name, and for the rest of her career readers wrote requesting details of Fern's appearance.[1] The extended, complex reaction activated by the early periodical writings of Fanny Fern marks cultural anxieties regarding female scripts of identity and agency located outside prevailing constructions of femininity in the nineteenth-century United States.

Chapter 1 focused on a single text that initially was privately circulated: Sarah Kemble Knight's constructions of conventions of women's voice and domain in the "amateur" genre of the journal. This second chapter considers Fanny Fern's early periodical writing in order to understand how the regularly recurring publication of an author's writing—its scheduled, familiar discourse—promoted repeated redefinitions and reconfigurations of the (female) self. The 1825 publication of and response to Knight's *Journal* reveal contours of a larger cultural discourse concerning gender and representation. This discourse, as I argue in the previous chapter, inflects subsequently published nineteenth-century U.S. women's texts. Chapter 2 extends my examination to detail the cultural moment that allowed publication of Fanny Fern's writing and made possible the establishment of a sustained relationship between Fern and her readers.

The discussion in this chapter draws on works from Fern's periodical writing beginning in 1851, when her work was first published, until 1854. In 1854 significant financial incentives led Willis to temporarily pause in her writing for periodicals while she added the genre of the novel to her hitherto exclusive writing of periodical pieces.[2] The publication of that novel, *Ruth Hall* (1854), coincided with public revealing of Fern's identity. Once Willis resumed periodical writing, her use of fictive female personae was transparent. My interest here is in early periodical writings in which Willis repeatedly enlists strategies of female representation. These works were published prior to Willis's crossing genres into the novel and prior to her public identification as Fanny Fern. This focus allows consideration of women's writing in a popular form and, given the anonymity that Willis then inhabited, enables exploration of gender flexibility permitted within that popular genre. Perhaps equally important is that, as Melissa Homestead notes, Fern's "*Olive Branch, Musical World & Times,* and *True Flag* columns (i.e. those published before her fictionalization of that portion of her career in *Ruth Hall*) remain largely unexamined" (151). My focus provides an important opportunity for consideration of this neglected period of Fern's writing. My investigation of Fern's early periodical writings magnifies then-current cultural practices displaying the modifications, anxieties, and penalties activated by women's published writing in the nineteenth-century United States.

This chapter discusses Fern's early periodical writing in four parts: first, a consideration of generic conventions of periodical writing and women's autobiographical writing, as well as the multiple representations enabled by the periodical piece; second, Fern's biographical and cultural contexts; third, a discussion of female elasticity and representations of the woman periodical writer in Fern's early writings; and finally, a concluding section regarding gender, genre, and voice.

I.

My reading of Fern's early periodical writing employs the poetics of women's autobiography to examine the poetics of women's periodical writing. Discussions of the former emphasize vexed issues of prevailing gender assumptions and corresponding authorial constraint and elision. Lauren Berlant's apt observation that "[s]entimental female autobiography ... raised the possibility that under the 'woman' lurked something horrible, a residual 'female' whose knowledge and desire was not entirely caught up in the patriarchal domestic economy" ("The Female Woman" 437) identifies the uneasiness and suspicion with which readers greeted female autobiographical writing. Nancy K. Miller's cogent reading of women's writing as "a defense and illustration," a negotiation of conventional ideas about women, and "a poetics calling for another, freer text" (263) points to the woman writer's suppressions in her text and to inherent difficulties of writing the (female) self under constraint. While mindful of such restrictions, Sidonie Smith foregrounds the power of publication to enable the woman writer to "establish the discursive authority to interpret herself publicly in a patriarchal culture" (*Poetics* 45).

In this chapter I extend such valuable considerations of the poetics of women's autobiography to considerations of women's periodical writing, and I situate women's periodical writing beyond an "iconic representation of continuous identity" (47). That is, I examine ways in which the regular, routine appearance of the periodical piece allowed the woman writer's repeated redefinitions and reconfigurations of self. I read this intersection of gender and publication as enabling the woman writer to profess various (self-) representations. Put another way, the poetics of women's periodical writing enabled gendered constructions beyond a single female self inventing assorted personae to suit her rhetorical purposes. I argue that rather than reinforcing a binary view of female selfhood and writing, one alternating between a putatively real self and the façade, the poetics of women's periodical writing provided a space for revisions of notions of unitary female selfhood. These revisions foregrounded a mutable self as vital for successful female navigation of patriarchal systems.

For Sara Willis, writing as Fanny Fern, a columnist whose sex-gender identity was the subject of readers' heightened conjecture, periodical writing encouraged her to construct multiple female representations. As Homestead has observed:

> Under the sign of the Fanny Fern pseudonym, Fern's early sketches offered a multiplicity of voices and identities to readers from sentimental to satiric and all shades in between narrated in the third person, "soliloquized" in the voice of a named character, spoken by an unidentified first person, or spoken in the first person voice of "Fanny." (176–77)

Homestead identifies the significance of the various personae Fern inhabits in her early periodical writing. These include an unfairly criticized stepmother ("The Model Stepmother"), a newly married wife ("The Tear of a Wife"), an observant passerby ("The Stray Lamb"), and a child ("Thanksgiving Story"), among many other selves. I supplement Homestead's observations by noting that within and across these assorted female representations, Fern persuasively appealed for readers' sympathy. Christine Ross's observation that Fern "appear[s] to have recognized, to some degree, the social construction of identity" (87) suggests Fern's understanding that audience interaction with her writing would be inflected by their assumptions regarding, for instance, the gender and situation of the personae she employed. Diverse declarations of identity in Fern's early periodical writing prompted the reader to rely on her or his subjective readings of the writer as accurate; that is, readers assigned varying identities to Fern based on their own assumptions and anxieties. Correspondingly, Fern's varied female representations helped establish a relationship between Fern and her readers as she activated their goodwill for the individual selves she sympathetically imagined.

At other times, Fern selected subjects for her periodical writing and adopted tones that provoked speculation about her sex-gender identity. For instance, one early column criticizes widowers who remarry quickly ("The Model Widower"); another piously prescribes a zealously self-sacrificial wifehood ("How Woman Loves"); and another features a dying husband who is worried that his wife will be unprotected after his death ("Dark Days"). The male-centered topics of such writings encourage an essentialist reading of the author (since the columns concern men, they must be written by a man). Also, the perspective employed in such writings is authoritative in tone and so suggests access to male agency. Periodical writing, then, enabled Fern to multiply present the (female) self and to write from an ambiguous sex-gender identity. Homestead clearly identifies central features of this part of Fern's early periodical writing as "Fern's self-conscious construction and promotion of a persona in dialect with her periodical context and her readers" (164). I would add to that mix by reinforcing the role of the wide range of brief prose forms Fern employed in her periodical writing—essays, letters, paragraphs, and soliloquies, among others. Such an array further enabled Fern to sustain that dialect among her periodical context and reading audience.

For Willis, Fanny Fern was a fictional representation of a self, authorized to speak to a series of real and imagined readers. Her weekly column was instituted in September 1852, fifteen months after her first periodical piece had been published. The subsequent regular publication of her writing permitted her to consider topics of cultural significance. Further, regular publication enabled her to revise expectations about what constituted appropriate female speech and behavior, all while writing anonymously and androgynously. Sidonie Smith's observation that "an autobiographer may shift the grounds of self-representation and respond to cultural expectations about appropriate female speech and behavior" (*Poetics* 54) underscores the potential generic flexibility within women's autobiographical writing. Correspondingly, I see Willis, in Fern's early periodical writings, extending from the sentimental to the satirical and from the conventionally feminine to the conventionally masculine, each piece promoting a self or selves represented by that specific topic. Multiple narratives of Fanny Fern emerge from Willis's representation of female and male selves and from her representation and modification of Fern's selves as manifest in voice. These diverse narratives provided Willis with effective strategies for reconfiguring female selfhood as necessarily multiple for women to negotiate patriarchal forms and practices.[3]

II.

Sara Payson Willis was born in Portland, Maine, on July 9, 1811, the daughter of Nathaniel Willis and Hannah Parker Willis. Her father was a strict Calvinist deacon and founder and editor of *The Recorder,* the nation's first religious paper. Fern attended Catharine Beecher's Female Seminary in Hartford, Connecticut. She married Charles "Handsome Charlie" Harrington Eldredge on May 4, 1837. Her daughter Mary was born in 1838, followed by Grace in 1841, and Ellen in 1844. Until 1846, when she was thirty-five years old, she led the conventional life of a privileged white middle-class woman.

A series of personal tragedies activated Sara Willis's voice as a periodical writer and led to the gender flexibility of Fanny Fern. First, her younger sister, Ellen, died of childbirth complications in February 1844. Soon after in March 1844 her mother died. A year later, in March 1845, her oldest daughter, Mary, died. These family deaths devastated Willis and significantly depleted her female community. It was, however, her husband's sudden death in 1846 that collapsed her domestic and economic security. Prior to his death Charles Eldredge had invested heavily in a risky business venture and had subsequently lost a related lawsuit. After he died, his creditors claimed his assets, leaving Willis virtually destitute. Her father (who had remarried after her mother's death) and her in-laws broke with established custom by refusing to provide financial support to Willis and her surviving daughters.[4]

In the absence of a male provider and family support, Willis initially worked within limited economic scripts available to a woman of her race and class status. She tried unsuccessfully to obtain a position as a schoolteacher. She attempted to earn money by sewing but could not make enough to support her children. In 1849, having exhausted other avenues and at her father's urging, she agreed to what turned out to be a disastrous second marriage. After two years she created a scandal by separating from her abusive husband; they were divorced two years later. Forced by poverty to grant custody of one of her daughters to her former in-laws (i.e., Charles Eldredge's parents), Willis, finally and desperately, began writing for periodicals. She appealed to her brother, well-known poet and editor Nathaniel Parker Willis, for help in publishing her writings. His curt refusal and criticism strengthened her resolve to succeed as a writer.

Willis's first periodical writings were published anonymously, but she soon began to use the pseudonym Fanny Fern. Over time her pieces were published in various periodicals and became increasingly popular: "Seventy thousand copies of her first book, *Fern Leaves from Fanny's Portfolio* (1853)," a collection of her periodical writings, "sold in America within a year of its publication, and another twenty nine thousand copies sold in England, making *Fern Leaves* one of America's first bestsellers" (Temple 131). A lucrative contact to write a novel resulted in the thinly veiled autobiographical text, *Ruth Hall* (1854), "Fern's second book, [which] sold equally well" (131). Upon publication of *Ruth Hall*, an angry editor who had lost the rights to publish Fern's periodical writings vindictively revealed her identity.[5] Rather than damaging her career, the sensationalistic exposure of her identity increased Fern's book sales and popularity. In 1855 Fern signed an exclusive contract with Robert Bonner's weekly paper, the *New York Ledger.* In 1856 she married biographer James Parton. For the rest of her life she continued to be a famous, very financially successful, prolific writer.[6]

Willis's gender-specific attempts at economic survival—family support, remarriage, teaching, sewing—had failed to provide her with more than, at best, a meager financial income. They had succeeded, however, in exposing her directly to class-inflected anxieties of women's restricted economic opportunities.[7] Had Charles Eldredge lived and prospered, Willis would have been much less likely to experience the harsh realities that often menaced the untethered middle-class woman. Alison Easton identifies prevailing assumptions that would have attended the widowed Willis's search for paid employment: "To work for money was to advertise one's lack of a male protector, without whom (such was deemed the threat of masculine sexuality) the female would only with difficulty remain 'pure'" (221). Willis was ultimately able to escape such gendered dangers as a result of the phenomenal literary success of Fanny Fern. However, having been sensitized to the complicated anxieties and perils with which the woman wage worker contended, she never forgot them and, it could be argued, never fully recovered from her experience of them.[8] Berlant observes that for the rest of Willis's life, Willis associated "her writing with other more typical women's work: that of housewives, seamstresses, prostitutes" ("The Female Woman" 431). I would add that Willis's continued alignment of her writing with more conventional women's work underscores the psychological trauma of gendered vulnerabilities associated with that work. Willis's literary success provided significant protection from the more material vulnerabilities such as sexually transmitted diseases, residence in tenement housing with its accompanying dangers, and physical threats faced by solitary working women at work and on the streets.

However, Willis's lifelong alignment of her writing with more conventional women's work also evokes the emotional resonance of her past terrifying experiences as a widowed, financially needy mother. When Willis had occupied that position, the middle-class white woman's cultural scripts she had initially turned to relied on customary aid for distressed women. Such charity was not legally codified, but to a significant degree it was culturally expected. After the failures of these class-specific female assistance models, Willis notably modified her negotiation of dominant cultural gender constructions by rejecting (failed) conventional avenues of assistance; she instead began to access the independent and androgynous. When known as a poor widowed mother, Willis was at best an object of charity. "Fanny Fern," perhaps male, perhaps female, was popular where Willis was shunned, and she was sometimes viewed as masculine where Willis was always viewed as feminine.[9] Through Fern, Willis gained entry to masculine agency and the opportunity to intervene in gendered and economic limitations.

Early success of Fern's writing for periodicals emerged partially from the popular growth in the mid-nineteenth-century United States of regularly published literary papers. These papers, published on daily or weekly schedules, resembled newspapers in appearance. Increasing literacy rates, growing urban populations, and national transformation of publishing technology had potently mixed to create a growing, lucrative market for periodical publication.[10] For example, as David Reynolds has detailed, U.S. newspaper publication increased from 200 newspapers in 1800 to 2,526 newspapers by 1850 (46). Correspondingly, as Mary Kelley has recently written, "By 1840, there were 1,500 periodicals in circulation. During the ensuing decade, the innovation of the penny press and the publication of weeklies prepared the ground for the emergence of weekly newspapers that contained little other than fiction" (*Learning to Stand* 58). The resulting greatly expanded readership prompted significant shifts in previously genteel agreements among periodical publishers and editors. Competition, often fierce, for readers and writers unsettled what had been the kinder, gentler world of male-dominated publishing.[11]

Kelley valuably summarizes the gendered aspect of the evolution of mid-nineteenth century U.S. periodical publishing:

> Women played an equally important role in the emergence and development of America's periodicals. Beginning in the last decade of the eighteenth century, the number of periodicals published in the United States increased sharply. This was also the decade in which periodicals dedicated to women's patronage entered the literary marketplace. (*Learning to Stand* 57)

A byproduct of these varied changes in periodical publishing was the assumption that female writers would attract female readers and so add to a periodical's popularity and circulation numbers. This assumption provided women writers with unprecedented access to periodical publication "within a burgeoning women's culture industry" (Berlant, "The Female Woman" 441).[12] Like Willis, other white middle-class women also discovered a desire to earn a regular income by writing for publication. As women's periodical writing was increasingly published, these writings provided additional models for other women to aspire to and to emulate. Berlant's recognition of women's desire to engage "the contested conditions of public enunciation under which Fern and many of her sister writers labored and profited" (429) identifies the attractions of public voice as well as of paid employment. For economic reasons as well as for less-material incentives, middle-class white women were drawn to respond to gendered cultural scripts expected by typically male periodical publishers and editors. Their resulting writings reshaped contours of nineteenth-century U.S. periodical writing. They created an accepted, highly visible public place for women writers, a place that has been sustained throughout the twentieth and into the twenty-first century in the United States.

Periodical writing served as a particularly appropriate site for Willis's literary sensibilities. Its required length allowed for brief commentary without extensive research or writing. Its regular publication invited immediate response to current topics. And periodical publication encouraged cultivation of a recognizable voice to expand a periodical's readership in a time of highly competitive circulations. Gale Temple's close analysis of Fern's skill at attracting readers individually and as a group asserts that "Fern successfully mines each individual reader's sense of being misunderstood and thwarted in her individuality, and Fern's popularity results from her ability to isolate and appeal to those individuals as a 'mass,' as a consumer group" (146). I would add that Fern's ability to appeal to a wide range of readers was importantly supplemented by the then-common practice of publishers freely reprinting work that had been initially published in other papers. Homestead details the practice of "newspapers routinely appropriat[ing] American-authored works first printed in other American newspapers or magazines," describing how editors "with scissors in hand . . . would review copies of the exchange papers and select items for inclusion in his (or, more rarely, her) own, giving the typesetters clippings from other papers from which to set type" (155). This practice resulted in the progression of Fern's early periodical writings from their initial publication in the Boston papers the *Olive Branch* and the *True Flag* to their "quickly mov[ing] beyond this localized audience through the mechanism of reprinting, finding their way into other weekly papers . . . and daily newspapers across the country" (Homestead 155).

While neither Willis nor her editors received monetary payment for such reprintings, both indirectly benefited from the increased popularity that resulted from national dissemination of Fern's name and writing. As Homestead writes:

> Although the circulation of the *True Flag* and the *Olive Branch* was largely local, they clearly saw the exchange system and Fern's wide reprinting as opportunities to attempt to build their subscription lists. As part of an informal quid pro quo, editors who copied from exchange papers were expected to "puff" the papers from which they copied and to publish information on how to subscribe to them. (158)

As a result of the familiarity of Fern's voice to readers, Willis was able to repeatedly increase the amount of money she was paid for her writing. In 1855, Robert Bonner, owner and editor of the popular *New York Ledger*, hired Willis at an unprecedented $100 per column to write exclusively for his paper. He then "paid $2,000 for a full page advertisement in the [rival] *New York Herald*" (McGinnis 6). That advertisement featured just one sentence printed repeatedly down the entire page: "Fanny Fern writes only for the *Ledger*." Bonner made it plain that Fern's voice was now exclusive to readers of his *New York Ledger*. That is, though the *New York Ledger* had registered copyrights of Fern's works (as had the *Musical World and Times,* but not, however, the *Olive Branch* and *True Flag*),

> the benefit to be gained from publishing Fern's sketches was the association of Fern's name with the name of the paper as an "original contributor." Copyright or no copyright, none of them [the various editors] expected or even desired that Fern's sketches appear "exclusively" in their papers, instead seeking the widest possible reprinting of her sketches through exchange. (Homestead 162–63)

Bonner also shrewdly publicized Fern's salary to his readership, reinforcing the emotional and monetary significance of that well-known female voice.[13] Readers responded to this promotion, "for years . . . mobb[ing] the offices of the *Ledger* on the day the paper came out, eager to be the first to see what Fanny Fern had to say" (Warren, Introduction xxxi). Such marketing strategies were (successfully) intended to cultivate connections between Fern and the *New York Ledger*'s readers in order to increase circulation numbers. Nicole Tonkovich's detailing of the intersection of the woman writer's public identity and public voice reads "the 'author's' name . . . [as] a trademark that guarantees a particular product and in the process marks itself as suitable for a particular reading constituency" (57). I would add that on another, less visibly commercial level, these tactics also served to develop an enduring relationship concerning (self-) representation between Fern and periodical readers. A primary component of this relationship was the pliable female self readers came to expect from Fern, one who in the elasticity that defined her provided a model for women's endurance of cultural norms.

III.

Fanny Fern's direct, engaging, polemical writing voice was immediately recognizable to nineteenth-century U.S. readers. Indeed, even today, reading through copies of the *New York Ledger,* one finds Fern's writing to be readily identifiable well before reaching her name at the end of a column. Fern's familiar voice enabled her to put pressure on and to expand certain conventional generic boundaries of periodical writing. Readers' recognition of Fern's voice and their desire to read more of what she had to say allowed Fern to discuss an extensive range of often transgressive subjects in her periodical writing. Robert Bonner, publisher of the *New York Ledger,* encouraged Fern's often outspoken stance and made it a policy never to edit or to condense her writing (Warren, "Uncommon Discourse" 64).[14] Because readers typically privileged Fern's voice over her subject matter, Fern was to a degree authorized by readers to consider and write on topics that extended beyond those viewed as appropriate for women writers. In early columns, for instance, Fern variously promoted rights of women and children ("All's Well"), criticized social hypocrisy ("Summer Friends, or 'Will is Might'"), and constructed multiple narratives of identity ("What Mrs. Smith Said"). Such subjects, in addition to being disruptive choices for a writer who might be female, worked to intensify reader interest in Fern's sex-gender identity.

Public attention to and questioning of Fern's identity encouraged Willis's investigations of female representation in her periodical writing. In Sidonie Smith's observation, in women's autobiography the process of "self-interpretation emerges rhetorically from the autobiographer's engagement with fictive stories of selfhood" (*Poetics* 47). Correspondingly, I argue that in women's periodical writing the process of self-representation emerges rhetorically from the woman writer's engagement with fictive stories of female selfhood. The autobiographer's collaboration, then, is between the created self and the constructed, imagined culture. For Willis the construction is between her multiple voices and her real and imagined readers. Fern consistently rejects the false notion of unitary female selfhood in favor of female elasticity.

For instance, in "Self-Conquest" (28 Feb. 1851, *Olive Branch*), Emma is simultaneously a happy bride, "a pretty young thing," a loving daughter, a nervous daughter-in-law subordinate to an oppressive mother-in-law, and an unruly woman admiringly viewed by her husband as "struggling with trial, day by day, suffering, enduring, gaining the victory over her own spirit, silently and uncomplainingly." Tensions among Emma's various selves are temporarily muted by her submission and then somewhat more permanently relieved by the purchase of a house distant from her mother-in-law. Similarly, in "The Invalid Wife" (16 Oct. 1852, *Olive Branch*), an unnamed woman is concurrently a wife, a female physically recovering from the birth of her ninth child, a mother, and a patient rendered helpless by an authoritative female nurse. The temporarily bedridden woman longs to assert her desires over the nurse's orders; unable to do so, she cries privately in frustration, enduring her situation until she regains or—in this open-ended piece—fails to regain her health.

Such scripts for representation of multiple female selves are extended in "Dark Days" (4 Dec. 1852, *Olive Branch*) where Janie Grey is a widow, prey to unscrupulous men, and a mother too poor to pay for the heat that would save her child's life. Again a woman inhabits multiple scripts, and again it is only her ability to flexibly inhabit these roles that allows her at least temporary survival. That survival is unflinchingly stark—her husband has died despairing that she will be dangerously vulnerable without him, and she has been helpless to prevent her child's death. Janie Grey continues to exist, for the moment, but her future is ominous. In all three of these early periodical pieces—"Self-Conquest," "The Invalid Wife," and "Dark Days"—Fern's women simultaneously inhabit multiple roles: none is a coherent female self. Indeed, the employment of manifold representations works to keep any one representation of a self destabilized. Constructions of these pliable multi-selved women contribute to the flexibility of Fanny Fern's own identity—she may be any or all of these roles—and to her taxonomy of female representations.

Just as Fern's representations of a female self are elastic, so too is the language of her early periodical pieces, which extends from the sentimental to the satirical. For instance, pathos dominates the child's speech that begins "Thanksgiving Story" (20 Nov. 1852, *Musical World and Times*): "'Mary!' said the younger of two little girls, as they nestled under a coarse coverlid, one cold night in December, 'tell me about Thanksgiving-day before papa went to heaven. I'm cold and hungry, and I can't go to sleep.'" The children speak quietly but are overheard by their mother who weeps onto "the coarse garment, upon which she had toiled since sunrise." This scenario corresponds with construction of the woman writer as a mother compelled by harsh economic circumstances to begin writing after her husband's death in order to feed her children. As such, it invokes a female script readily recognized by nineteenth-century U.S. readers: the domestic, delicate woman whose maternal feelings force her—as nothing else could—to violate middle-class strictures by revealing herself publicly. The piece's beginning activates readers' constructions of femininity regarding the woman writer. As Alison M. J. Easton argues, it also reflects that Willis "knew from personal experience the fragility of that middle-class life and understood it as a construction" (223). In contrast to her more satirical writings, Fern's voice in her sentimental writings often reflects self-consciousness regarding assertions of conventional femininity. Having violated cultural norms, a woman may find that unexamined reinscription into these norms is impossible.

Months earlier, "Hints to Young Wives" opened with "Shouldn't I like to make a bon-fire of all the 'Hints to Young Wives,' 'Married Woman's Friend,' etc., and throw in the authors after them?" (14 Feb. 1852, *Olive Branch*). In this piece Fern's beginning disparages texts and authors that appear to promote some of the same narratives she herself cultivates in her sentimental periodical writings. However, Fern quickly moves beyond titles to focus on social conditioning performed by these texts. She describes her "little neighbor who believes all they tell her is gospel truth" and so rushes to greet her husband "the minute she sees [him] coming up the street . . . as if she hadn't another minute to live." Fern compares the young woman's frenzied attentions to her husband to those of "a cat in a fit" and with brusque sympathy calls her a "poor little innocent fool!" whose excessive devotion results in her husband's contempt for her. Fern ends with an anecdote in which her younger self, mending her husband's coat, found in the pocket a

> *love-letter from him to my dress-maker!!* I dropped the coat, I dropped the work-basket, I dropped the buttons, I dropped the baby (it was a *female*, and I thought it just as well to put her out of future misery) and then I hopped up into a chair in front of the looking-glass, and remarked to the young woman I saw there, "F-a-n-n-y F-e-r-n! if you—are—ever—such—a—confounded fool again"—and I wasn't.

From the first sentence to the last, this brief periodical piece inscribes a female community (the young neighbor, Fern's younger self, her infant daughter, her female readers, and by extension all women) inevitably vulnerable to received notions of female self-sacrifice. When Fern's younger self "hopped up into a chair in front of the looking-glass" to address her image, she rejected such subservience and literally and figuratively stood to recognize and to educate herself. Fern portrays zealous female marital devotion as destructive self-denial that soon results in male contempt, disloyalty, and disrespect. The essay serves as a cautionary lesson for women, one illustrating dangers of entering marriage ardently ready to sacrifice the self.

Other early periodical writings by Fern cultivate similar stances. For instance, "Everybody's Vacation Except Editors" (14 Aug. 1852, *Olive Branch*) and "The Tear of a Wife" (28 Aug. 1852, *Olive Branch*) feature a sarcastic woman writer deriding the unacknowledged privilege of (male) editors and of husbands. "Everybody's Vacation Except Editors" is fronted with the unattributed quotation, "Everybody is having a vacation except editors." Fern then assertively begins the piece with "I should like to have the editor who wrote that, look me in the face, answer the following 'catechize,' and then dare whine after that fashion!" The subsequent catechism itemizes perquisites and special attentions an editor receives, such as invitations to "railroad celebrations, water excursions, balloon ascensions, anti-slavery fights"; tickets to "circuses, concerts, and theatres"; fruit ("pears and nectarines, strawberries, grapes, peaches and melons"); pies and slices of wedding cake; enough free books for "a magnificent library"; flattery from "all the big and lesser literary lights, male and female, constantly revolving round him"; and "pretty bouquets when he is sick from his lady contributors." The privilege accorded the male editor is measured here in material goods and sycophantic attention presented to him at no monetary cost. Within the essay's default codes of patriarchy and capitalism, to receive goods free of charge marks one's (male) status. Just as husbands in "Hints to Young Wives" devalue the marital devotion they do nothing to earn, so here male editors similarly devalue goods they do nothing to earn and discontentedly remark solely on what they do not receive (a vacation). Only Fanny Fern, by implication doubly devalued as a woman not a man and as a writer not an editor (i.e., a member of labor rather than management), recognizes, itemizes, and protests such unequal treatment.

"The Tear of a Wife" serves as the site of yet another facet of assumptive male privilege. The piece opens with the unattributed quotation, "The tear of a loving girl is like a dew-drop on a rose; but on the cheek of a wife, is a drop of poison to her husband." The essay begins by addressing new brides, sarcastically cautioning that "whether you have anything to smile at or not; one thing is settled—you must not cry! Never mind back-aches, and side-aches, and head-aches, and dropsical complaints, and smoky chimneys, and old coats, and young babies! Smile! It flatters your husband." Fern's quick list sketches the conditions of these women's lives and recognizes the degree of false cheer required for them to ignore such realities. She then shifts her address to the portrait of an ungrateful, weeping young wife implied by the essay's opening quotation:

> Besides, you miserable little whimperer! What have you to cry for? A-i-n-t y-o-u m-a-r-r-i-e-d? Isn't that the *summum bonum,*—the height of feminine ambition? You can't get beyond that! It is the jumping-off place! You've arriv!—got to the end of your journey! Stage puts up there! You have nothing to do but retire on your laurels, and spend the rest of your life endeavoring to be thankful that you are Mrs. John Smith! "Smile!" you simpleton!

Fern's precise critical reading of the quotation uncovers the absolute rejection of any self demanded by the movement from "loving girl" to "wife." A sign of a self as slight as one tear—prior to marriage prosaically read as "a dew-drop on a rose"—is, postmarriage, no less than a toxic reproach to a husband. Months earlier in her "Hints to Young Wives," Fern argued that such wifely subsuming of self leads to a husband's disrespect. Here Fern goes further, savagely mocking the proscription that with marriage a woman has "got to the end of [her] journey"—that is, that a wife exchanges whatever limited selfhood she may have been perceived as having for the single, subordinate identity of her husband's grateful wife.

Within such acerbic pieces from her early periodical writing, Fern frequently returns to falsely romanticized notions of marriage. In "A Whisper to Romantic Young Ladies" (12 June 1852, *True Flag*), Fern enlightens unmarried young women who trust the portrayal of marriage that they read in romance novels. Fern tells them that after marriage if a husband "*smile*[s] on anything short of a 'sirloin' or a roast turkey, you are a lucky woman." After deriding ways that romance novels leave out wearisome realities of middle-class domestic life, Fern cautions, "But this humdrum life, girls, is another affair, with its washing and ironing and cleaning days, when children expect boxed ears, and visitors picked-up dinners. All the 'romance' there is in it, you can put under a three-cent piece!" (qtd. in Warren, *Fanny Fern* 296). In all four early periodical pieces—"Hints to Young Wives," "Everybody's Vacation Except Editors," "The Tear of a Wife," and "A Whisper to Romantic Young Ladies"—Fern employs sarcastic language and an exasperated tone of lived experience. Elizabethada Wright argues that in such essays "Fern's irony is particularly difficult to read" largely due to Fern's "provid[ing] nudges and winks everywhere in her work; thus everything would seem to be ironic" (102). Indeed, in such columns Fern's use of irony is extravagant and even omnipresent. Fern ironizes in her early periodical writing in the service of provoking young women to recognize and comprehend restrictive realities of socially sanctioned positions typically assigned to women.

The thread of multiple and elastic female representations running throughout Fern's early periodical writings is foregrounded in a series of essays published in the *Olive Branch* with "model" in the title, including "The Model Beau," "The Model Lady," and "The Model Grandmamma," among other "models"—female and male, positive and negative. For instance, the woman in "The Model Widow" and the man in "The Model Widower" (both 26 June 1851, *Olive Branch*) are each callous, vain, inattentive parents fixated on remarrying quickly. The woman in "The Model Step-Mother" (7 Aug. 1852, *Olive Branch*), however, is loving, caring, selfless, and vilified, particularly by other women. Each essay provides a separate female model for women readers to either emulate or reject. Taken together, the model essays form a guidebook of recommended (sometimes by negative example) pliable female scripts in nineteenth-century U.S. culture. That Fern continued the model series of essays over a period of months suggests their resonance and popularity with gendered assumptions of her audience.

These representations throughout the early periodical writings sustain an ongoing narrative between Fern and her readers. Willis regularly confronts cultural representations of women in her early periodical columns, at various moments evaluating, rejecting, embracing, and sympathizing with them. At the same time, these representations enable Willis to portray the woman periodical writer's own multiple narratives of selfhood.

The success of Fanny Fern's self-representations figures in the response of a Salem woman who wrote to the *Olive Branch* "that she did not care about Fern's identity: 'I know what you are to *me* . . . a kind, loving sister, with a flashing smile that breaks through the drolleries, making me long to shake hands with you'" (28 Aug. 1852; Warren, *Fanny Fern* 100). Fern's unwavering refusal to provide one unified self for her audience authorizes readers to "know" Fern in accordance with their own beliefs and desires. As Berlant writes, "By providing a formal structure of identification through the example of her own 'personal journalism,' the expression of Fern's personality becomes the model for that kind of individuated expression she aims to enable the reader to imagine in herself" ("The Female Woman" 445).

An 1853 editorial in the *Olive Branch* trivialized gendered speculations that circulated around Fern's early periodical writing:

> It makes not one iota of difference whether Fanny Fern is a *he* or a *she*, it cannot be denied that she (we call her *she* in virtue of her *nom de plume*,) has written some of the most beautiful fragments and "prose poems" in her piquant off-hand style, to be found in the English language, to say nothing of the dashes of genuine humor which some of them contain. Crusty, crabbed and sour anatomical specimens of editors may say what they please, Fanny Fern is, and will continue a popular writer, for she writes from the *heart,* and it will reach the hearts of those who read. (5 Mar. 1853)

By 1853 Fern's various positionings of a self in relation to nineteenth-century U.S. social arrangements worked to refigure gendered restrictions regarding her writing. Fern's early periodical writings opened a cultural space for Fern and for every female reader to envision herself as a person as well as a woman, a mother, and a writer. The editorial proclaiming that "it makes not one iota of difference whether Fanny Fern is a *he* or a *she*" refers directly to Fern but at the same time speaks indirectly about/to all women when it privileges an emotive "heart" over sex-gender identity. In addition, the fictive stories of female selfhood that Willis employs, as well as the gender flexibility of her writing, work to aid her in investigations of the woman writer's voice. In Miller's precise observation, "female autobiographers know that they are being read as *women*" ("Women's Autobiography" 262). Correspondingly, I argue that Willis knows that readers desire to read Fanny Fern as a woman. Her rhetorical acknowledgment of "the fact of her femininity as a social reality" ("Women's Autobiography" 263) is initiated with her invention of the feminine yet ironic name Fanny Fern.

Willis publicly constructs Fanny Fern as multiple, destabilizing any one self-representation of Fern; each representation is then incorporated as a possible aspect of Fern's self. For instance, Willis mixes her early periodical publications with notions of the middle-class family when she writes about articles that have been falsely published under her name: "'Never wrote one line of the above-named articles, which are traveling round the country, with a host of others like them. The way that *illegitimate Ferns* are smuggled into *my well-regulated family*, while *my own mental children* are kidnapped and baptized by aliens, is very curious to witness'" (23 April 1853, *True Flag;* italics mine). Willis constructs Fern as an attentive mother ("well-regulated family") and her columns as her offspring ("my own mental children"). Writings falsely attributed to Fern are presented as aspects of a self and as children who are born out of wedlock ("illegitimate Ferns"). Columns of Fern's that have been pirated and assigned to other authors are portrayed as permanently abducted children ("my own mental children are kidnapped and baptized by aliens"). Individually and collectively, all personae in this dizzying familial mix of a mother and her variously legitimate, illegitimate, and abducted children constitute "Fanny Fern." Appropriately, no father—as persona, metaphor, patriarchal agent, or anything else—is listed as a member of this "family" or as part of "Fanny Fern."

A few months later in the *Musical World and Times,* Fern writes of encountering a boy selling copies of her essay collection *Fern Leaves from Fanny's Portfolio.* He "assured me it was '*the* book of the season—forty thousand already sold!—presses running night and day, but the demand not supplied,' etc., etc.

> "Who wrote it?" I asked.
> "Fanny Fern," the boy replied.
> "Who is she?" said I.
> "Don't know," said the peripatetic little bookseller. "She's first this person, and then that: now a man, and then a woman; somebody says she's everybody, and everybody says she's *some.*" (13 Aug. 1853)

Fern's strategic use of a young boy (a "peripatetic little bookseller"), one of the lowest and youngest laborers in the market economy, enables her to illustrate how common awareness of her provocative ambiguity has become. Her popularity is such that "'everybody says she's *some.*'" That Fern herself (as always, incognito) is able to question the boy regarding authorship of her own book without his realizing who she is further underscores the ambiguity of her identity. Readers who have imagined a "real" Fern stage-managing fictive personae to suit her needs are again confronted with Fern's ambiguous multiple selves.

Fern's early periodical writings repeatedly render a single "true" self-representation impossible, often in response to readers' conjectures regarding Fern's identity. Just as authenticity of Sarah Kemble Knight's *Journal* was questioned for years after its 1825 publication, so Fern's identity was repeatedly contested. For example, a reader wrote an inquiry in verse to the *Olive Branch* (10 Apr. 1852) that began:

> Oh mirth-provoking Fanny,
> Pray tell me if you will,
> What sort of being you really are,
> And whether a Jack or a Jill.

The reader's desire to know "what sort of being you really are" implies a single answer to that question if only Fern will choose to provide it. But for Willis, female identity must be multiple. To promote a unified female self is not only false but also dangerous. Confronted with the culture's gendered demands, white middle-class women are forced in self-defense to perform the multiple and pliable. Willis's rhetorical insistence on the necessity of a performative female identity signifies her view of female identity in general as well as her perception of her own identity. Though many women will fail to successfully navigate the larger culture, for Willis an elasticity of representation is crucial for even the chance to survive. Willis's constructions of Fanny Fern in her early periodical writing serve as her workshop for arguing, cajoling, considering, lecturing, and testing on the subject of female identity as well as on the subject of her own identity.

An editorial (28 May 1853) in *The Musical World and Times* joined the national conversation regarding gendered complications signaled by Fern's voice. (In another Fern-related layering of identity and anonymity, *The Musical World and Times* was then edited by Willis's brother, Richard Storrs Willis. Though Storrs Willis had not initially known that his sister was "Fanny Fern," he had learned of her identity by this point.) The editorial defended Fern against those who argued that "the writer of such searching, forcible, and, withal, common-sense articles as sometimes came from the unknown pen, must be a man;—the public being unwilling to give femininity credit for the power and courage necessary for their production" (Warren, *Fanny Fern* 101). The editorial's rendering of "power and courage" as qualities readily available to both women and men points to the gendered work that had already been accomplished by Fern's early periodical writing. In this editorial, public discussion of Fern's identity served as the occasion for considerations of what was and what was not definitionally female and male.

Nineteenth-century U.S. advertising campaigns for Fern's writing collections and novels (*Ruth Hall, Rose Clark*) later capitalized on the multiplicity of representations active in Fern's early periodical writing.[15]

Ranney's, a New York bookstore, used an advertisement titled "Fanny Fern Blown Up But No Bones Broken" in *Harper's Weekly* (27 Feb. 1858):

> People start in great amaze,
> From their eyes they wildly gaze,
> Crying as they hurry past,
> "Fanny Fern is gone at last!"
> Keep cool, people—'tis not so—
> Fanny Fern is still the go [*sic*].
> 'Twas a Fanny Fern afloat,
> Name bestowed upon a boat.
> Read the choicest works of Fanny
> Get a book and gift from Ranney. (McGinnis 20)

Indeed, as Fern's iconic cultural status evolved, a range of objects were named after her, including, among others, babies, cigars, an opera libretto, perfume, a steamboat, and a train car. The mix of things named for Fern was as wide and as various as her audience had become. Given that diverse audience, objects named after Fern benefited by being perceived as at least potentially more desirable. Fern's name was assigned to marketable commodities in order to attract the purchasing attention of the many consumers familiar with her name, writing, and popularity. Babies named after Fern received her name as well as the popular currency that her name carried. By their existence, such varied namesakes further extended Fern's many identities as well as her discourses of publicity and self-fashioning. I would argue that particularly in these early years of her literary popularity, Sara Willis was no more or no less a namesake of Fern's than, for example, the steamboat or the opera libretto. Indeed, in retrospect, it seems overdetermined that in 1856 Sara Parton would be forced to go to court to establish sole legal ownership of the name "Fanny Fern."

Early periodical writings reflect Willis's awareness of her readers' assumed scripts regarding white middle-class women in general and Fanny Fern in particular. At times the tone and subjects of her early periodical writing reinforce readers' gender expectations. At other times the tone and subjects evade or problematize those expectations. The shifting voice and topics of Fern's early periodical writing support Willis's suggested revisions of women's cultural narratives. Unlike the female autobiographer, the female periodical writer may repeatedly interpret and reinterpret the female voice. Willis's audience lends her authority to interpret the woman writer's role in nineteenth-century U.S. culture.

Consequently, a mutual, extended dialogue develops between writer and readers. Fern provokes, readers imagine, Fern responds, readers re-imagine. Fern and readers of her early periodical writing jointly attempt to navigate the complexities of female positioning. Within the single text of her *Journal,* Sarah Kemble Knight insisted repeatedly and contradictorily on her status as a conventional woman. Within the repeated texts of her early periodical writing, Fern insists on her status as an unconventional and ambiguous (wo)man.

Mutability is essential to Willis's construction of Fanny Fern. It marks her conviction that a performative female identity is crucial. Further, multiple roles that Willis assigns to Fern signify Willis's perception of her own identity. It is Willis's generic choice of periodical writing that enables her multiple and repeated representations of female identity. However, periodical writing forces Willis to recognize the dismaying truth of what is required for middle-class U.S. white women to survive. Were Willis writing a novel, for instance, the novel would provide generic space for development and resolution. Even if the resolution were to be falsely positive, Willis would still have had the therapeutic exercise of writing such a possibility. Instead, Willis's early periodical writing functions individually and collectively to compel her to comprehend the reality of women's negotiations of repressive culture. The regular publication of periodical writing is such that Willis cannot even momentarily elide the truths she rehearses.

Willis draws on a combination of fiction and autobiography for her early periodical writing. The next chapter in this study will show Louisa May Alcott also mixing the fictional and autobiographic in *Hospital Sketches.* Other nineteenth-century U.S. white female authors write nonfictional, almost realist accounts of their lives. This should not suggest that undue emphasis be placed on the constructed, permeable line between the fictional and the putatively nonfictional. However writers or readers may classify a text or parts of a text as fictional or "true," all women in this study engage degrees of autobiographical writing. In all cases, as Willis would have clearly recognized, women—in their lives, in their writing—had to practice an elasticity of self-constructions to survive.

IV.

Periodical writing served as a site for a woman writer to experiment with notions of a self without that self becoming perceived as an immutable subject position. The sometimes complex and coded intersection of gender and voice allowed for disclosure of a self without corresponding private exposure. In the mid-nineteenth-century United States, the meeting of gender and publication marks complicated and sometimes deeply desired divisions among women's various selves. Fern's voice in her early periodical writing revealed ambiguous body contours under her pseudonymous "veils." As I have argued, the scheduled, familiar discourse of the periodical piece and the fictive stories of selfhood imagined of Fern by readers engendered investigations and articulations of various representations of a female self.

Though my discussion in this chapter concerns Willis's early periodical writing, I wish to turn briefly to recent critical responses to *Ruth Hall*, which interestingly read the characterization of the novel's main character, Ruth/Floy, against multiple personae of Fern's early periodical writing. Homestead observes that the "multiplicity and instability of 'Fanny' as a print phenomenon" seen in the early periodical writing "is missing from Fern's fictionalization of that experience" in *Ruth Hall* (177). Likewise, Kristie Hamilton's close analysis of *Ruth Hall* maintains that by employing a single fictive persona in the book, Fern

> escaped the contemporary censure of being classed as a "political writer" by creating a character, Ruth Hall, who embodied at once middle-class, "feminine" respectability and American individualism, even as Ruth's consciousness and values were transformed by a growing recognition of the collective vulnerability and subjection of women. (89)

Homestead and Hamilton identify the character Ruth Hall as a single, somewhat coherent fictive persona adopted by Fern. Their readings point to Willis's rhetorical movement away from the multiple personae seen in her early periodical writing. Such curtailing of the multiple and varied to the singular and consistent is further discussed by Homestead, who argues that "Fern created that stable proprietary self [that is, of Ruth Hall] only after successfully exploiting a different mode of authorship and circulation in her early years writing for weekly periodicals" (153). Homestead sees the character of Ruth Hall representing "a new, more stable Fern who would author-ize future book and periodical manifestations" (153).[16] I agree with Homestead's reading and further suggest that Willis's approach to performative aspects of female identity insisted upon in her early periodical writing was recast as she wrote *Ruth Hall*. In the turn to the genre of the novel, Willis gained length and extended development. The range of female mutability enabled by briefer forms of periodical writing was to a degree displaced by portrayals of penalties assigned to women who had failed to adequately perform required aspects of female identity. Homestead recognizes this movement in her reading of the character of *Ruth Hall* as "a new, more stable Fern."

Correspondingly, Hamilton reads *Ruth Hall*

> as a record, critique, and partial analysis of the mechanisms by which bourgeois domestic ideology effected the in-group surveillance and policing that would ensure the continued identification of womanhood with certain narrowly defined activities and with a particular socioeconomic status. All women who fell, or were forced, outside these limits could be dismissed as deviant. (103–4)

Once in the genre of the novel, Willis used the length and development of the novel to extend her brief periodical discussions regarding the necessity of female mutability. Hamilton's reading of *Ruth Hall*'s notions of female deviance underscores what I argue is Willis's perception of her own identity as potentially fragile. That perception needs to be viewed through the experiential trajectory of Willis's adult life. In a sweep of death, tragedy, and grief, Willis had been changed from a complacent, economically secure wife and mother of three living children to a culturally stigmatized, poverty-stricken, widowed mother of two living children. Whatever Willis had accepted as secure about her family, husband, class status, and reputation was at best destabilized, at worst dismantled, within the space of months. The gendered deviance assigned to her, especially by other women, educated Willis regarding female fragility, particularly her own. The genre of the novel allowed Willis to write her way from requirements of female mutability seen in her early periodical writing to typically dire consequences for women who one way or another were deemed to have failed to perform well enough.

In autobiography, as Sidonie Smith observes, "there have always been women who cross the line between public and private utterance, unmasking their desire for the empowering self-interpretation of autobiography as they unmasked in their lives the desire for publicity" (*Poetics* 44). Nineteenth-century U.S. women's periodical pieces written across boundaries of female utterance configure this generic form as a means of self-interpretation. However, unlike the female autobiographer, the female periodical writer simultaneously unmasks and masks the self, repeatedly representing and revising a voice. Separation between the woman writer's public and private voice was not, as modification of the periodical piece by Willis and others suggests, arbitrary and binary, though nineteenth-century U.S. women writers may have felt it as such in their attempts to declare a consistent "I" in a repressive patriarchal culture. Rather, a spectrum of female self-representation occupied the space between public and private voice.

Fern's nineteenth-century U.S. women's early periodical writing allowed Willis to reveal herself through her writing and also to represent herself as a woman her culture wanted her to be. Michel Foucault's discussion of the confession's production of truth leads to an individual being "authenticated by the discourse of truth he was able or obliged to produce concerning himself" (58). Fern produced her confessions, her discourses of truth, to authenticate, transform, and disguise concepts of self and gender. For readers, in Berlant's reflection, "one woman's disclosure of the frustrations of everyday life ennobles the lives of other women: moreover, the complaint installs woman's writing as a part of an ongoing pedagogy about how to negotiate the contested life of femininity" ("The Female Woman" 445).

After Willis crossed generic boundaries to write *Ruth Hall* and *Rose Clark,* and after Fern's identity was revealed, Willis continued to write as Fanny Fern until days before she died. The lengthy *New York Ledger* editorial on her death, written by her long-time editor and friend Robert Bonner, reads in part:

> Who was Fanny Fern? began to be the question of the day. The secret of her identity was so well guarded that the most inquisitive could not get track of her and the myriad suppositions, guesses, announcements, denials and discussions which were published on the subject greatly enhanced the public interest. (9 Nov. 1872)

Having reprised the sensation regarding Fern's identity that had been activated by her early periodical writing, Bonner praises Fern's character, lists her book publications, and then, throughout the second half of the editorial, includes quotations from a range of personal notes Willis had written to him "during the many years of Fanny Fern's connection with the *Ledger.*" Rather than selecting from among Fern's periodical pieces, two novels, essay collections, or indeed any of her published writings, Bonner instead quotes from her personal correspondence to him.[17] The quotations drawn from Fern's notes to Bonner foreground her opinions regarding motherhood, charity, religion, and gratitude. Such subjects and Bonner's selection of Fern's remarks on them implicitly inscribe Fern as a conventional white middle-class woman. Though Bonner's editorial on Fern's death recalls the earlier furor over her gender, it also insists on construction of Fern as what Bonner, in the second sentence of the editorial, names "the embodiment of American womanhood." Bonner's editorial on Fern's death maintains the discourses of publicity and self-fashioning that Fern had begun to evoke early in her literary career. It is fitting that the editorial concludes not with Bonner's writing but with a quotation from Willis's writing in a 25 January 1870 note to Bonner signed, "Yours Fanny Fern."

Long after the anonymity and androgyny provided by her pseudonym and capitalized upon in her early periodical writings had collapsed—when Sara Willis (by then Parton) signed personal letters "Fanny Fern" and had sued for and won exclusive rights to the name—Parton continued to write as Fern.[18] Though the pseudonymous veil was now transparent, it still enabled her to write, to figure, and to refigure a self. Willis had initially discovered female agency and representation through her composition of Fern's early periodical writings. Ultimately, she modified the periodical writer's project for her personal project, using it to reflect and transform concepts of self, gender, and women's voice.

In the next chapter I continue my examination of women's autobiographic writing and female representation, turning more explicitly to constructions and explorations of sex-gender identity. Using Louisa May Alcott's early work *Hospital Sketches,* I consider intersections of form and gender that Alcott discovers in her work as a writer and as a nurse in a Civil War hospital. In a moment when Sarah Kemble Knight's *Journal* and Fanny Fern's periodical writings were in print and continued to provide un/conventional representations for and of women, the outbreak of the Civil War resulted in possibilities and opportunities for women in a changing nineteenth-century U.S. culture beyond what either Knight or Fern had imagined.

CHAPTER 3

"How Could You Leave Me Alone When the Room Was Full of Men!"

Gender and Self-Representation in Louisa May Alcott's *Hospital Sketches*

> [Civil War narratives feature] metaphoric transfer of civil war from an external, political realm to inner conflict over sexual choice and the proper gender roles.
>
> —Margaret R. Higonnet, "Civil Wars and Sexual Territories" (1989)

IN LOUISA MAY Alcott's *Hospital Sketches* (1863), a text that mixes the travel narrative, letters, and sketches based on her Civil War nursing experience, the hospital is a gendered location of voyeuristic observation: wounded male soldiers stare passively at female nurses who maternally bathe them and observe the weakened male body with little fear of sexual interpretation or interaction. The form of the hospital sketch freed Alcott—as the hospital itself freed the woman nurse—to handle male bodies and to have male/female physical contact without directly invoking male and female sexuality for herself or her nineteenth-century U.S. readership. The hospital sketch positioned the woman writer to consider culturally constructed, significantly desexualized notions of gender in ways prohibited by less clinical, and so potentially more sexualized, narrative forms. As the published author of a collection of children's tales (*Flower Fables* [1854]) and adult stories—her work had appeared in the *Atlantic*, the Boston *Commonwealth*, and the *Olive Branch*, among others—Alcott had consciously striven to learn literary strategies of successful writing in order to have her stories published, particularly in the *Atlantic*.[1] Though these rhetorical strategies valuably allowed experimentation with form and audience, they did not furnish a model for a woman writer to explore sociosexual complications of a woman nursing hospitalized men. Just as conventions for transporting food and treating the wounded required adaptation in wartime (Jones xix, xxi), so did literary conventions of more peaceful times.

As part of her pioneering work on Alcott, Madeleine B. Stern has shown that Alcott's writing in this period—*Hospital Sketches* was published the same year as the first of Alcott's pseudonymous gothic thrillers—was "especially productive for an author essaying a variety of genres" (*Critical Essays* 2). In my reading, Alcott's use of a pseudonym for those thrillers and her use of the hospital location in *Hospital Sketches* show her experimenting with gender and literary forms. In the thrillers Alcott, as the ungendered A. M. Barnard, could write about sex without anyone knowing it; in *Hospital Sketches* Alcott, by controlling representation of the hospital, could avoid writing about sex without anyone missing it. In both, the generic choice gave authority to write: a woman writer could anonymously invent gothic thrillers or relate a somewhat fictionalized account of her maternalistic nursing experiences without disrupting readers' comfortable view of her sociosexual status.

The first chapter of this study focuses on Sarah Kemble Knight's early-eighteenth-century *Journal*, its constructions of women's voice and domain, and the relation between the text's 1825 publication and other nineteenth-century U.S. women's texts. The second chapter employs Fanny Fern's early periodical writing to shed light on intersections of genre, reconfigurations of the (female) self, and establishment of a sustained relationship between Fern and readers. Knight's writing privately and Fern's writing anonymously allowed them at times to write transgressively. Alcott, whose authorship of gothic thrillers was undiscovered in her lifetime, wrote *Hospital Sketches* under her own name. Like Knight and Fern, Alcott wrote autobiographically and was aware of the choice to write privately or anonymously. But unlike Knight and Fern, in *Hospital Sketches* Alcott wrote publicly as—more or less—herself.

Alcott's generic choice of the hospital sketch and her use of a fictive persona in *Hospital Sketches* occur at the intersection of form, gender, and agency, a location familiar to other women writers in this study. For example, as discussed in chapter 2, Fern's pseudonymous writings combine the autobiographical and fictive for greater authority, even though readers' generic expectations of literary papers—where Fern's periodical writing typically appeared—might well have prompted them to read Fern's work as strictly nonfictional. The next chapter in this study, following this discussion of *Hospital Sketches*, examines S. Emma E. Edmonds's use of an often bewildering mix of the fictive and autobiographic, as well as Mary Livermore's and Annie Turner Wittenmyer's choices to write fairly straightforward nonfictional accounts of their war experiences. Such movement between the fictive and autobiographic in these women's Civil War reminiscences suggests choices made by female writers regarding how they wished to be heard and viewed by audiences. Extending previous chapters' examinations of women, self-writing, and nineteenth-century U.S. publication, and with attention to discussions conducted in subsequent chapters, in this chapter I investigate Alcott's uses of the fictive and autobiographical in her considerations of female (self-) representation and sex-gender identity.

Criticism of Alcott's works has noted her prolific literary output and use of a range of literary forms. Elaine Showalter calculates Alcott's output at "at least 270 works in every genre from poetry to tragedy" (Introduction x). Alcott's productivity and wide use of genres have been linked to the double-voicedness that feminist literary criticism has identified in women's writing. Discovery and subsequent publication of Alcott's anonymous sensational writing revealed Alcott's dual literary life and supported readings of her double-voicedness. The result has been that literary critics typically locate Alcott's sensational tales in one category and her works in other popular forms—children's books, domestic texts, fairy tales, historical essays, sentimental texts—in another (Cappello; Douglas; Showalter, Introduction). These binaries are tempting: how many readers of *Little Women* have read one of the anonymous gothic thrillers for the first time and thought that the secret, passionate voice must be Alcott's "real" voice?

I depart from such readings, however, in my belief that this categorization obscures generic contours of the body of Alcott's writings. Alcott's literary productions are too varied—and the narrative voice of works such as *Little Women, Eight Cousins, Rose in Bloom,* and other children's books too strong, despite Alcott's own ambivalence about these and other works—to be reduced to such uncomplicated binary categories. Alcott's extensive writings are, I think, less adequately contained by double-voicedness than by generic multivocality, a resistance to writing solely in any one style and a gift for writing across generic boundaries. Additionally, I see these movements across forms as enabling Alcott to portray a range of female representations.

Richard H. Brodhead, contextualizing Alcott's career, described her inclination toward generic multivocality as aided by her "com[ing] to her career at the time when literary boundaries were being socially organized," a moment when writers had "an array of literary possibilities and had several publics and several models of authorship equally available to them." A rise in publishing "outlets she personally had access to reflects, more generally, the proliferation of literary vehicles . . . that helped make literary writing a commercially viable career" (*Cultures of Letters* 106, 80, 77). Despite early use of these opportunities, Alcott later poignantly recognized family and cultural strictures regarding her writing: "To have had Mr. Emerson as an intellectual God all one's life is to be invested with a chain armour of propriety. . . . And what would my own good father think of me . . . if I set folks to doing the things I have a longing to see my people do?" (Madeline B. Stern, *Critical Essays* 42). Such remarks can be used to support readings of the anonymous voice of the gothic thrillers as the "true" voice, the one that could not be spoken by the Alcott constructed by her family, their Concord circle, and the many readers of her popular, signed works. I would add, however, that they also reflect Alcott's anxieties of publication and weary awareness of public expectations and scrutiny of her writing/self. Working in a range of genres expanded Alcott's possibilities for writing out fictive stories of selfhood.

Alcott's extensive choice of literary forms—available through her inclination and through literary circumstances of the time—allowed her to reveal, in a Foucauldian sense, more than she would in any single literary form.[2] Yet Alcott's mix of fiction and her own experiences as seen in *Hospital Sketches* also allowed her to elide (self-) examination of her sexuality. Alcott experimented with gender and form in order to privately write or publicly not write about male and female sexuality. Martha Saxton sees Alcott's nursing experience as deeply fearful, forcing her to "repress her terrors [of men] and be physically intimate with many males," trauma which led, during her recovery from illness, to hallucinations that revealed "hideous fears of rejection and violence" (257). Saxton relates an incident of Alcott's recovery when Alcott, delirious and momentarily left alone, crashed out of bed. When her sister May came to help her, Alcott berated her, yelling, "'How could you leave me alone when the room was full of men!'" (257).[3] Alcott's use of the hospital sketch permitted her to evade issues of sexuality, especially when the room was full of men. This intersection of gender and form freed Alcott to construct an alternative sex-gender identity for a white middle-class woman in the nineteenth-century United States.

Much has been written and conjectured about the ambiguous, contradictory constructions of sexual identity and gender in Alcott's life and writing.[4] Alcott herself complicates conjectures, having told Louise Chandler Moulton: "'I am more than half-persuaded that I am a man's soul, put by some freak of nature into a woman's body . . . because I have fallen in love in my life with so many pretty girls and never once the least bit with any man'" (49). In this 1882 interview Alcott seems to construct herself on the then-emerging Krafft-Ebing biological model of sexual orientation as an "invert," a woman whose body is occupied by a man's soul.[5] Such sexological models and studies would, as Joseph Bristow writes, eventually play "a major role in enabling sex to be debated more widely and seriously at all levels of society" (15). A crucial legitimacy would be provided by sexological studies that would later authorize public discussions of sex and sexuality. Alcott's remarks in 1882 imply a gender definition based on sexual attraction and suggest that her attempts to find a coherent gendered subject position were lifelong ("so many pretty girls" over the years) and persistent ("more than half-persuaded" by recent theories of sexual orientation). The maternal, chaste figure of Tribulation Periwinkle whom Alcott had scripted twenty years earlier in *Hospital Sketches* marks an early moment of Alcott's considerations of gender construction.

My discussion of Alcott's work in *Hospital Sketches* is followed by consideration in chapter 4 of other manifestations of U.S. female alternative sex-gender construction in women's Civil War writing. The chapter 4 discussion of S. Emma E. Edmonds's *Nurse and Spy in the Union Army* examines Edmonds's living and writing as "Frank Thompson" as a much more potentially disruptive alternative sex-gender identity of the kind that we see Alcott tentatively beginning to explore in *Hospital Sketches*. Further, chapter 4's subsequent examination of two other women's Civil War memoirs—Mary Livermore's *My Story of the War* and Annie Turner Wittenmyer's *Under the Guns: A Woman's Reminiscences of the Civil War*—unpacks wartime observations of self-defined conventional women as they represented and responded to less conventional women who cross-dressed as male soldiers. Taken together, these texts situate the U.S. Civil War as, among other things, a cultural workshop for experimenting with and writing about female cross-dressing. Alcott's work in *Hospital Sketches* serves as a preliminary stage of this exploration.

I.

I never began the year in a stranger place than this . . . leading a life of constant excitement in this greathouse surrounded by 3 or 4 hundred men in all stages of suffering, disease & death.

—Louisa May Alcott, January 1863 journal entry

Sections of *Hospital Sketches* that draw on the travel narrative reflect Alcott's familiarity with and revisions of literary conventions of the female traveler role. As Mary Suzanne Schriber writes in her study of women's travel, "[t]ravel mattered in nineteenth-century America for both men and women, but it mattered particularly for women and their observers because of gender" (45). With few exceptions, antebellum women's travel narratives characteristically had partaken of then-current discourses for treating gender by "present[ing] the narrator as feminine" and using "lengthy descriptions of the domestic" (Mills 4). Such narratives also typically marked the female traveler as eschewing unconventional experiences. The antebellum U.S. woman's narrative of travel in Europe and the Near East focused on well-known historical sites. Nina Baym observes that these narratives privileged the familiar and avoided "experiences nobody had ever had before" in favor of "see[ing] what others had seen, know[ing] what others had known, feel[ing] what others had felt" (*American Women Writers* 132).

Alcott's construction of the train and steamboat journey of Tribulation Periwinkle, her fictive persona in *Hospital Sketches,* to Washington, DC, furnishes an informative contrast to Sarah Kemble Knight's travel narrative. Separated by over 150 years, Knight and Alcott are nonetheless linked by their ability and inclination to write about their journeys on the way to then-uncommon experiences for women. Differences in cultural and geographical travel conditions of the eastern United States (or for Knight what will become the United States), between the eighteenth and nineteenth centuries emerge starkly in a comparison of Knight's and Alcott's descriptions. For example, Knight's narrative of her trip involves more danger and autonomy than does Alcott's construction of Trib's travels. In Knight's portrayals of her bargaining to hire a guide, traveling alone or as the only woman among male travelers, and journeying through the wild, we see the travel conditions available at the time to a white woman of some economic means and class status. Knight's descriptions of other travelers (as opposed to people living in places through which she passes) appear fairly infrequently because the New England landscape had not yet been subjugated to provide for regular middle-class travel. Indeed, Knight's journeying via postal routes points to the somewhat more established travel of mail than of people at that time. As I argue in the first chapter, women and men who observed Knight on her journey had limited means for understanding how to correctly classify a white woman of some identifiable status who traveled alone. For their understanding and also for her own self-understanding, Knight had to classify herself for them, in her behavior and in the pages of her *Journal.*

Over a century and a half after Knight's travels, Alcott began her own journey at a time when travel for white women had become both more common and more restrictive. Alcott's construction of Trib's behavior on her journey, as well as the way Alcott wrote about that journey, emerges from strictures that then implicitly governed female travel. Compared to Knight's eighteenth-century trip, Trib's journey reflected significantly improved travel conditions in the nineteenth-century United States as well as—despite increased travel restrictions—greater acceptance of white women's travel. Trib's journey by train and steamboat did not take her into the wilderness or along routes designated more for mail than for people. Nor is Trib mistaken for a prostitute. However, the range of behavioral possibilities available to Alcott in her writing about Trib's journey was, perhaps ironically, much more limited than those available to Knight as she wrote about her own trip. Unlike Knight, Alcott had to fit Trib's behavior within fairly narrow parameters precisely because travel had become more conventional.[6] That is, appreciably more fellow travelers observed Trib's behavior at any given moment than were present to observe Knight's travel behavior. Trib was visible to her numerous fellow travelers as a white woman of a certain class status. Beyond that, however, she was marked by the invisibility—a quality rarely if ever assigned to Knight on her travels—of a white woman classified as conventional traveling during a time when female travel was somewhat acceptable. Taken together, travel sections of Knight's *Journal* and Alcott's *Hospital Sketches* reveal in broad terms that as female travel became to some degree more common, more convenient, and less dangerous—and so to some extent socially sanctioned—cultural restrictions governing such travel increased correspondingly.

Not surprisingly, concerns of gender and conformity inform travel portions of *Hospital Sketches* and Knight's *Journal*. As discussed in the first chapter, Knight uses what she perceives as disruptive behavior of other women to aid in her self-construction as a proper woman. In Knight's portrayals of women, she is almost always more conventional and of higher class status than they are. In the travel section of *Hospital Sketches,* Alcott only briefly gestures toward Trib's fellow female travelers. In both texts the main female traveler (Knight, Trib) exhibits little or no sympathy with other women. No like-minded, democratic union of females is activated by shared travel in these texts. This is not to suggest that such temporary female communities might not have formed in Federalist America at various times and for various reasons. However, Knight and Alcott, both of whom reached womanhood with uncommon qualities and desires for women of their times, constructed female travels as solo journeys largely independent of the support of women. If a travel-generated alliance of females existed in Knight's or Alcott's experiences, it appears to have been untranslatable, and indeed unrepresentable, for them in their autobiographic narratives.

In *Hospital Sketches* Alcott multiply deploys and defies conventions of the travel narrative. The travel section of *Hospital Sketches* is a conventional preparation for the less conventional hospital sketch to come in the text, one less bound by fixed gender roles. Alcott constructs Trib, her Dickensian fictive persona, as the stereotypical spinster traveler whom critics would later characterize "as indomitable, eccentric and mostly rather crazy" and as a revision of that stereotype (Mills 32). Trib has conventionally feminine and masculine characteristics, and she describes the domestic as well as the political, personal, and public. Further, Trib confidently travels alone. Alcott's portrayal of Trib's unaccompanied journey recognizes, as Schriber rightly observes, that "female vulnerability, codified in conduct books, fiction, and the press, was a rhetorical and actual obsession in Victorian America" (79). By "satiriz[ing] the need for escorts," in Jane E. Schultz's reading, Alcott mocks that obsession ("Embattled Care" 116). Alcott's revision of the women's travel narrative intersects with the nursing narrative in *Hospital Sketches:* opening with and then interrupting the more familiar form of the women's travel narrative works to unsettle readers with humor and to prepare them for the unfamiliar, unsettling nursing narrative that follows. Schriber writes that Alcott's use of the travel narrative corresponds with other "women's texts of travel [that] make gender visible at certain sites as women work their way into the world of travel writing and around the constraints of gender" (61).

Reading the nursing sketch that follows Trib's travels in *Hospital Sketches* in conjunction with the travel narrative of Knight's *Journal* makes plain that both literary forms serve as sites for women to write their autonomous behaviors. In each case the generic circumstances necessary (travel and nursing) allow the woman writer to position herself or her female persona as superior to or independent of other women. In both literary forms uncommon experiences away from home are employed in an attempt to make the female self legible on its own among or without other women. In Alcott's *Hospital Sketches* and Knight's *Journal,* as well as in other works discussed in this study, the compulsion to write the female self emerges from and is abraded by prevailing gender assumptions inhabited, promoted, and resisted by other women.

Other women's Civil War nursing experiences were published, but Alcott's was one of the earliest accounts.[7] This absence of an immediate literary model is matched and explained by the absence of an experiential model. In antebellum America, only women affiliated with religious orders were permitted to nurse professionally. Schultz provides valuable context in her discussion of women beginning to figure into an increasingly professionalized medical discourse before the Civil War, having been "excluded from medical networks on the basis of a biological determinism that cast them as unfit" ("The Inhospitable Hospital" 366). Additionally, as Carroll Smith-Rosenberg argues in her groundbreaking work on Victorian sex and class roles, the mid-nineteenth-century movement by "well-connected physicians . . . to upgrade standards within the medical profession and simultaneously to defend their practices against rural and irregular physicians" also served to limit women's roles in professionally practicing medicine as doctors, midwives, or nurses (230). The next chapter's reading of Civil War reminiscences by S. Emma E. Edmonds, Mary Livermore, and Annie Turner Wittenmyer supplements this discussion in its examination of women's public and private roles in the war effort despite—and at times because of—their tightly restricted participation in the medical professions.

At the time of *Hospital Sketches,* forty-two-year-old Florence Nightingale embodied the figure of the female army nurse.[8,9] Her Crimean War service as well as her influential works *Notes on Nursing* (1859) and *Notes on Hospitals* (1859) led contemporaries to identify her "with the reform of hospitals and military medicine as much as with nursing" (Charles E. Rosenberg 1). Nightingale had a compelling "concern with cleanliness and ventilation" in hospitals, as well as a passionate commitment to advocating her nursing philosophy and methods in writing (2). Her texts authorized female nurses to practice these methods and to promote them in writing. Alcott read Nightingale's *Notes on Nursing* in preparation for nursing, and her remarks about hospital conditions in her writing align with Nightingale's views and convictions (Hawkins 4).[10] In *Hospital Sketches* Trib approvingly notes "the long, clean, warm, and airy wards" of a neighboring hospital and the "draft of fresh air flowing in."[11] From her position as a self-described "used up nurse," she rebukes "any hospital director" who disagrees with these practices. She also lovingly describes Dorothea Dix, Superintendent of Union Army nurses, as "our Florence Nightingale" (55).

Conventions established by Nightingale's writing also contributed to the breakdown of convention afforded by the Civil War. When war broke out, entrenched resistance from the federal government and male medical establishment seriously hampered women's early efforts (more than twenty thousand women applied for work in Confederate and Union military hospitals) to earn money, seek adventure, or express patriotism by volunteering to nurse the wounded (Schultz, "The Inhospitable Hospital" 363). Mary Livermore in her nursing retrospective, *My Story of the War: A Woman's Narrative* (1889), discussed in the next chapter, explicitly compared early stages of the Civil War with the Crimean War: "'All (there) were tied up with official formalism until Florence Nightingale, with her corps of trained nurses and full power to do and command, as well as advise, landed at Scutari, and ordered the store houses opened'" (qtd. in Thompson 76). Nightingale's groundbreaking representation of effective female nursing in her writing facilitated the U.S. government's and the male medical establishment's eventual capitulation to women's war nursing.[12]

Alcott would also have been familiar with the July 1862 visit of Ralph Waldo Emerson's daughter, Ellen Tucker Emerson (for whom Alcott had first imagined the stories of *Flower Fables* [1854]), to Portsmouth Grove Army Hospital (which housed "1700 or more sick and wounded soldiers") in Newport, Rhode Island, several months before Alcott left for Washington. Alcott probably would have read Ellen's at times lengthy letters to family members about her visit ("It took me all day to write it [her previous letter], and my arm ached"). Ellen's observations of and conversations with soldiers ("How well they talk!") reflected her Union zeal: "They are, so many of them, patriotic and fiery through their sickness that I was wholly satisfied with them, and very much elated after my talks with them." She also recorded a parenthetically clarified gendered moment when tea was distributed "to nurses (soldiers of course) who carried it to their men" (Gregg 291, 284, 291, 275).

Hospital care of male soldiers by female nurses is seldom as central in other Civil War nursing narratives as it is in *Hospital Sketches*. Subsequent nursing narratives are longer, written by women whose war service was not quickly cut short by illness as was Alcott's, and more extensive, including descriptions of travel to battles and hospitals, fundraising, administration of nursing efforts, distribution of supplies, and difficulties in obtaining appropriate food for the wounded. Narratives written after the war tend to be self-consciously aware of the historical moment in accounts of meetings with Ulysses S. Grant, postassassination retrospectives on Lincoln, and focus on the war's end.

Hospital Sketches most obviously sets the tone for subsequent women's nursing narratives in S. Emma E. Edmonds's *Nurse and Spy in the Union Army* (1865), discussed in the next chapter. *Nurse and Spy* twice quotes "Miss Periwinkle" (75–77, 237) and in at least two other sections plagiarizes parts of *Hospital Sketches* with minor alterations and without attribution (238–39, 250–51).[13] However, aspects of *Hospital Sketches*—for instance, constructions of wounded soldiers as boys by the nurse/writer and constructions of the nurse/writer as mother or sister by soldiers (and the writer herself)—that may seem to set the tone for subsequent nursing narratives are so prevalent in Civil War narratives generally that *Hospital Sketches* seems more representative than initiating of a discourse for treating gender that resulted from opportunities for female travel, work, and self-invention provided by the war. Women's energetic Civil War involvement is documented in works such as Frank Moore's *Women of the War* (1866), which contains over forty chapters on individual women and women's war efforts (with no mention of Alcott), and Linus P. Brockett and Mary C. Vaughan's *Woman's Work in the Civil War* (1867), nearly eight hundred pages of small print with sections on individual women administrators, organizers of aid societies, and volunteers in non-nursing capacities, which briefly mentions Alcott (her first name misspelled as "Louise") and *Hospital Sketches* in an extensive list in the book's final section (793). Focusing on female Civil War hospital nursing, *Hospital Sketches* accurately captures an emerging discourse for treating gender that is perpetuated and sustained in subsequent nursing narratives.[14]

II.

[The nurse] must have a respect for her own calling. . . . [S]he must be a sound, and close, and quick observer; and she must be a woman of delicate and decent feeling.
—Florence Nightingale, Notes on Nursing

In late 1862 Alcott wrote in her journal: "November. Thirty years old. Decided to go to Washington as a nurse if I could find a place. Help needed, and I love nursing and *must* let out my pent-up energy in some new way" (Myerson et al., *Journals* 110). Arriving at the Union Hotel Hospital in 1862 immediately after the bloody Battle at Fredericksburg,[15] Alcott served as a nurse for six weeks and then contracted typhoid fever. She returned home to New England, near death. Once recovered, she edited and revised her war letters to her family, also drawing on the brief private journal she had kept while in Washington.[16] For her fictive self she used Tribulation Periwinkle, a woman who goes to Washington to nurse in a Civil War hospital. The resulting sketches, published in the antislavery Boston *Commonwealth* in spring 1863, "met with instant success and were copied in papers all over the North" (Jones xli). After their serial publication Alcott added two new chapters; the collection was then published as a book, which was also well received. The success of *Little Women* (1868, 1869) led to a new edition, *Hospital Sketches and Camp and Fireside Stories* (1869), which contained *Hospital Sketches* and eight stories. The version of *Hospital Sketches* available in *Alternative Alcott* (1988) emerged during these multiple generic adaptations.[17]

In the first chapter of *Hospital Sketches,* Trib's hectic self-definitions as she decides to enlist invoke a sisterhood of nurses led by both Miss and Mrs. Generals ("we hear no end of Mrs. Generals, why not a Miss?" [4]). Once she has been accepted and is ready to leave for Washington, however, sex-gender identity is foregrounded in her comparing herself to "boys going to sea" (4) and to "the soldier who cries when his mother says 'Good-bye'" (6), as well as her hugging her family "without a vestige of unmanly emotion" (5). As Trib boards the train, her presexual nature is established in a partial assertion of conventional femininity: "I clutched my escort in a fervent embrace, and skipped into the car with as blithe a farewell as if going on a bridal tour" (6). Aligning herself with a prehoneymoon bride, Trib draws on social approbation afforded women who marry. Her comparison likewise signals impending loss of virginity and initiation into sexual matters. Lest this female persona be confused with Alcott—and suggest Alcott's own sexual nature—the text assures us of Trib's authenticity. The "remarkably elastic" nature of the travel narrative allows Alcott to include travel notes to "convince the skeptical that such a being as Nurse Periwinkle does exist, [and] that she really did go to Washington" (Schriber 58, 12). Trib, intended to veil Alcott from the public, is, however, a temporary fictive representation. At the end of the text Alcott mixes irony and femininity to end Trib's "bridal tour." Self-conscious in her retrenchments from Trib's unconventional experiences, Alcott then writes Trib's epitaph.

On her journey Trib defines herself as subject to misreading, sometimes by others ("I'm a bashful individual, though I can't get anyone to believe it" [6]) and sometimes by herself ("I'm a woman's rights woman . . . [but] I was now quite ready to be a 'timid trembler,' if necessary" [9]). Once she arrives at the hospital, she observes that it is a place of observation, where she will be subject to close (mis)reading by male strangers, "all staring more or less at the new 'nuss,' who suffered untold agonies, but concealed them under as matronly an aspect as a spinster could assume, and blundered through her trying labors with a Spartan firmness" (21).[18] That Trib reads male scrutiny as sexual is revealed by her response. She attempts to protect herself (a self-defined "spinster") from gazes she reads as sexualized by promoting a false reading of herself as a matron—that is, according to her implicit definition, as a non-spinster—a sexually experienced, though asexual ("Spartan"), woman.

Alcott's adoption of multiple roles in *Hospital Sketches* (beginning on the first page with Tribulation Periwinkle) aligns with Fanny Fern's use of a range of personae in her early periodical writing. However, while Fern and Alcott assume a variety of roles in their texts, they diverge regarding use of a conventionally understood feminine voice (a heightened version of what Trib names a "'timid trembler'" [9]). Fern nimbly adopts such a voice—with varying degrees of the sexual and flirtatious—when it suits her subject and perceived audience. Indeed, Fern relishes her ability to perform the feminine convincingly and so to persuade readers, or at least give them pause, regarding her identity. A not insignificant portion of Fern's pleasure in this act is her understanding that the persona of a demure woman can be as authoritative as the various male personae she adopts at other times.

In *Hospital Sketches*, however, while Alcott exhibits her own glib fluency with a range of personae, the role of the sexual female is markedly absent. In its place Alcott assigns an asexual mutability to Trib. Though her use of the asexual can be understood in a variety of ways, I read it as a substitution for the sexual that is pivotal to her project in *Hospital Sketches*. To even briefly feminize and so sexualize Trib would critically interrupt Alcott's considerations of gender construction in the text. The feminine performance that Fern is amused to (de)activate invokes the type of female that Alcott/Trib is not (and cannot, will not, be). The inability to occupy feminine cultural spaces without dis/ease motivates Alcott/Trib's desire to nurse in the war. That temporary national location is where she hopes to explore—as she cannot at home—an alternative sex-gender identity for a white middle-class woman in the nineteenth-century United States. I do not mean to suggest, however, that the personae Alcott adopts in *Hospital Sketches* conceal a coherent self. Though Fern and Alcott differ significantly in their uses and inhabiting of a feminized role, the "I" Alcott declares in *Hospital Sketches* is as multiple and as performative as Fern's.

Other authors in this study negotiated demands of compulsory femininity with choices that are compelling in their own right. For instance, Knight adopted a feminine voice in her text in an attempt to conventionalize her unconventional behaviors. S. Emma E. Edmonds wrote of temporarily passing as a man and so was able to avoid those gendered demands for a time. Mary Livermore and Annie Turner Wittenmyer wrote texts invested with insistence on their conventional behaviors and womanhood. In all cases, these white women writers negotiated a desire to publicly declare a self with their vexed awareness of prevailing constructions of femininity.

After Trib fears she was being eroticized in the male gaze and tries to desexualize herself in response, she attempts to desexualize wounded men with her own gaze and rhetoric, seeing them as "'our brave boys,' as the papers justly call them," their suffering making "one glad to cherish each as a brother" (22). Drawing on authority of news reports, Trib moves from constructing the wounded patients as boys to embracing them as brothers, both readings seeming to allow only nonsexual adult affection. When subsequently told to order the men to strip and to bathe them ("'Come, my dear, begin to wash as fast as you can. Tell them to take off socks, coats and shirts, scrub them well, put on clean shirts, and the attendants will finish them off, and lay them in bed'" [23]), Trib is confronted by the near-naked (and potentially sexualized) male body. The itemizing of garments makes clear the men will keep their pants on, but at the same time suggests how much of the male body will be exposed. Though references to amputated male limbs are common in *Hospital Sketches* as well as in other Civil War nursing narratives, the male body in its entirety—as opposed to severed parts of that body—is rarely invoked. Its provocative presence here suggests Trib's (and Alcott's) thinly suppressed anxieties and fearful interest concerning physical contact with men. These concerns are somewhat muted by the comic examples Trib prefers to the reality that leaves her at a loss for words ("If she had requested me to shave them all, or dance a hornpipe on the stove funnel, I should have been less staggered; but to scrub some dozen lords of creation at a moment's notice, was really—really—" [23]). Trib again turns to rhetoric that endeavors to desexualize ("there was no time for nonsense" [23]) in order to reconfigure the potentially sexual reality of a woman bathing half-naked male strangers. She chooses "a withered old Irishman" (23) to bathe first, and his comic remarks result in

> a general grin, at which propitious beginning I took heart and scrubbed away like any tidy parent on a Saturday night. Some of them took the performance like sleepy children, leaning their tired heads against me as I worked, others looked grimly scandalized, and several of the roughest colored like bashful girls. (23–24)

Trib's proffered reading of herself has moved from bride to matron to parent, while her renderings of male patients have moved from boys to brothers to children to female children. These constructions resist desexualization except for the "grimly scandalized" men who, like Trib, recognize the erotic potential of their situation but, ill-positioned to prevent it or protest against it, are unable to reconfigure it. Unlike Trib—and unlike men who are not wounded and hospitalized—they are not in command. As male patients they forfeit authority over their bodies and the sexual sensibilities that they held in the more overtly sexualized world outside the war hospital.

By the time she has finished bathing the men, Trib has taken rhetorical control of their (chaste) physicality ("having got the bodies of my boys into something like order" [29]). She basks in what she now views as their unerotic gaze, their faces "lighting up, with smiles of welcome, as I came among them, [I] enjoy[ed] that moment heartily, with a womanly pride in their regard, a motherly affection for them all" (29, 32). Trib's construction of herself as mother and woman is at least temporarily established as Alcott ironically and self-consciously reintegrates Trib into sex-gender conventions. In her satisfaction Trib is convinced that the stripped men have been desexualized by/for her. Likewise, the act of her bathing them has, by her implication and by what she assures herself is the now nonsexual nature of their observation, desexualized her for them.

Earlier in the text, Trib reads passive observation by male patients as predominantly sexual and responds by attempting to revise the men and herself in their eyes. She confesses, however, to her own surveillance while the men sleep, gazing at them more closely than she would dare when they could return her stare and limiting her gaze to their faces:

> Many of the faces became wonderfully interesting when unconscious. Some grew stern and grim[;] . . . some grew sad and infinitely pathetic, as if the pain borne silently all day, revenged itself by now betraying what the man's pride had concealed so well. Often the roughest grew young and pleasant . . . letting the real nature assert itself. . . . I learned to know these men better by night than through any intercourse by day. (34–35)

Observation of individual male patients in other Civil War narratives is typically limited to brief, pious deathbed scenes. However, in Alcott's hands, clinical conventions of the hospital sketch and her use of them to endeavor to desexualize male patients allow Trib to consider culturally constructed notions of gender ("man's pride") while staying away from male sexuality. For Trib, sleep frees men from prevailing gender constraints that require them to conceal pain and what she constructs as their "real nature[s]." During waking interaction, compulsory gendered behaviors prevent her (and, ostensibly, any observer) from knowing the men in this way. In nighttime observation, however, gender constraints are temporarily loosened by sleep, allowing Trib to more fully "know" the men. Her nighttime observation is not a Foucauldian regulatory gaze of surveillance policing a captive population. Rather, Trib covertly studies men to determine how gender figures into their identities and, by implication, into her own identity. She may limit her reading to the men's faces rather than their full bodies because the bodies are covered (and so less readable) or because such observation in the absence of professional necessity (bathing, bandaging) could provoke a sexual reading and could resexualize the male bodies she has been at pains to desexualize. Her privileging and reading of men's faces is a private act, stripping the men of emotional concealment, just as public bathing stripped them of physical concealment.

Trib fears sexual implications in the daytime gazes of male patients. Her initiation of the nighttime gaze marks her reading of the gaze as sexually chaste, while also signaling the agency the hospital encourages in her. Moving beyond her previous limited experience of women and men, Trib recognizes an opportunity to explore gender construction—a subject central to her tentative self-definition. Her monologic nighttime gaze at the men begins the emotional interaction for which Trib traveled to Washington. That intercourse must be fully realized for Trib to lose her emotional virginity. To accomplish this, Trib must engage in dialogic, emotional intercourse with a conscious, mature man who, like her, evades issues of (his) sexuality.

This male counterpart, John, soon arrives, preceded by praise from another patient, which increases Trib's desire to observe him:

> I had some curiosity to behold this piece of excellence, and when he came, watched him for a night or two, before I made friends with him; for, to tell the truth, I was a little afraid of the stately looking man, whose bed had to be lengthened to accommodate his commanding stature; who seldom spoke, uttered no complaint, asked no sympathy, but tranquilly observed what went on about him. (38)

Trib refrains from immediately approaching him due to the implicit maturity of his imposing height and dignified behavior. His silent observation and his lack of complaint or supplication are read by Trib as a withholding that resists her construction of male patients. Her physical description of him contains none of her characteristic humor and instead anticipates the pain that for her will desexualize him:[19]

> A most attractive face . . . as yet unsubdued by pain; thoughtful and often beautifully mild while watching the afflictions of others, as if entirely forgetful of his own. His mouth was grave and firm, with plenty of will and courage in its lines, but a smile could make it as sweet as any woman's; and his eyes were child's eyes, looking one fairly in the face, with a clear straightforward glance, which promised well for such as placed their faith in him. (39)

John's being seriously wounded, and thus stationary, allows Trib again to take advantage of her professional status and gaze at the male face, this time in repose if not in sleep. Trib observes the captive mature maleness that she would otherwise avoid and studies that maleness further. Her examination reveals a face combining typified qualities of man ("grave and firm," "will and courage"), woman (a mouth "as sweet as any woman's"), and child ("child's eyes"). The reading Trib imposes on John's face crosses boundaries of gender and age, suggesting John's face as Trib's ideal human face. Trib's reading of John's face promotes a belief in natural human goodness, a quality heightened by the lack of human goodness that has resulted in the need for the war hospital.

Descriptions of John in *Hospital Sketches* as a "dying statesman or warrior," and in death as "a most heroic figure," modify Alcott's more class-specific observations in the journal she kept while in Washington, which see John as "what we call a common man, in education and condition, to me [he] is all I could expect or ask from the first gentleman in the land. Under his plain speech & unpolished manner I seem to see a noble character" (Myerson et al., *Journals* 39, 45). Alcott's journal typically records experiences later significantly expanded in *Hospital Sketches,* except in this instance where, in the move from private journal to published sketches, references to John's class status are condensed and coded. In Amy Lang's considerations of class status in the mid-nineteenth-century United States, Alcott's editing of her original comments regarding John corresponds with "the new awareness of class distinctions among Americans at midcentury and the increasingly problematic nature of social classification" (3). The journal comments signal Alcott's awareness of class divisions and recognition of John's class status as lower than her own. Subsequent abbreviation and revision of Alcott's class-specific descriptions of John in *Hospital Sketches* point to subordination of class issues, reflecting, as Lang correctly argues, "the characteristic, even definitive, denial of class by the nineteenth-century middle-class" (10). This editing is crucial to Alcott's establishment of shared class status between John and Trib that will enable her to develop their emotional intercourse. Class difference, coded as it is, functions as an essential component of Alcott's literary ability to violate conventional norms of femininity.

After Trib learns that John is dying, visible signs of his suffering allow her to embrace him physically and emotionally. He looks "lonely and forsaken," and he weeps, but this does "not seem weak, only very touching, and straightway my fear vanished, my heart opened wide and took him in, as, gathering the bent head in my arms, as freely as if he had been a little child, I said, 'Let me help you bear it, John'" (40). When he responds gratefully, Trib asks why he had not sought comfort earlier, seeking (and receiving) reassurance that his emotional independence was not a rejection of her and her nonsexual nursing aid. Satisfied, she concludes with a significant step in self-characterization, seeing herself in his eyes as "the poor substitute for mother, wife, or sister[,] . . . a friend who hitherto had seemed neglectful" (41). For the first time, Trib characterizes herself as wife, as sexual partner, and touches a male patient for emotional reasons. Trib participates in what Harriet Blodgett defines as "*womanliness* in culturally approved terms [that] carries the satisfaction of being needed, of having others dependent upon oneself for nurturance'" (159). Had Trib touched John outside of her professional duties before she knew he was dying, her touch could have been (self-) read as erotic. Now, as a result of her knowledge and emotional reaction to his impending death, her touch can be (self-) read as female tenderness, allowing Trib to characterize herself as a wife substitute.[20]

Generic boundaries of the hospital sketch authorize an emotional intercourse between Trib and John. Less clinical, and so necessarily more sexualized, genres would resist or further complicate such interaction. Even so, in referring to John as "the manliest man among my forty" who nevertheless said, "'Yes, ma'am,' like a little boy" (41), Trib veers from man to boy and sexual to less sexual in her characterizations of him. Trib's intimacy with John is complicated by her fear-inflected binary of sexualized and desexualized. As she attempts to construct a female/male friendship that extends beyond the body and emphasizes comradeship between a man and a woman of like spirits, her reading reveals John as a male rendering of Trib herself. Both John and Trib are thirty years old; both are described as "bashful" (41, 6); Trib's androgynous physical description of John could also serve as a description of herself. John is a son essentially married to his mother (John wears her ring that "'she gave [him] . . . to keep [him] steady,'" and he "'must be father to the children and husband to the dear old woman, if I can'" [42]), while Trib is a daughter whose mother wails at her leaving and sees her off to war as though she were a son. Both go to war for primarily personal reasons that suggest their gendered roles: Trib because she "wants something to do" (3), John because "'I wanted the right thing done'" (42). Trib asks John if enlisting wasn't as bad as marrying—that is, since either would result in his leaving the family that relies on him. Because soldiering had long been a choice for men, while women volunteering for wartime nursing in the nineteenth-century United States had only recently become acceptable, Trib needs John's gender-specific reading of (male) enlisting to arrive at her own reading of (female) volunteer nursing. By her question Trib seeks affirmation from John for the social worth of military service. Alcott makes it plain that Trib connects the act of enlisting to the act of marrying, suggesting that, to her, enlisting to serve in the war—as soldier or nurse, as man or woman—could be understood as a culturally sanctioned, asexual substitute for marriage.

Similarities between John and Trib that cross or elide gender boundaries culminate in John's death. John's doctor assigns Trib the task of telling John he is dying, because "'women have a way of doing such things comfortably'" (39). The male doctor's choice of Trib is appropriate, but not for his gendered reasons. Both Trib and John privilege toughness and independence, seeing these as valuable qualities that have allowed them to negotiate life's hardships successfully. The strength and self-reliance they share make Trib the fitting bearer of the information that these serviceable qualities cannot save John from fatal wounds that resulted from his choice to enlist. Likewise, Trib's strength and independence will not save her from physical risks associated with her choice to nurse. After John weakens and dies at the end of chapter four—in a scene abstaining from religious pieties and sentimental language repeatedly found in deathbed scenes of subsequent Civil War nursing narratives—chapter five begins with Trib's own near-fatal illness.

The literal death of John the soldier parallels the professional death of Trib the wartime nurse. John is the last person Trib nurses before she falls ill, becomes a hospital patient herself, nearly dies, and returns home, "end[ing] my career as an army nurse" (60). The primarily asexual (and so for Trib mostly nonthreatening) emotional exchange between John the patient and Trib the nurse within the wartime hospital allowed Trib to consider similarities between cultural positions of white, nineteenth-century U.S. adult women and men. Implicit comparisons between female nursing and male soldiering, and between roles of devoted adult daughter and devoted adult son, suggest a larger exploration of gender construction. However, this exploration occurs in the temporary location of the wartime hospital where women are permitted to work only because the need is dire and where all men and women are at high risk of illness and death. If Trib's considerations of gender construction are related to the site and conditions that allow her to think them, then such thoughts are as unconventional, temporary, and dangerous as the war hospital itself.

Trib's exploration of gender construction depends on Alcott's foregrounding of asexuality. While gender and sexual power regularly drive nineteenth-century U.S. social and cultural arrangements, in the world of *Hospital Sketches* the asexual shapes Trib, Alcott, and the fragmenting nation. In Alcott's hands, the neglected, disdained asexuality commonly assigned to spinsterhood (Alcott's, Trib's, and other women's) and to the emerging role of the female nurse is a transformational force. Asexuality brings Alcott's authorship into being, is essential to Trib's loss of emotional virginity, and expands the role of nurse/author. Indeed, the asexual nurse/author is activated in the text as crucial to the divided nation. In *Hospital Sketches* Trib's nurse/author role is extended "into the larger symbolic one of the guarantor, like her patient John, of democracy itself. Like Whitman, but in a somewhat less erotic way, Trib and John are the wound-dressers of the nation." In her inspired recognition of the latent potency of asexuality and, correspondingly, in her rejection of its habitual disparagement, Alcott revises "asexuality into a stance of national sympathy."[21]

The U.S. Civil War served as the de facto workshop for such revision. Though masculine sexual power determined social control, wartime disorder resulted in a temporary lessening of hegemonic vigilance. Thus, even while cultural agents (officials in the federal government and the male medical establishment, among many others) remained alert for deviations from the normative, slippages nonetheless occurred. My next chapter discusses S. Emma E. Edmonds's successful wartime performing of the masculine and Mary Livermore's and Annie Turner Wittenmyer's observing and recording of other women's failed attempts at such performances. The comradely friendship between Trib and John emerges from and is allowed by this same wartime moment. Trib and John are Americans from different U.S. geographic regions who travel to war to serve the Union. Their asexual, patriotic bond gestures toward the common equality Abraham Lincoln once imagined for the post–Civil War United States. After her rich but brief and interrupted war participation, Alcott in *Hospital Sketches* imagines how the asexual might contribute to, might be valuable in, and indeed might be essential to the next stages of democratic nation building.

That vision, as well as Trib's nursing, ends abruptly when, during her illness, Trib's father arrives to take her away from the hospital: "at the sight of him, my resolution melted away, my heart turned traitor to my boys, and, when he said, 'Come home,' I answered, 'Yes, father;' and so ended my career as an army nurse" (60). The presence of Trib's father soon after John's absence through death demonstrates the father's replacement of John as the man with whom Trib is most closely associated. The text self-consciously retreats from Trib's emerging independence and professionalism. John was not a relative by blood or marriage, was unknown to Trib's family and friends, was of lower class status than Trib, and was unmarried and so potentially sexualized, all of which made Trib's close connection to him unconventional and inappropriate when viewed by the world outside the hospital. Her father's much more conventional and acceptable authority likewise conventionalizes Trib, returning her to her subordinate role of child (non-adult, non-nurse). The arrival of the father—just "the sight of him"—leads Trib to reject her patients as well as her newfound understanding of herself.

Trib's behavior after her father appears (she yields fully to him; she "melts" into physical and emotional weakness) indicates recognition that she is returning, willingly if not happily, to an accepted female norm. While I do not wish to unduly emphasize the progression of female autonomy followed speedily by debilitating illness, this sequence of events invites speculation. That Trib's illness occurs directly after liberties afforded her by the war hospital suggests severe penalties for female independence. Significantly, Trib's war experiences closely mirror Alcott's own. Alcott, while nursing in Washington, DC, wrote letters home, kept a journal about her experiences, and then contracted typhoid. To put it plainly, Alcott nursed, wrote about it, and, as a result, almost died. She never regained her prenursing good health or that measure of autonomy. In the text of *Hospital Sketches* that Alcott assembled and wrote after she recovered from illness, she meticulously replicates that punitive progression.

The disciplinary in Alcott's life was soon augmented by the terrifying when, as cited earlier in this chapter and referenced in the chapter title, during her recovery Alcott experienced a delirious fear of being left alone (that is, without another woman) "'when the room was full of men'" (257). A few months later, however, Alcott would write of Trib's satisfied viewing of rooms full of men as sons/brothers in *Hospital Sketches*. Trib's platonic self-construction as mother/sister to men is destabilized by Alcott's postnursing panic. Near-fatal illness rendered as punishment for female independence mixes with a hallucination of men so threatening as to cause fearful agitation. Without diminishing the force of these gendered scenes, I argue that they are lesser symptoms that emerge from the larger governing disorder of Alcott's lifelong domination by her egotistic father, Bronson Alcott. In Alcott's wartime experience and in *Hospital Sketches*, the father arrives unannounced, uninvited, unwelcome.[22] He not only disrupts Trib's/Alcott's independence; he peremptorily ends it ("When he said, 'Come home,' I answered, 'Yes, father;' and so ended my career as an army nurse" [60]). His very appearance terminates Trib's/Alcott's rich participation in possibilities of gender, asexuality, and nation building.

Though Trib agrees to leave with her father, this rejection of the hospital and of nursing is ultimately emotionally incomplete. She "shall never regret the going, though a sharp tussle with typhoid, ten dollars, and a wig, are all the visible results of the experiment; for one may live and learn much in a month" (60).[23] Her pensive naming of nursing as an "experiment" points to her return to conventionally gendered (i.e., non-experimental) life.[24] Trib's remark, implying that wartime nursing produced other, less visible results than illness, money, and a wig, suggests that the living and learning she experienced remain alive to her, private and unavailable for glib listing. Alcott's mix of humor, irony, and wistfulness problematizes the overt content of her text as she approaches and yet retreats from an alternative sex-gender identity for a white middle-class woman in the nineteenth-century United States.

A child's deferring to the parent and a woman's loss of hair are conventional forms of disempowerment.[25] Thus, the arrival of her father at the hospital coupled with her hair loss due to illness work to diminish Trib. Previous attempts to desexualize in the text were reactions to the unsettling possibilities of Trib or her patients being viewed as sexual. Here, neither the arrival of her father nor the loss of her hair is presented as a reaction to sexuality, a need for Trib to be seen as asexual. Instead, both are reminders of Trib's subordinate place (to her father, to the gender-specific ways women are read) in the hegemonic structure that tolerates the temporarily necessary aberration of the war hospital. Trib partially scripts female hair loss as a wartime sacrifice, an injury not unlike a wound that she has sustained in service to her country: "though a sadly womanish feeling, I take some satisfaction in the thought that, if I could not lay my head on the altar of my country, I have my hair" (61). Still, Trib has lost possibilities of soldiering and war nursing on some sort of equal level. Her feeling is "sadly womanish"; she has been denied the patriotic opportunity to give her life for her country. Like Susan B. Anthony, Trib must learn that "women can neither take the ballot nor the bullet" (qtd. in Young, *Disarming the Nation* 15).[26] Alcott's comments on the sacrifice of Trib's hair are inflected with characteristic wryness and irony, again complicating the text. Having positioned Trib to temporarily evade cultural assumptions, Alcott can only uneasily reinscribe her in those norms.

Revision—and resistance to revision—of Trib's wartime nursing continues with the poem concluding the "Off Duty" chapter of *Hospital Sketches* on the "death" of Nurse Periwinkle:

Oh, lay her in a little pit,
With a marble stone to cover it,
And carve thereon a gruel spoon,
To show a 'nuss' has died too soon. (61)

Alcott employs ironic humor in this mock epitaph as she self-consciously retreats from the (self-) representation of Trib and its value to her. The four-line verse, with its rhyming couplets, indirect diminutive portrayal of Trib (her body requires only a "little pit"), and slang rendering of "nurse," attempts to return to the more lighthearted tone of prehospital sections of *Hospital Sketches*. This rhetorical movement fails, complicated as the text is by the serious treatment of John's death and—despite the poem's insistence on equating Trib's leaving the hospital with Trib's death—by Nurse Periwinkle's recovery. The Trib/nurse identity, now promoted as a no longer useful, fictive self-representation, is dismissed with mock mourning. Trib the nurse who went on the equivalent of a bridal tour begins to be conflated with Alcott the self-identified spinster.

The denial of Trib must not obscure the chain of events in and out of *Hospital Sketches* that preceded it: Alcott's illness cut short her nursing experience, killing her possibilities for nursing and for assuming a larger role in the world opened to her in the war hospital. As Alcott's possibilities died with her contracting typhoid, Trib, the fictive representative of those possibilities, dies, too. Alcott has recorded and now silences another female representation. However, Trib's voice, as with the range of female voices recorded in texts by Sarah Kemble Knight and Fanny Fern discussed in earlier chapters, remains available in the text itself. The poem's "too soon" points not only to the short tenure of Trib's nursing experience but also to the premature death of possibilities that ended with illness and a return to conventional life. The self-conscious playfulness of the ending poem is contradicted by pressures that combined to make Trib leave the hospital. Only when debilitated by disease, confronted with her father's compelling presence, and unable in her illness to draw strength from her fragile new identity does Trib succumb to the comforting lure of her old identity. Only then is Tribulation Periwinkle reconfigured into Louisa May Alcott.[27]

The personae of Trib—nurse, patriot, woman at large in the wider world—served to veil Alcott from the public, to ensure that Trib's freedoms were not confused with Alcott's acceptance of her own social restrictions. Once the use of the nurse as a representation of the self had been forced to end, the text produced about that experience needed to be realigned with conventional cultural values of readers if it were to succeed. Serial publication of the sketches privileged Trib's hospital experience. However, when the sketches were collected as a book, Alcott added two new chapters—"Obtaining Supplies" and "A Forward Movement," which became the first and second chapters—describing Trib's journey and reinforcing the more conventional travel narrative aspect of the text.[28] For instance, a *Commonwealth* reader would have been introduced to Alcott's hospital writings with the first published sketch, "A Day," which opens as Trib is called to bathe the wounded; a *Hospital Sketches* reader would have begun with Trib's decision to "enlist" and the description of her travel to Washington, not reaching the sexually complicated scene of "A Day" until the book's third chapter. Such revisions reshape the original sketches' predominant focus on the autonomy of the nursing experience of this middle-class white woman. These alterations display Alcott's understanding of genre as what Frederick Jameson has described as a "social contract" between any "writer and a specific reading public" (160). Alcott's modifications of *Hospital Sketches* recognize the efficacy of generic adaptation and demonstrate her awareness of readers' assumptions.

Later revisions continue these strategies, showing Alcott's successive use of letters, sketches, travel narrative, book, and collection, each gradually modifying and reframing her nursing experience. For the 1869 *Hospital Sketches and Camp and Fireside Stories,* Alcott followed advice to edit a description of a negligent hospital chaplain—"by taking out all Biblical allusions . . . the book may be made 'quite perfect,' I am told. Anything to suit customers" (Myerson et al., *Journals* 164). She also agreed to the reissue of the "nonfictional" *Hospital Sketches* with "fictional" stories that challenge the experiential authenticity of her original sketches. The first stories—"The King of Clubs and the Queen of Hearts" and "Mrs. Podgers' Teapot"—which follow *Hospital Sketches* are light-hearted, peacetime romances, situating *Hospital Sketches* as fiction among other fiction. Later, the war hospital death of wounded Murray in "The Blue and the Gray" and Nurse Hale's attitude in "A Hospital Christmas" mirror John's death and Trib's experience, further penetrating *Hospital Sketches*'s permeable boundaries between fiction and nonfiction. From the first sign of the sketches' success, Alcott's revisions steadily conventionalized her unconventional female experiences so that reader-customers would purchase her product. A portrait of Alcott's economic reliance on income from her writing and her concomitant status as family breadwinner emerges from these modifications. Incisively alert to readers' generic expectations and gender assumptions, Alcott progressively, pragmatically, and ironically conventionalized the text of *Hospital Sketches*.

However, this rhetorical movement to align the text with common gender biases should not be overrated or misread. To unduly emphasize these revisions may obscure *Hospital Sketches*'s multiple alignments of the nineteenth-century U.S. white woman writer and woman nurse. This compelling conflation was initially activated by the professional guidelines of female nursing and female writing that permitted a significantly desexualized approach to female/male interaction. That is, the female nurse attended to hospitalized men whose illnesses enabled others to view them as childlike in their physical infirmity. The nurse served in a professional capacity (not private, not conventionally feminine) and was, by regulation, typically a matron or a spinster. Presented as a matron or spinster professionally interacting with men solely because they were patients, the female nurse could be perceived to be as chaste as the men to whom she tended. This dual desexualization of male patient and female nurse afforded an uncommon space in nineteenth-century U.S. culture where a white woman could asexually participate in and observe female/male interaction. Correspondingly, the female author could write about men whose physical and/or emotional characteristics led her and readers to perceive such men as weak and so sexually disempowered. The female author wrote in a professional capacity (like the female nurse, not private, not conventionally feminine) and so in her texts could use her authorial license to render herself or her persona(e) chaste. Dual desexualization of female writer and male subject enabled the woman writer, like the woman war nurse, to asexually participate in and observe female/male interaction.

Second, in their professional relations with men, the female nurse and female writer were less likely to be viewed as defiant in their behaviors. The female nurse selflessly served and attempted to save men's lives. After establishment resistance to women's nursing was overcome, subsequent decades would come to see nursing as a socially sanctioned profession for women. In Civil War women's nursing, we see very early stages of this progression toward eventual cultural acceptance of the female nurse. The female writer's profession allowed her opportunities in her work to conceal her identity, mix the fictive and the autobiographical, and promote her behavior as conventional. These camouflaging strategies confounded (dis)approving classification of the female writer. In both cases, degrees of acceptance and pretense partially liberated the female nurse and female writer from the most pressing anxieties of social censure regarding their professional work with men.

Finally, in nursing and writing, women could evade considerations of their sexuality. In their work, in the ways detailed above, the female nurse and female writer could substitute the asexual for the sexual. The asexual allowed the female nurse and the female writer to work outside conventional feminine cultural spaces. Asexuality thus enabled expansion of roles of the female nurse and the female author. In both cases, then, such women could observe women and men together without foregrounding the sexual.

Taken together, the professional and the asexual mixed for the female nurse and the female writer, enabling a rare and valuable exploration of men and women outside an insistence on the sexual. To return to *Hospital Sketches,* just as readers saw Trib considering similarities of men enlisting, women volunteering to nurse in wartime, and either men or women choosing not to marry, so the text finally suggested similarities between women who could nurse men without necessarily sexualizing them and women who could write about men without necessarily sexualizing them. The hospital sketch appropriated the war hospital and representation of the female war nurse for the woman writer. This use of a liminal location where men and women could read each other without eroticism enabled Alcott more freely to explore nineteenth-century U.S. gender construction and the complex network of powers that constrained and defined white middle-class women and Alcott herself.[29]

Alcott's enlistment as a nurse enrolled her directly into the assembly of liminal locations caused by the Civil War. Within the divided national space, elements of the professionalization of nursing and the transformation of the sex/gender system met in the temporary war hospital and conflated with Alcott's nurse/soldier/mother self-definitions to invite her examination of her gendered identity. Alcott, just turned thirty years old, was, like the nation, also negotiating liminality, attempting to locate herself within a larger patriarchal, heterocentric culture. Turning to her investigations of literary categories and her reliance on the writing act, in *Hospital Sketches* Alcott feminized the Civil War narrative for herself. Individualizing the war narrative as she individualized her male patients, Alcott reconfigured possibilities of gendered identity. For her, the work of that reconfiguration would ultimately do no more than contribute to her disappointment and frustration at the circumscribed and conflicted life she later led—devoted daughter, exhausted writer, driven breadwinner. However, for some readers—women and men fettered by prevailing sex-gender assumptions—*Hospital Sketches*, with its sometimes masked gendered reconfigurations, can be read as doing its own kind of work. Though distanced from other women and races in its most immediate discourse, *Hospital Sketches* contributes to the larger dialogue of gendered writing on systems of domination by marking Alcott's wartime testing of middle-class cultural confines during a moment in the nineteenth-century United States when previously fixed boundaries—between states, genders, and races—suddenly seemed mutable.

The next chapter's discussion moves from the more tentative considerations of sex-gender identity seen in *Hospital Sketches* to representations of white women who more fully inhabited such roles by cross-dressing as male soldiers during the Civil War. I first draw on S. Emma E. Edmonds's record of her military service as "Frank Thompson" in *Nurse and Spy in the Union Army* to examine cultural implications of white women's successful wartime cross-dressing. I then turn to scenes of women's cross-dressing in post–Civil War reminiscences by Mary Livermore in *My Story of the War* and Annie Turner Wittenmyer in *Under the Guns: A Woman's Reminiscences of the Civil War* to analyze differences in public responses to representations of women's cross-dressing in decades following the war.

CHAPTER 4

"I Am Other than My Appearance Indicates"

Sex-Gender Representation in Women's Nineteenth-Century Civil War Reminiscences

> *"And so that was the way by which you came to put yourself in male attire?"*
> *"Yes, sir! and the only thing that made me feel sorry, was to see what a fool I had been, not to turn to a boy before, when it was so easy! And from that day forth I was happy and prosperous!"*
>
> —E.D.E.N. Southworth, The Hidden Hand, 1859

READING S. EMMA E. Edmonds's contemporary Civil War memoir, *Nurse and Spy in the Union Army* (1865), against two later Civil War histories by well-known women's war effort organizers—Mary Livermore's *My Story of the War* (1889) and Annie Turner Wittenmyer's *Under the Guns: A Woman's Reminiscences of the Civil War* (1895)—provides a lens through which to view moments of gender flexibility in restrictive nineteenth-century U.S. sex-gender conventions.[1] The presence of cross-dressed women in these narratives can be seen as emerging from a discourse of sex-gender representation that resulted from opportunities for female travel, work, and self-invention provided by the Civil War.[2]

Cross-dressing, gender construction, and authenticity intersect in nineteenth-century U.S. Civil War narratives that record cases of women who disguised themselves as male soldiers.[3] Women's war narratives in particular register the provisional autonomy and transgressive nature of cross-gender impersonation. Written during and after the war by Northern and Southern women, these texts have prompted investigations of authenticity and historical veracity regarding gender imposture. For instance, Betty Fladeland uses a Union soldier's diary to suggest that some female wartime cross-dressing may have been less successful than was previously believed, while C. Kay Larson links women's Civil War military service with late-twentieth-century issues of women in the military and so strives to authenticate her nineteenth-century examples. Richard Hall's *Patriots in Disguise,* a general overview, proclaims its concern with "issues of credibility and authenticity" (205).[4]

Elizabeth Young's influential approach to women's Civil War cross-dressing texts purposely diverges from such readings:

> My concern is less with the documentary recovery of the lives of women soldiers than with the symbolic significance of stories about them. . . . Civil War cross-dressing narratives suggest the particular symbolic opportunities the war afforded for the representation of female boundary-crossing. . . . [T]he woman soldier functioned as a figure of rhetorical excess, violating the literary boundaries of identifiable fact along with the socials limits of appropriate femininity. (*Disarming the Nation* 150)

Young's work has reshaped critical response to such texts in its articulations of their significance beyond questions of authenticity. My approach is largely in agreement with Young's. As these war narratives discuss women who impersonated men, they may, at times, cross generic lines into the fictive, just as their subjects cross gender lines. Following Young, my reading of three of these texts recasts usual oppositional categories of historical veracity and fictionalization, considering instead the resonance of these historical/fictive cross-gender scripts in nineteenth-century U.S. Civil War and Reconstruction cultures. However, I depart from Young in my deliberate decision to allow the possible experiential accuracies of these texts to remain uncontested. That is, my critical approach neither relies on nor resists notions of authenticity. Rather, I follow current autobiographical studies by remaining mindful of gendered difficulties women have repeatedly encountered at the vexed intersection of self-construction and life writing. As Felicity Nussbaum has written regarding women's issues of representation and voice, "cultural constructions of self and gender intermingle with the individual subject's interest and engagement in taking up the particular discourses available at given historical moments" (149).

Where Young's critical focus is on "the symbolic significance of stories about" cross-dressing Civil War women and not on "documentary recovery of the lives of women soldiers" (*Disarming the Nation* 150), Jane Schultz's approach embraces documentary recovery—not recovery per se of women's lives but of the cultural moment they occupied, the gendered context of the U.S. Civil War.[5] Her archival work provides a fascinating, wide-ranging statistical frame for such texts. In particular, Schultz's extensive recovery of previously uncollected data expands the gendered contexts for works written by and about women during a time when "over twenty thousand women sought work in the military hospitals of the Confederacy and the Union," pursuing paid employment, adventure, or patriotic action through war nursing ("The Inhospitable Hospital" 363). I supplement and depart from Schultz's readings by drawing on results of her invaluable archival work as I conduct a cultural analysis of selected women's Civil War narratives and of ways in which the energetic war efforts of such women contributed to representation of gender issues of access and authority.

Civil War narratives written by S. Emma E. Edmonds, Mary Livermore, and Annie Turner Wittenmyer extend identity explorations in texts considered in previous chapters. For instance, in Sarah Kemble Knight's *Journal,* Knight's independent travels intersect with her (contradictory) insistence on her identity as a conventional woman. By sharply critiquing women whom she identified as acting unconventionally, Knight fostered a view of herself as a woman who, unlike women she observed on her travels, readily conformed to gendered expectations. Though Knight herself was a woman speaking and acting with a significant measure of autonomy, she allowed herself exploration of that identity only by presenting herself as a conservative woman traveling among women who behaved badly.

In her early periodical writing, Sara Willis, writing as Fanny Fern, used the concealment of her pseudonym to construct multiple female representations. As Fern explored various identities in her writing, her sex-gender identity became the subject of readers' heightened conjecture. Willis used the public anonymous and androgynous persona of Fanny Fern to revise audience expectations as well as her own understanding of conventional female speech and acts.

The third chapter's discussion of Louisa May Alcott's *Hospital Sketches* details Alcott's considerations of alternative sex-gender identities. Unlike Knight, Alcott was not compelled in her text to insist on female conformity. And unlike Fern, Alcott did not write anonymously, though she did use a transparent fictive persona in Tribulation Periwinkle. Prompted by the dramatic experiences of her six weeks of nursing in a war hospital, Alcott revised the asexuality associated with spinsterhood, using it to explore and develop female identity roles of nurse and author. Across the Federalist period to the Civil War and, turning to texts by Mary Livermore and Annie Turner Wittenmyer, to the post–Civil War period, women represented women operating with varying degrees of cultural access and authority.

In *Nurse and Spy in the Union Army*, Edmonds, disguised to readers and fellow soldiers as "Frank Thompson," occupied an alternative sex-gender identity that gradually developed across texts by Knight, Fern, and Alcott. In *My Story of the War* and *Under the Guns*, Livermore and Wittenmyer, self-defined conventional women, retrospectively recorded their wartime observations of women who appeared to violate gender boundaries. In all three texts, these women, like Knight, Fern, and Alcott, wrote autobiographically, often disruptively, and attempted to negotiate complexities of nineteenth-century U.S. female positioning.

This chapter discusses sex-gender representation in women's nineteenth-century Civil War reminiscences in four parts: first, Edmonds's biographical contexts, a close reading of her wartime impersonations in *Nurse and Spy*, and her postbellum history; second, an examination of Mary Livermore's observations of cross-dressed women in *My Story of the War*; third, an analysis of an extended cross-dressing description in Annie Turner Wittenmyer's *Under the Guns*; and finally, a concluding section regarding representations of women's wartime cross-gender impersonation.

At the same moment the U.S. Civil War was breaking out, nineteenth-century sexology was attempting to codify identity within the sex-gender system. This emerging sexual science attempted to order, contain, and stabilize ambiguous and contradictory sex-gender constructions "into medicalized categories of deviant identity—hysterics, onanists, homosexuals" (Fradenburg and Freccero vii). Joseph Bristow has argued that "sexuality became such a significant topic of scientific investigation" in the latter half of the nineteenth century due to "multiple sources that constellated together . . . evolutionary and eugenic thought, the intensification of women's campaigns for the suffrage, and the development of sexually dissident subcultures" (57).[6] These disparate sources and others disrupted and threatened social and cultural arrangements. The desire to codify sexuality emerged in response to such fears.

In the latter half of the U.S. nineteenth century, as cultural assumptions regarding sex and sex-gender identity were challenged, strategies to impose boundaries on such assumptions emerged. For instance, the Krafft-Ebing biological model of sexual orientation, popularized in the late nineteenth century, pathologized homosexuality with the "invert," a woman whose body is occupied by a man's soul. This codification labeled a wide and hitherto unnamed middle ground between perceived binaries of female and male. As Christina Matta notes, "[f]rom their first appearance in U.S. medical literature, homosexuals had been included in the broader category of sexual inverts—a category that encompassed transvestites; women who smoked, whistled, or preferred sports and masculine dress"; men vain about their physical appearance; and men "who had effeminate voices" (78–79).[7] Subsequently, inversion was listed in the American Surgeon General's index as one of many female pathologies.[8] Such scientifically supported cross-gender identification gestured toward real (a man's soul) though limited (still a woman's body) access to masculine agency for women. Sexological studies eventually "played a major role in enabling sex to be debated more widely and seriously at all levels of society" (Bristow 15). That is, sexological studies bestowed a legitimacy upon cultural discussions of sex and sexuality.

Though this chapter focuses on women's nineteenth-century Civil War reminiscences, this is not to suggest that it is only during the war that gender, identity, and sex began to intersect. Androgyny, hermaphroditism, homosexuality, inversion, and lesbianism among other sex-gender constructions emerged at various times for various reasons. I agree with Julia Epstein and Kristina Straub's assertions that

> distinctions between male and female bodies are mapped by cultural politics onto an only apparently clear biological foundation. As a consequence, sex-gender systems are always unstable sociocultural constructions. Their very instability explains the cultural importance of these systems; their purpose is to delimit and contain the threatening absence of boundaries between human bodies and among bodily acts that would otherwise explode the organizational and institutional structures of social ideologies. (2)

Having said that, however, I also note that the U.S. Civil War provided a particularly fertile moment for considerations of sexuality. As Young writes:

> Sexuality is consistently unstable in the disruptive Civil War moment recreated in these texts. Both lesbian possibilities and fantasies of male homosexuality surface, often in dynamic interplay with weakened heterosexual formations. Both orthodox and heterodox sexuality frequently operate as allegorical languages for describing national and regional relationships. (*Disarming the Nation* 19)

Women's Civil War narratives that recorded moments of cross-gender impersonation were thus permitted to begin to discuss the previously undiscussable. These narratives coincided with emerging theories of sexual orientation and helped reconfigure gender possibilities within dominant cultural imagination. Their wartime examples of women who tested gendered confines when they "laid aside, for a time, [their] own costume, and assumed that of the opposite sex" (Edmonds 6) and their ambiguous and mediated treatments of such women contributed to a larger national dialogue on gender and identity.

I.

In *Nurse and Spy in the Union Army* (1865), an immediate bestseller, S. Emma E. Edmonds's war impersonations cross boundaries of gender, race, class, and region as she passes as a male contraband, female contraband, Irish peddler, Confederate soldier, Canadian boy, and male Union orderly.[9] Edmonds also disguises herself to readers, writing as a female nurse and spy who sometimes disguised herself as a man, when in reality she had enlisted as a male nurse ("Frank Thompson"), already in male disguise. Twenty years after publication of *Nurse and Spy*, Edmonds revealed her past identity as Frank Thompson and exposed the narrative deception (that her wartime employment was based on the perception that she was a man, Frank Thompson, and not, as her text maintains, a woman), a deception that was central to her book.

Sarah Emma Evelyn Edmonds was born in 1841 in Canada. At age seventeen, she disguised herself as a boy and ran away from home to avoid marriage. She eventually lived in Michigan, where she enlisted as a private in the Union Army under the name Franklin Thompson. Successfully disguised as a man, she fought in the war for two years. When she contracted malaria in 1863, she deserted to avoid discovery as a woman when hospitalized. Resuming conventional female clothing and behaviors, Edmonds later married and had children. She died in Texas in 1898.[10]

The "Publisher's Notice" framing *Nurse and Spy* (which indicates no knowledge of Edmonds's initial cross-dressing as Frank Thompson) promotes Edmonds's courage and skill—"in the 'Secret Service' as a 'Spy,' which is one of the most hazardous positions in the army—she penetrated the enemy's lines . . . no less than eleven times; always with complete success and without detection" (5)—while recognizing cultural anxiety regarding a woman disguised as a man: "Should any of her readers object to some of her disguises, it may be sufficient to remind them it was from the purest motives and most praiseworthy patriotism, that she laid aside, for a time, her own costume, and assumed that of the opposite sex" (6). The "Publisher's Notice" anticipates cultural resistance by linking cross-gender disguises to "patriotism" and "purest motives." In this preemptive defense of Edmonds's cross-dressing, "patriotism" is employed as a gender-neutral term, a motivating, commendable nationalistic response that, the statement implies, transcends gender. The use of "purest," however, is freighted with more implications: it gestures toward the pure/chaste woman of the cult of true womanhood as well as refutes readers' suspicions of impropriety—for instance, promiscuity or other sexual acts then read as violations—in a woman disguised as a man. Thus, patriotic men and women, a category that includes traditional women, all acting from "pure" motives and, all, assumably, within the white monoculture, may be permitted to cross-dress.

Additionally, to dress as a man "for a time" indicates temporary cross-dressing, implying that a woman's permanent passing as a man is what truly threatens the culture, which should recognize that

> whether [a woman's] duty leads her to the couch of luxury, the abode of poverty, the crowded hospital, or the terrible battle field—it makes but little difference what costume she assumes in the charge of her duties. Perhaps she should have the privilege of choosing for herself whatever may be the surest protection from insult and inconvenience in her blessed, self-sacrificing work. (6)

The publisher's assertion that woman's "costume" "makes but little difference"—that her dress is indeed a costume, a disguise—attempts to define dress as only superficially related to gender. That is, a woman performing her duty is womanly no matter how she is "costumed." Male attire is chosen for protection as she pursues her duty; a true woman, the paragraph reassures readers, would not pass as a man for any other reason. This sex-gender assertion is ironized by the reality of Emma Edmonds, who began passing as a man as early as 1858, when she ran away from home.

The notice prepares readers for the moment in the text when Edmonds learns that "one of the Federal spies had been captured at Richmond and was to be executed" (105) and decides that, as she is "dissatisfied" with nursing (104), she will apply for this "situation of great danger and vast responsibility" (105). Passing to interviewers as Frank

Thompson, she continues to pass to her readers as an undisguised woman applying for work as a federal spy. Questioned about her patriotism and use of firearms, she then has "a phrenological examination, and finding that my organs of secretiveness, combativeness, etc., were largely developed" (106), she is granted the position.[11] She is instructed to disguise herself as a Black man in order to cross enemy lines:

> I commenced at once to remodel, transform, and metamorphose for the occasion.... I purchased a suit of contraband clothing, real plantation style, and then I went to a barber and had my hair sheared close to my head. Next came the coloring process—head, face, neck, hands and arms were colored black as any African, and then, to complete my contraband costume, I required a wig of real negro wool. (107)

Edmonds's verb sequence accurately represents her view of stages of changes in gender, class, and race: clothing remodels her, a haircut transforms her, and darkened skin coloring metamorphosizes her. Standard rhetoric about regretfully sacrificing her hair—a conventional form of female desexualization—is absent from this businesslike account, unintentionally revealing changes in sex-gender appearance that Edmonds had already made to become Frank Thompson.

Though Edmonds had few resources that would have enabled her knowledge of the codification of the sex-gender system then in progress, her self-construction as a model soldier nonetheless resisted the pathology of inversion. That construction destabilized sexology's definition of so-called androgyny as an illness that diminished female identity: Frank Thompson was demonstrably healthy and energetic. Edmonds's self-construction also rejected sexology's belief that women were able to engage in physical activity and/or violence only by becoming male—that is, that there existed no wholly female physical activity or violence. As Schultz writes, "androgyny implies a merging of masculine and feminine qualities, a collapsing of sexual distinctions" ("Embattled Care" 104). Edmonds's construction of herself was neither androgynous nor male. Instead, her aptitude for soldiering was not masculine but appeared as natural to her as conventional aspects of the code of pure womanhood.

Yet Edmonds's cross-dressing was not as absolute as her descriptions at times may have implied or as she herself might have hoped. Schultz reads "the wish [of Edmonds and other Civil War female cross-dressers] to cross-dress as a man" as "closely related to the wish to escape womanhood, at least for a time. Even if Edmonds had no intention of denying her femininity in masculine cross-dress, the fact that she assumed a male identity must be seen in larger cultural terms as a critique of the restrictions upon mid-century womanhood" ("Performing Genres" 89–90). Young goes further, taking the title under which "Edmonds's memoirs were first published"—*Unsexed*—and reading it as "a word that succinctly captures the extent to which she not only assumes masculinity but abandons femininity" (*Disarming the Nation* 151). While I agree with Schultz that Edmonds's cross-dressing "must be seen in larger cultural terms," I differ with Young's assertion that Edmonds "abandons femininity." Indeed, I remain unconvinced that such abandonment was possible for a woman in Edmonds's circumstances and cultural moment. The act of a woman's passing as a man among men layers rather than abandons femininity. The abandonment Young reads in the title she references is, I suggest, more a reflection of a mix of dominant-culture fears regarding cross-dressing, sensationalistic marketing strategies, and the desire for high book sales in the struggling Civil War publishing industry than it is a reflection of Edmonds's femininity.

Edmonds's awareness that cross-dressing violated prevailing assumptions led her to follow her description of her disguise with contextualization of it as a patriotic act:

> Do my friends wish to know how I felt in such a position and in such a costume? I will tell them. I felt just as happy and as comfortable as it was possible for any one to be under similar circumstances. I am naturally fond of adventure, a little ambitious and a good deal romantic, and this together with my devotion to the Federal cause and determination to assist to the utmost of my ability in crushing the rebellion, made me forget the unpleasant items, and not only endure, but really enjoy, the privations connected with my perilous positions. (121)

The war opened a location for Edmonds to explore "natural" interests in adventure, ambition, and romance, qualities not typically encouraged in cultural constructions of women. Further, the federal government implicitly valued these qualities, resulting in the federally sanctioned occasion for a disguised white woman to pass as a Black man. Such an opportunity would have been unavailable in peacetime, except perhaps on the stage, where wartime danger would have been replaced by a different sort of daring and audience. Edmonds was indeed "happy" and "comfortable" as she "enjoy[ed]" her transformation: it legitimated qualities typically discouraged in women and supported her role and purpose in the great Federal cause, while eliding cultural disruption.

The women writers discussed in earlier chapters detailed similar pleasure and well-being regarding their occupying less normative female positions. In her *Journal* Knight's enjoyment of her travels, her observations, and the wit that her travels inspired in her is clear on every page. Fern's delight in the playful and varied literary impersonations enabled by her pseudonym and anonymity is equally apparent. Even in the more serious sections of Alcott's *Hospital Sketches,* Trib is consistently represented as vibrantly and deeply engaged in her experiences.

Edmonds's impersonations invert conventions of nineteenth-century passing narratives which characteristically use disguise to pass higher (whereas Edmonds was lower) in the class hierarchy and which typically portray deceiving the less observant upper class as easier than deceiving the watchful underclass. According to Edmonds's narrative, she—a white, literate female—passes undetected as a Black, ignorant boy when viewed by Rebel soldiers and by male and female slaves. The components of the putatively successful passing are uncomplicated: skin dye, "a wig of real negro wool," and "a suit of contraband clothing, real plantation style." Here, skin color and hair transform race; clothes transform class; and their combination transforms gender.

However, Edmonds's passing identity is contested in a scene in which her skin dye has begun to fade:

> [O]ne young darkie looked up at me in a puzzled sort of manner, and turning round to one of his companions, said: "Jim, I'll be darned if that feller aint turnin' white; if he aint then I'm no nigger." I felt greatly alarmed at the remark, but said, very carelessly, "Well, gem'in I'se allers 'spected to come white some time; my mudder's a white woman." This had the desired effect, for they all laughed at my simplicity, and made no further remarks upon the subject. (116)

The narrative suggests boundaries of race, class, and gender ("'I'll be darned if that feller aint turnin' white'") are permeable, easily crossed and recrossed. If challenged, the impersonator may employ accented speech and strategic humor to deflect questions. Yet the Black man who speaks in this scene knows better: he relies on authority of his own racial identity ("then I'm no nigger") to suggest an impermeable boundary being unimaginably breached. The laughter, then, is perhaps directed not at Edmonds's feigned "simplicity" but rather at this non-Black stranger explaining her deteriorating appearance with the (laughable) notion of beginning Black and subsequently "coming white." (That

Edmonds's impersonation would be detected by a Black audience without her realization seems more likely than her passing undetected.) This possible penetration of her disguise, however, may be less important than its ultimate success: she remains unexposed, gains information she needs, and returns safely to Union camp. Though Edmonds's secret may have been detected, her passing was not revealed. Because her identity as white, female, literate, and Northern remains concealed enough for her safety, Edmonds has, to a significant extent, successfully crossed race, gender, class, and geographic lines in this impersonation.

After she returns to camp, Edmonds abandons the disguise because "it was not safe for me to palm myself off again on the rebels as a colored boy. . . . I should be in danger of being recognized" (147). She subsequently appears "in military uniform" (177). This impersonation as a young white male Union orderly necessarily begins without explanation. Were Edmonds to explain to readers why she is, seemingly inexplicably, in disguise to her Union employers, she would have to reveal that she enlisted as a man, Frank Thompson, and that she has continued to pass as a man. This information would be far too disruptive of cultural assumptions as well as the narrative established in the text. Rather than provide such an explanation, Edmonds instead abruptly appears in the guise of a male orderly.

Community perception of her as a boy and the attendant dangers of her participation in battle free memories of an earlier self: "I remembered that when I was a child . . . [my mother] was afraid I would meet with some violent death, for I was always in some unheard of mischief, such as riding the wildest colt on the farm, firing off my father's shotgun, and climbing to the highest point of the buildings" (218). Childhood and now adulthood dangers are identified by a lack of social and spatial confinement. Edmonds's connecting these stories of selfhood points to gender issues of access and authority. Her mother's gendered experience suggests to her that such acts will result in violence, while Edmonds's own unexamined experience leads her to conclude that she lives a charmed life—after all, "bullets seemed quite harmless as far as I was personally concerned" (218). She attributes her survivals and successes to individual luck, eliding the suspension of gender roles (a girl allowed to roam freely, a woman disguised as a man) that resulted in her access to masculine agency.

This elision is underscored when Edmonds asks a dying soldier on the battlefield if she can help him. She looks at him and is "*satisfied* . . . that my suspicion was well-founded" (271; emphasis added). He in turn examines her with "an earnest gaze, and, as if *satisfied* with the scrutiny" (272; emphasis added) confides to her: "I can trust you, and will tell you a secret. I am not what I seem, but am a female. I enlisted from the purest motives, and have remained undiscovered and unsuspected. . . . I wish you to bury me with your own hands, that none may know after my death that I am other than my appearance indicates" (272). Edmonds, a woman disguised as a man, hears the dying confession of a woman whom she initially believes to be a man but, with scrutiny, identifies as a woman.[12] The dying soldier initially believes Edmonds to be a man and may or may not then identify her as a woman. Despite these dual impersonations and their suggested detections, the text partially encourages an ungendered reading: Edmonds honors the confession and gives the woman "a soldier's burial" (272)—one soldier respecting the dying wishes of another.

This battlefield encounter of two women—one fatally wounded, one for whom bullets are harmless—secretly impersonating male soldiers suggests an alternative narrative of selfhood for Edmonds. The two women gaze at each other until both are "satisfied." The possibility of mutual though unstated recognition is implied, as well as another female representation and the opportunity for Edmonds as Franklin to record the voice of another disguised woman. The soldier's confession that she enlisted from "the purest motives" recalls the "Publisher's Notice" proclaiming Edmonds's disguises as also stemming from "the purest motives." In recognizing the soldier as a woman, hearing her confession, and protecting her sex-gender identity, Edmonds discovers and rejects (buries) a cross-gendered alternative self. Her burial of the woman inters her recognition of the dangers of cross-gender impersonations, just as she evaded the realizations that slaves may have detected her contraband impersonation and that suspended gender roles in childhood and adulthood have allowed her significant freedoms.

Young's analysis of this passage disallows its authenticity and instead reads it an invented scene that allows Edmonds to contemplate wartime cross-dressing:

> Improbable as an actual event, this encounter between the two women offers a covert symbolic meditation on Edmonds's own experience "passing among the wounded." In this moment of mutual identification, the cross-dressed soldier not only recognizes Edmonds as a kindred cross-dresser but provides a mirror-image to describe Edmonds herself. Edmonds's account of the other woman reveals her own "looks"—idealized as "sweet face," "golden locks," purest motives—to an astute reader. (*Disarming the Nation* 153–54)

I agree with Young's reading up to a point, diverging, however, from her emphasis on improbability and actuality. This battlefield encounter between these women provides rich implications—actual and imaginary—of crossed-dressed women soldiers scrutinizing other soldiers for revealing sex-gender markers, as well as male soldiers viewing other male soldiers for similar markers. In the life Edmonds was then leading as a cross-dressed woman soldier, all other soldiers would have been potentially female, potentially—with careful scrutiny—like Edmonds herself. She was surrounded by and an active participant in wartime blurrings of probability and improbability.

A variety of readings, some contradictory, are prompted by this scene. The burial enables multiple forms of identification for Edmonds: she identifies the soldier as a woman, she identifies *with* the soldier, and, as Young asserts and Schultz implies, she identifies *as* the soldier. Yet the scene also allows for rejection of such literal and metaphorical identification as the cross-dressed soldier is buried and so cast off. In both readings burial of the cross-dressed soldier occurs—as rejection and as reluctant abandonment of a fulfilling self. If the wo/man in the uniform of the U.S. Army standing over the grave is, by some definitions of the time, an androgyne, then androgyny here is American, nationalistic, and patriotic. The icon of the U.S. soldier as the "true" American is joined by the androgyne and also by Alcott's nurturing female soldier. The latter two representations are each compelling in their own right as figures who depend on, yet challenge, gender roles.

The scene also invites speculation regarding lesbian impulses. Young interestingly reads the "intimations of same-sex intimacy" as signaling that "the sustained adoption of male dress . . . [also allows] pleasures of masculine agency and romance with women" (*Disarming the Nation* 155–56). While these women do indeed share intimacies, such intimacy is seemingly allowable only because one of the women is dying. To this mix of fascination, identification, scrutiny, and desire, Schultz adds a "spiritual affinity" that emerges from cross-dressing:

> The soldier's twice repeated words of trust communicate the cross-dresser's code to Edmonds, who knows, before the wounded soldier tells her, that he is a woman. Likewise, the code obviates the need for Edmonds herself to be revealed. The resonating experience of the cross-dressers brings them into rare alignment: their spiritual affinity silently promises confidentiality and affirms labor in the third space, the invisible space between, where conventional gender identity does not figure. ("Performing Genres" 86)

The scene offers compelling possibilities of same-sex attraction (two women recognizing each other, immediately trusting each other, one begging the other to "bury me with your own hands") while resisting others (whatever this attraction is, it will certainly have a brief duration, with one woman dying and the other likely to be killed at any moment).

In all cases, for Edmonds, cross-gender impersonation results in autonomy and authority (even disguised as a male contraband in proslavery territory, she has authority to deceive). Yet to access masculine agency and elide nineteenth-century U.S. restrictive sex-gender conventions, she must put off fears of detection and death as she puts on male clothing. Despite her cross-gender impersonation—or perhaps because of it—her text must subordinate issues of gender under the guise of duty and pure motives. Here, "radical notions of gender do not secure radical gender politics" (Young, "Confederate Counterfeit" 210). Edmonds tests confines of gender in her cross-dressing and her narrative. She also consistently reinforces cultural constructions of gender (e.g., duty, pure motives, individual luck) that guard her self-definition as a heterosexual woman. She thus allows herself to maintain a somewhat coherent subject position in her text and, correspondingly, in her life. Such moments reflect Edmonds's awareness and manipulation of sex-gender ideology and rhetoric.

The women writers discussed in previous chapters exhibit similar awareness of social expectations regarding female behaviors. Across the various genres adopted by these women, all mix the genuinely uncommon with the overtly conventional in their female (self-) representations. Their generic choices of degrees of fiction and nonfiction, while interesting and significant, are nonetheless subordinated to their keen recognitions of what may be publicly expected from white middle-class women.

In a later disguise as a rebel boy, Edmonds is conscripted into the Southern Army and crosses multiple boundaries with bewildering rapidity: a white woman passing as a Northern spy passing as a Southern boy fighting as a Confederate soldier and then crossing Union lines and passing immediately as a Union soldier. Fighting her way to the Union side in battle, she turns and "discharg[es] the contents of my pistol" (316) in the face of a Southern officer. Afterward, informed "that I would not be permitted to go out again . . . in the capacity of spy" for fear she would meet with "those who had seen me desert their ranks, and I would consequently be hung up to the nearest tree," she "turned [her] attention to more quiet and less dangerous duties" (318). But when a shell explodes outside Edmonds's tent, she is, as Schultz writes, "unmanned by . . . the sudden ferocity of what appears to be a benign shell [which] reprises the immediate danger that she herself has always been in through potential detection" ("Performing Genres" 89). As a result, Edmonds becomes ill and feverish. Regarding this breakdown, Schultz writes that "[h]ere detonation and detection are linked: something finally explodes inside of Edmonds (her successful performance of masculinity perhaps) and she is returned to a feminine reality consonant with loss" ("Performing Genres" 89):

> All my soldierly qualities seemed to have fled, and I was again a poor, cowardly, nervous, whining woman; and as if to make up for lost time, and to give vent to my long pent up feelings, I could do nothing but weep hour after hour, until it would seem that my head was literally a fountain of tears and my heart one great burden of sorrow. (359)

Edmonds's alertness regarding sex-gender ideology again emerges in this rhetoric. She invokes another female representation and voice—in this case putatively her pre-cross-gender impersonation self ("I was again poor, cowardly, nervous, whining"). This characterization points to Edmonds's initial attraction to a role that would allow her to engage fictive stories of selfhood and to the overwhelming consequences that readers would expect for a woman who had had such alarming access to and (ab)use of male power. Yet, crucially for my reading, Edmonds's earlier weak self is only putatively suggested. Edmonds, after all, was never a subservient, weeping female. Indeed, largely by her own account, she was a fearless child who grew into a cross-dressing salesman and later a successful soldier. Her tears may emerge as grief for her soldier identity as she embraces femininity with its accompanying restrictions. She may also construct herself as a weak, sobbing woman to provide a favorable substitute in her readers' minds for the soldier who had coolly used power and, mere lines earlier, had detailed the bloody damage her shot did to the Confederate captain—"his handsome face was very much disfigured, a part of his nose and nearly half of his upper lip being shot away" (317). Instead, she represents herself as powerless, as any conventional woman would be, able only to "do nothing but weep hour after hour" (359).

Her liminal gender progression continues as she was released from "further duty as 'Nurse and Spy' in the Federal army" and "procured female attire, and laid aside forever (perhaps) my military uniform; but I had become so accustomed to it that I parted with it with much reluctance" (360). (In reality, Edmonds, fearing detection, deserted the hospital and Army.)[13] Clothing initially characterized as "costume," only superficially related to her identity as a woman, has now become customary—that is, a significant part of her self-representation that she lays aside yet lingers over. Finally unwilling to permanently pass as a man or a woman, Edmonds concludes her book by rhetorically returning to possibilities of her previous cross-gendered identities: "I am about to return to the army to offer my services in any capacity which will best promote the interests of the Federal cause—no matter how perilous the position may be" (384).

The text's illustrations participate in Edmonds's vacillation regarding typically oppositional categories of male and female.[14] The page that lists the illustrations is subtitled "Disguises and other scenes," which emphasizes cross-gendered visual representation. A range of female representations and potential female voices appear in the illustrations. Of thirteen engravings, seven are of Edmonds disguised as a man (one as a male contraband, five as a Union orderly, and one as a rebel boy). In contrast, the frontispiece shows Edmonds in female riding attire, posed next to a horse; though she is dressed as a woman, her activity-specific clothing and her hand on the mane of the saddled horse (which paws the ground in anticipation), suggests readiness for action at a moment's notice. These illustrations visually extend female scripts of the written text.

In the end Edmonds's *Nurse and Spy* made public a wider variety of gender representations—woman as male contraband, orderly, soldier. Though modified by their temporary nature, their liminal wartime location, and their patriotic rhetoric, these representations, imbued with the authority and wider distribution of print, contributed to the larger national discourse on sex-gender identity. Edmonds reentered this cross-gender conversation in 1883, when she publicly revealed herself as "Frank Thompson," seeking Congressional action to receive a military pension and to have Frank Thompson's desertion charge dismissed (Richard Hall 83). Edmonds related that in the twenty years since the war, she had "resumed my own proper dress, and have never worn any disguises since, except when sitting for pictures" (83). Before the Civil War, Fanny Fern's identity was revealed through male acrimony and was intended to humiliate her publicly and damage her economically. Decades after the Civil War, Edmonds revealed her identity herself, intending to gain necessary and valuable publicity in order to benefit economically. Edmonds's revelation resulted in interviews, articles, and testimonials concerning her past and current identities, as well as the authenticity of her claims. The paper trail responding to her disclosure extended the dialogue on sex-gender identity begun in *Nurse and Spy*. During the war her sustained passing as Frank Thompson so violated sex-gender assumptions that she fled the hospital, deserted the Army, and wrote it out of her narrative rather than have it exposed. Twenty years later in the post-Reconstruction United States, when she revealed her former male identity, Edmonds subsequently corresponded with and met her soldier comrades, was awarded a pension, and was "formally inducted into the Grand Army of the Republic" (Young, *Disarming the Nation* 150).

The resulting publicity identified such sustained cross-gender impersonation as notable and unusual but, by the 1880s, no longer an unthinkable disruption of nineteenth-century U.S. sex-gender conventions. In the postwar decades, those conventions had been reconfigured to recognize gender possibilities outside rigid binaries of female and male. The sexological project to classify sex-gender categories recorded and legitimized gender ambiguity within the public imagination. In the 1860s for Frank Thompson to be revealed to be S. Emma E. Edmonds would have been, in Edmonds's later words, "'far worse than death,'" that is, only transgressively representable in the public imagination (Fladeland 455). In the 1880s, by the time Edmonds chose to declare that she had been Frank Thompson, institutions of representation had expanded to recognize and contain cross-gender imposture. Edmonds's disclosure was at once culturally allowable (it made the newspapers as well as the Congressional Record) and, given the years she subsequently spent repeatedly authenticating her identities for official purposes, disruptively uncommon.

II.

The reception of Edmonds's revelation concerning her life as Frank Thompson (1883) and subsequent successful actions to grant her a pension (1884), to have desertion charges dismissed (1886), and to receive back pay (1889) can be aligned with Civil War reminiscences by Mary Livermore and Annie Turner Wittenmyer that appeared during this same cultural moment. Unlike Edmonds's text, an account of her cross-dressing experiences written during the war, Livermore's *My Story of the War* (1889) and Wittenmyer's *Under the Guns* (1895) are dually distanced from their subject: they write decades after the war's end from the distance of self-defined conventional women who had observed women who appeared to violate gender boundaries.[15] Their conflicted retrospective responses to cross-dressed women they encountered reflect the voyeuristic curiosity and limited acceptance of the cultural reaction to Emma Edmonds/Frank Thompson.

Mary Ashton Rice (1820–1905) was born and educated in Boston. From 1839 to 1842 she lived with a slave-owning family in Virginia, working as a schoolteacher for their children (Venet 146). After her marriage to Daniel Livermore, a minister and temperance activist, Livermore began to write on religion, temperance, and antislavery issues for the newspapers. She was the author of "seven books, more than forty magazine articles, countless newspaper articles and over ninety speeches" (Gayle and Griffin 59). During the Civil War, Livermore worked as a volunteer with the U.S. Sanitary Commission, collecting food and clothing for soldiers and very successfully fund-raising for the war effort. After the war Livermore devoted her considerable energies to regular lecturing and to suffrage and temperance organizations.[16]

In an early section of *My Story of the War*, Livermore recalls visiting a Union regiment as part of her war work, and she begins to construct a narrative that subordinates cross-gender impersonation by privileging instead the motivation for such transgressions: "One of the captains came to me . . . and begged to know if I noticed anything peculiar in the appearance of one of the men, whom he indicated. It was evident at a glance that the 'man' was a young woman in male attire, and I said so" (113). As in the "Publisher's Notice" to Edmonds's text, this scene suggests that for women, male clothing is no more than a costume, and in this case an ineffective one. First, the soldier's "peculiar appearance" is easily ("evident at a glance") read correctly by another woman (seemingly by virtue of her own sex an authority on female sex-gender identity) who, without hesitation—as though this is a decision no one would need to weigh—promptly reports the impersonation to authorities. Next, the soldier, confronted by the captain, responds in conventionally female fashion: "speaking in tones of passionate entreaty, she begged him not to expose her, but to allow her to retain her disguise" (114) so that she may remain in the regiment with her enlisted husband. Her emotional "plead[ing]" (114) and the reason for her impersonation are conventionally female. She is not a woman who wishes to pass as a man in order to access male power or liberty; rather, she is an emotional, needy woman, so dependent on her husband that, she says, "it would kill her if he marched without her" (114). Unlike Sarah Kemble Knight, this woman desires to travel only to be with her husband; she desires neither to travel alone nor to be alone.

This female voice may or may not be fully or even partially authentic. The woman's speech is recollected by Livermore (not the unnamed woman herself). Additionally, the speech was recorded in 1889, decades after it was ostensibly spoken. However, what remains more reliable is what this scene reveals about Mary Livermore. As with many supporters of women's rights in the late nineteenth century, Livermore advocated relational feminism, a view of sex roles that promoted "women's distinctive contributions to society as mothers and wives and located these contributions within a system of education, legal rights, and increased social responsibilities that promoted a better society" (Gayle and Griffin 56). In private, Livermore disparaged "cloying portrayals" of women as "pious blarney" (56). Livermore's public speeches "supported feminine ideals of motherhood, the nurturing of children and family, and the duties of wives while simultaneously arguing for women's increased participation in public life" (57). Long after the war had ended, this unidentified female voice had retained enough significance for Livermore to include it in her text and carefully align it with normative female rhetoric. Further, Livermore—a well-known women's rights activist and orator—publicly established her own conventional womanhood as she proceeded to detail her response to this woman whom she had encountered a quarter of a century earlier.[17]

Livermore makes clear that such a woman must be responded to authoritatively (she must accept that her role is to remain behind), but kindly (she is presented as misguided in her implicit challenge of gender divisions, but misguided in a recognizably female way). She is "quietly conducted outside the camp" where Livermore "[takes] her in charge. . . . wish[ing] to take her to my home" (114). That is, she is escorted from the male wartime location and committed to the domestic care of another white woman. Livermore implicitly assumes that this woman shares her class status—that she will be easily contained by pressures that ostensibly control all white middle-class women (in this case, being "taken charge of" by another woman). However, Livermore has overread her own gendered authority and underread the woman, who "leap[ed] suddenly from the carriage . . . and in a moment was lost amid the crowds" (114). Though the extent of her desperation is unexpected, the woman's reasons for behaving as she does are still within conventionally female boundaries. The woman's despair and desire to remain with her husband dominate Livermore's narration in this section:

> That night she leaped into the Chicago river, but was rescued by a policeman. . . . It was impossible to turn her from her purpose to follow

her husband. "I have only my husband in all the world," she said, "and when he enlisted he promised that I should go with him; and that was why I put on his clothes and enlisted in the same regiment. And go with him I will, in spite of everybody." The regiment was ordered to Cairo, and the poor woman disappeared . . . the same night. None of us doubted but she left to carry out her purpose. (114)

"Leaping" both from the carriage and later into the river, she is physically and emotionally resolute—she will be with her husband or die. The script in which Livermore incorporates the woman suggests agoraphobic dependence on her husband; the woman cross-dresses not to access masculine agency but to remain close to it. In Livermore's reconstruction the woman is desperately determined, a "poor woman" whose crossing of gender boundaries is a pathetic female attempt to cling to the only coherent subject position she can imagine. Further, Livermore's descriptions of the woman's desire to be with her husband serve to register her heterosexuality and fidelity, writing less conventional sexual implications of women's cross-gender imposture out of the text.

Livermore extends her discourse on motivations of women soldiers by next invoking "half-soldier heroines" (119), women who "followed the army as nurses, and divided their services between the battle-field and hospital" (116). By providing named examples of such women—making them known and potentially knowable—she attempts rhetorically to dismantle the cultural disruption of women successfully passing as men. However, Livermore's "half-soldier heroines" are not women who impersonated male soldiers, though they may have performed some of the same wartime duties. Her examples are women whose motivations (to be near one's husband, to nurse the wounded), as she constructs them, significantly partake of prevailing gender assumptions. While Livermore's representations of women do extend female behaviors, they also simultaneously limit gender possibilities by evading the motivation that lies at the heart of women's cross-gender impersonation—that is, that a woman may choose to pass as a man in order to access autonomy and authority that the dominant culture would otherwise deny her due to her sex-gender identity.

Alcott certainly would have recognized the limitations Livermore rhetorically imposes on female representations in *My Story of the War.* Indeed, they are the very limitations that Alcott had ultimately imposed on Tribulation Periwinkle decades earlier in *Hospital Sketches.* Additionally, Alcott herself acceded to these same restrictions in later editions of *Hospital Sketches* that progressively modify and conventionalize her wartime nursing experience. However, Livermore's later text significantly exceeds Alcott's earlier one in imagining possibilities of women's cross-gender imposture. Livermore's conclusion to this section of her text reflects her uneasy knowledge that some women did use the occasion of war to successfully—and perhaps permanently—impersonate men for reasons she can barely imagine:

> Some one has stated the number of women soldiers known to the service as little less than four hundred. I cannot vouch for the correctness of this estimate, but I am convinced that a larger number of women disguised themselves and enlisted in the service, for one cause or other, than was dreamed of. Entrenched in secrecy, and regarded as men, they were sometimes revealed as women, by accident or casualty. Some startling histories of these military women were current in the gossip of army life; and extravagant and unreal as were many of the narrations, one always felt that they had a foundation in fact. (119–20)

Livermore's equivocation ("for one cause or other") suggests a multiplicity of motivations on the part of these unknown women that would have ranged from wishing to nurse the wounded and following one's male partner to seeking opportunity for sexual acts then viewed as transgressive. Her estimation expands the number of cross-dressing women soldiers; indeed, she implies (more women enlisted "than was dreamed of") an army rich with disguised women. The titillating descriptions—"entrenched in secrecy," "startling," "extravagant," "unreal"—that mark her interest in these female narratives also reveal that for her these women are so exotic as to be nearly unrepresentable. In her desire to believe in some reality of these rumors ("one always felt that they had a foundation in fact"), she constructs an army of unknown, unknowable women (not seeking their husbands, not wishing to nurse) secretly disguised as male soldiers.

Having rhetorically discovered her desire, Livermore ends this section by rejecting her curiosity as well as these alternative female scripts:[18] "Such service was not the noblest that women rendered the country during its four years' struggle for life, and no one can regret that these soldier women were exceptional and rare. It is better to heal a wound than to make one" (120). Her remarks subordinate the sacrifices of women's battlefield combat ("making wounds") in favor of maintaining female gender boundaries ("healing wounds"). Though the final sentence may seem to preach wartime pacifism, its piety is located not in peace but in gender: men's province is to make wounds, women's to heal them. Not unlike S. Emma E. Edmonds, while Livermore considers cross-gender impersonations in her text, she also reinforces cultural constructions of gender that allow her to maintain a coherent female subject position, one distant from the "exceptional and rare" soldier women she has imagined for the past twenty years. *My Story of the War* inscribes in print the existence of such women, and while Livermore does not (cannot, will not) write the "startling histories of these military women" (120), she does record wartime private gender flexibility beneath dominant gender constructions.

The inclusion of these sections in Livermore's text resonates with the expanded national dialogue on nineteenth-century U.S. sex-gender conventions. In its ambiguous and contradictory negotiation of cross-gender imposture, *My Story of the War* reflects a great deal of late-nineteenth-century confusion. The text explains women's cross-dressing (to follow one's husband), promotes it ("a larger number of women . . . than was dreamed of"), and denies it ("exceptional and rare"). Indeed, *My Story of the War* reveals as much about Reconstruction sex-gender assumptions as it does about Civil War sex-gender assumptions. Decades after the surrender at Appomattox, Livermore's narrative engages in its own civil war over gendered issues of identity and authority.

III.

Reformer, editor, journalist, author, and temperance advocate Annie Turner (1827–1900) was born in Ohio. At age twenty-three she married William Wittenmyer and moved to Iowa, where her subsequent Civil War relief work and reform activities would be largely based. William Wittenmyer's death before the war left her a rich woman, able to advance reformist projects with her substantial wealth. Wittenmyer spent the rest of her life engaged in work to improve lives of children, men, and women disenfranchised by war and its devastating effects. Among her many accomplishments were the founding of homes for children orphaned by the war, the organizing of an aid system to collect hospital supplies, and later the development of special hospital kitchens and the training of women in their organization and use. Like Livermore, Wittenmyer later in the century became active and influential in temperance organizations and was elected the first president of the Women's Christian Temperance Union (WCTU).[19]

Annie Turner Wittenmyer's *Under the Guns* (1895), a late-century history of the Civil War, includes the chapter "A Woman Wounded in Battle," concerning a Union soldier wounded behind enemy lines and hospitalized there, "her sex . . . [un]discovered till she was under a surgeon's care" (17). The woman is sent back to the Union army with a message:

> "As the Confederates do not use women in war, this woman, wounded in battle, is returned to you." There was great indignation in the regiment to which this woman belonged; and officers and men hastened to protest, that, although she had been with them for more than a year, not one in the regiment suspicioned that she was a woman. She stood the long, hard marches, did full duty on the picket-line and in camp, and had fought well in all the battles in which the regiment took part. (18)

The men's "great indignation" emerges from their own sex-gender identity—that is, they are implicitly being identified as men so unmanly (so fearful of death or defeat) that they would (ab)use a woman in combat. Beneath their indignation is the disruptive awareness that a woman may pass successfully, perhaps permanently, as a man. Their hasty protests mark the evidence assumed to constitute sex-gender identity: a person who serves successfully as a soldier, whose clothes and hair conceal outward female gender signs, is assumed to be male. That only an examination of her unclothed body proves her to be female challenges social insistence on female gender confines.

Wittenmyer questions the woman concerning her motivations for enlisting, asking if she had a husband, lover, or friend in the regiment—conventional heterosexual motivations for her unconventional behavior. After being told, "'No, I didn't know any of them,'" Wittenmyer, unwilling or unable to imagine other reasons for a woman to disguise herself as a male soldier, plaintively asks why the woman enlisted. She is told, "'I thought I'd like camp-life, and I did'" (18). Wittenmyer's assumption that romance and dependence drove the woman to cross-gender impersonation is displaced by the woman's straightforward confession that autonomous personal preference led her to disguise herself. Her choice to enlist proves so appropriate that, even wounded as she now is, the wartime fear she names is detection and subsequent banishment—"'I was awfully afraid they would find me out, and then I'd have to go'" (18). Expanded possibilities allowed by wartime cross-gender impersonation will now be denied her, and the confinement of her former circumscribed gender conduct will reemerge.

First, the woman is wounded; then, when her sex is discovered, she is commodified ("this woman . . . is returned to you"). Next she is institutionalized in the hospital, and finally, as Wittenmyer relates, she is ordered by the male surgeon—here the cultural agent of gendered assumptions—to dress in women's clothes:

> We women from the North, by gift and by purchase, provided the necessary outfit for a woman's wardrobe. To raise some funds for her we had her photograph taken, first in the uniform of a private soldier, and then dressed as a woman. She sold them to soldiers and visitors for twenty-five cents each, and raised considerable money. I have the two I purchased, which I have treasured in my war album all these years. She was stout and muscular, with heavy features, high cheek bones, and her black abundant hair was cut very close. She was perhaps twenty-six or twenty-eight years old, but when in her military rig looked like a beardless boy. (19)

Just as the Confederate army arranged the woman's return over the line that was crossed in combat, so the women in camp arrange her return over the gender boundary that was crossed when she successfully disguised herself as a male soldier. The threatening liminality resulting from discovery of the woman's cross-gender identification motivates the camp women to unite to assist her. Combining their resources to donate and buy female clothing for her, they re-cover her in outward female gender signs and also (by use of their own clothing) incorporate her into their social class.

This association is further reinforced by the women's devising the dual photographic cross-dressing exhibit. The success ("She . . . raised considerable money") of arranging for the woman to capitalize on her cross-gender impersonation by posing in a soldier's uniform and then in women's clothing suggests the camp women's accurate gendered assessment that such performance would be viewed as a sex-gender curiosity—titillating enough to turn a profit but not sufficiently shocking, now that the woman's sex has been revealed, to repel buyers. Wittenmyer's scrutiny decades later of these now-treasured visual artifacts which she helped to contrive shows her, like Edmonds and like Livermore, still negotiating alternative gender possibilities (she muses that the woman "was stout and muscular, with heavy features") and cultural disruptions resulting from women's wartime cross-gender impersonation.

Ultimately, the woman is compelled to divulge her name to Wittenmyer ("I was commissioned by the officers to find out all I could about her, and where she lived, as she had been more friendly to me than to the others" [19]), in order to obtain a pass and transportation. (The woman's location in Nashville, within military lines, is metaphorically appropriate: in the liminal region of the war, she needs an identifying pass to cross its boundaries.) Wittenmyer withholds particulars of the conversation ("The interview was a long one. I can give only the main points" [19]), recording her own persistence and the woman's final reluctant question: "'If I tell you my name, and the place I wish to go to, will you keep it a secret?'" Accustomed to closely guarding her identity, the woman is loath to disclose information that, were it to become known, would make her return to regular dressing in women's clothing scandalously public. Were Wittenmyer to reveal this information, the woman (who cannot resume her soldier identity) would be unable to reappear quietly in her former identity; trapped in a liminal cross-dressing location, she would no longer be a man (her soldier identity exposed), but would also no longer be a culturally acceptable woman.

It is an act of faith—risking her remaining possibilities for a coherent female subject position—when, after Wittenmyer agrees to honor her confidence, the woman tells her, "'I will trust you' . . . and she whispered her name and residence. Two days after that she was on her way to her home in the Northwest. I never knew what became of her" (20). As with Edmonds and the disguised, dying soldier (and in strikingly similar language: "'I can trust you, and will tell you a secret'" [271]), trust between women results in information revealed, secrecy maintained, and practical dilemmas (burial, returning home) arising from cross-dressing resolved. The woman's disappearance from Wittenmyer's sight and experience corresponds with her unconventional behavior. Given significant cultural penalties for disruptive female behavior, such women do not publish narratives about these experiences. Three decades later, however, this woman who chose to pass as a man because it suited her is seen and heard in Wittenmyer's text. The lingering curiosity of Wittenmyer's last sentence ("I never knew what became of her") leaves open the prospect that the woman, like Edmonds, may have resumed conventional female existence or—tantalizingly—that she may have returned to cross-gender impersonation, ending this section with the possibility that women passing as men could be living undetected among late-nineteenth-century U.S. readers.

Wittenmyer's recognition of the arbitrary nature of gender construction links the cultural moment of her post-Reconstruction text with that of the Civil War. The sex-gender identity of the woman Wittenmyer describes was discovered, at least temporarily, because of her involvement in the war. Without the battlefield and its attendant possibilities for discovery due to wounds, death, or scrutiny, such women will perhaps continue to pass as men. In *Under the Guns,* the postwar period permits the possibility of (more) successful female cross-dressing. Wittenmyer's representation of this woman makes available an alternative sex-gender identity for readers. Such a model would not otherwise be readily available from the cross-dressing women themselves who concealed their autobiographic experiences as well as their class status and sex. As with the multiplicity of female representations and voices recorded by Knight and Fern, portions of these women's lives survive only because more conventional women felt compelled to record them.

IV.

The high sales of Edmonds's *Nurse and Spy*, Livermore's *My Story of the War*, and Wittenmyer's *Under the Guns*, along with publicity that resulted from Edmonds's revealing herself to be Frank Thompson, can be read as examples of "capitalism allow[ing] marginalized or stigmatized forms of sexual behavior and identity to filter into consumer culture packaged in disguised forms which take away the edge of political threat posed by those sexualities" (Epstein and Straub 10). Through the various rhetorical alignments, impersonations, and (self-) representations in these three war narratives, female cross-dressing and constructions of alternative sex-gender identity are allowed to enter (and to produce profit in) more normative public realms. Such "recuperative, appropriative modes of capitalism" (10) can also be seen at work in postwar national stage performances by (in)famous female U.S. Civil War spies.

After the war, Pauline Cushman and Belle Boyd, who had both worked as spies during the war, separately recast their life-threatening exploits as popular dramas. Dressed as a soldier, Cushman "regaled audiences in large cities throughout the country with tales of her days as a Union spy" (Dannett 242). Likewise, beginning in 1886 and continuing until her death in 1900, former Confederate spy Boyd performed in popularly acclaimed recitals "usually billed as a thrilling war narrative entitled 'North and South; or The Perils of a Spy'" (Sigaud 196). Onstage, Cushman and Boyd (re)presented themselves as dramatic players in public entertainment for which viewers were required to purchase tickets. Their performances obscured what had been the reality of successful female wartime cross-dressing. In exchange for the ticket price, audiences were captivated and titillated rather than directly confronted with alternative sex-gender possibilities. Presentations of Boyd and Cushman as flag-waving U.S. women diverted audiences from the disruptive realization that any "man"—sitting in the theater, passing by on the street, living in one's home—could, in fact, be a woman in disguise. Such stage acts were simulacra where boundaries of North and South were subsumed under the commonality of war and where battle was sanitized as theater. The same institutions of representation that modified slavery into sharecropping and then praised it as racial equality repackaged cross-gender identification as womanly and patriotic.

In all cases nineteenth-century gender flexibility was significantly underwritten. Its representations were compromised and marketed as works of loyalty and piety. These modifications did, however, allow woman's wartime gender reconfigurations to appear more visibly in nineteenth-century U.S. culture. Amended and revised as such texts were, they nonetheless marked, however obliquely, alternative sex-gender configurations. As a result, possibilities were suggested for women and men restricted by current sex-gender scripts.

The mid-nineteenth-century national space divided by the Civil War provided a location for reconfiguration of the sex-gender system. In their liminality, the cross-dressed women who appeared in Civil War narratives replicated to some degree the national experience as they endeavored to position themselves within dominant social and cultural arrangements. Such women investigated gender identities separate from restrictive notions of proper female behavior and from conventional sex-gender ideas of the world outside the possibilities of the war. Their reconfigurations, incorporated accurately and inaccurately in war narratives written by themselves or by others, in engravings, photographs, newspaper articles, testimonials, military gossip, and postwar legend, resonated over the decades with other war women like Mary Livermore and Annie Wittenmyer and with Civil War and Reconstruction culture more broadly. The mixed cultural responses that allowed representations of women's wartime cross-gender impersonation to appear without full censure highlight a false rigidity of conventional sex-gender roles for women and men both for that culture and for our own present-day one. During a moment when sexological studies strove to classify sex-gender identities more inflexibly and minutely, audiences voyeuristically considered possibilities of women who had crossed gender boundaries when they passed as men. Civil War narratives of Emma Edmonds, Mary Livermore, and Annie Wittenmyer participated in central cultural discussions of women's writing on normative ordering systems, signaling a wartime investigation of sex-gender restrictions that emerged as prevailing assumptions regarding statehood, gender, and race appeared open to revision.

In the next chapter, the Conclusion, I turn from the white middle-class women's autobiographic works that up until this point have been under consideration to African American Harriet Jacobs's compelling record of life in and after slavery in *Incidents in the Life of a Slave Girl*. In her text Jacobs, like the white women discussed in earlier chapters, positions herself as a conventional woman despite and within her circumstances—circumstances immeasurably more complicated and dangerous than those confronted by Knight, Fern, Alcott, and Edmonds. A reading of Jacobs's narrative in the context of this study underscores the amplified struggle for women like Jacobs to write the autobiographic—women whose race, class, or sexuality marked them as deviant from white middle-class standards. This final chapter's movement from white women's autobiographic writing to a foundational Black woman's autobiographic text tests the ways in which conclusions in previous chapters operate across ethnic/racial lines, and it further expands this book's discussion and analysis of women, writing, and representation.

CONCLUSION

"I Found It Hard to Preserve My Self-Control"

Race, Women, Representation

> *The author is a quick-witted, intelligent woman, with great refinement and propriety of manner. Her daughter, now a young woman grown, is a stylish-looking, attractive young person, white as an Italian lady.*
>
> —Lydia Maria Child to John Greenleaf Whittier (4 April 1861)

THIS STUDY ENDS with a discussion of *Incidents in the Life of a Slave Girl* (1861), Harriet Jacobs's account of her life in and after enslavement. In a scene from *Incidents*, "Linda Brent," Jacobs's thinly veiled autobiographic persona, describes a raced encounter that occurs when she is traveling by steamboat in the North with her white female employer, Mrs. Bruce, in the capacity of nursemaid to Mrs. Bruce's child:

> We went to Albany in the steamboat Knickerbocker. When the gong sounded for tea, Mrs. Bruce said, "Linda, it is late, and you and baby had better come to the table with me." I replied, "I know it is time baby had her supper, but I had rather not go with you, if you please. I am afraid of being insulted." "O no, not if you are with *me*," she said. I saw several white nurses go with their ladies and I ventured to do the same. We were at the extreme end of the table. I was no sooner seated, than a gruff voice said, "Get up! You know you are not allowed to sit here." I looked up, and, to my astonishment and indignation, saw that the speaker was a colored man. If his office required him to enforce the by-laws of the boat, he might, at least, have done it politely. I replied, "I shall not get up, unless the captain comes and takes me up." (136)[1]

In this scene Jacobs's construction of Linda Brent largely privileges genteel female behavior. Brent would rather go hungry than be insulted;

she expresses herself respectfully ("'if you please'"); and she expects others to be equally courteous ("he might, at least, have done it politely"). Jacobs's self-consciously normative representation of Brent's female gentility reflects her awareness of values and assumptions of her middle-class white Northern female readers.[2]

Harriet Jacobs wrote *Incidents* at night between 1853 and 1858 while she worked as a nursemaid for and lived with Nathaniel Parker Willis; his second wife, Cornelia Grinnell Willis; and their child (the family was fictively named the Bruce family in *Incidents*).[3] Jacobs's identity during this time was rich with contradictions of what W. E. B. Du Bois would later famously and influentially detail as the "peculiar sensation" of "double-consciousness," "the two-ness" of being "an American, a Negro; two souls, two thoughts, two unreconciled strivings; two warring ideals in one dark body" (35). Jacobs was a Southern woman living in the North; a mother living away from her children, serving as nursemaid to another woman's child; a fugitive slave working for a white man who edited a proslavery journal;[4] and a Black woman living with and among whites.[5] As Sidonie Smith has argued regarding Jacobs's double consciousness, "[f]rom her position on the margins, however, Jacobs can 'see' both inside and outside white culture, inside and outside 'true womanhood' and its supporting ideology" ("Resisting the Gaze" 99). It was from this vexed, disenfranchised position that Jacobs attempted to write an autobiographical text for publication.

In *Incidents* Jacobs uses the persona of Linda Brent to align herself and her text with white middle-class female Northern readers. For this association to succeed, Jacobs must complicate the condemnation that she anticipates will be directed toward her by her female audience when they read Brent's confession regarding sex with a white man. The text primarily responds to Brent's perceived disruptive sexual acts by foregrounding the cherished nineteenth-century middle-class construction of devoted motherhood. Throughout the text Brent's singular sacrifices—particularly her seven-year concealment in order to remain near and protect her children—are depicted as innate to any loving, dedicated mother. Further, the introduction to and editing of *Incidents* by well-known white abolitionist Lydia Maria Child serves to authorize a reading of Brent as a respectable, compliant, and contrite Black woman.

Critical readings of *Incidents* have centered on scenes of Brent in the South, typically the tenth chapter in which Brent confesses her sexual transgressions, and chapters detailing her seven-year concealment.[6] In the text Brent admits that she had sex with Mr. Sands, "a white unmarried gentleman" (46), in an attempt to protect herself from continued sexual persecution by her owner, Dr. Flint. Brent's sexual "headlong plunge" (47) is described as the result of her "shudder[ing] to think of being the mother of children that should be owned by my old tyrant" and her belief that Mr. Sands would arrange for her children's freedom (47). Brent's confession is located at an intersection of motherhood and a female gentility defeated by raced oppression. Her shamed plea for forgiveness, "Pity me, and pardon me, O virtuous reader!" (47), both informs white middle-class female readers that Brent respects and has endeavored to attain their moral standards and laments her failure to do so. That failure, however, is carefully positioned in the context of devoted motherhood. As Hazel Carby writes, Brent is "a demonstration of the consequences for motherhood of the social and economic relations of the institution of slavery" (54).

Jacobs's text directs critics and readers to considerations of motherhood primarily with the account of Brent's seven-year concealment, which foregrounds her maternal sacrifices. Jacobs lived for seven years in a hidden garret of coffin-like dimensions, giving up her health and all but minimal physical movement in order to remain near but never touch or speak to her children ("Season after season, year after year, I peeped at my children's faces, and heard their sweet voices, with a heart yearning all the while to say, 'Your mother is here'" [117]). Jacobs's extended narration of Brent's acute physical pain and emotional despair is embedded in the script of the sacrificing mother revered by the larger culture:

> I could have made my escape alone; but it was more for my helpless children than for myself that I longed for freedom. Though the boon would have been precious to me, above all price, I would not have taken it at the expense of leaving them in slavery. Every trial I endured, every sacrifice I made for their sakes, drew them closer to my heart, and gave me fresh courage to beat back the dark waves that rolled and rolled over me in a seemingly endless night of storms. (73–74)

Brent's sacrifices for her children do not result in resentment or in a lessening of her affection for them over time. Rather, Jacobs constructs Brent as a mother granted the priceless opportunity to forfeit her life for her children and in so doing to love them even more devotedly. With each ennobling sacrifice, Brent's love for her children is strengthened and her selfless courage is renewed.

My reading of *Incidents* foregrounds Jacobs's (self-) constructions of female gentility. This critical approach constitutes a fresh rereading of Jacobs's text. Jacobs's treatment of female gentility has received little scrutiny, which is understandable given the text's rich locations of, for instance, motherhood and captivity, both of which have garnered major critical attention. I turn to considerations of gentility in *Incidents* in order to test the unstable ground of the work's correspondence with white women's texts discussed in my study. Reading *Incidents* through a lens of gentility underscores Jacobs's violations of the normative while—as with the white women discussed in this study—also drawing attention to her alignment of herself with conventional gendered assumptions. This critical approach additionally reveals complexities of women's self-writing and agency, as well as inadequacies of heterosexual constructions. Through my use of gentility, I attempt to make transparent ways in which *Incidents* contests constraints of the feminine, puts pressure on categories of race and class, and works to forestall reactions against its uncommon discourses. These aspects of Jacobs's writing point to greater degrees of difficulty in writing the autobiographic encountered by women like Jacobs whose race, class, or sexuality identified them as outside the normative. Reading Jacobs's *Incidents in the Life of a Slave Girl* through the lens of gentility complicates generalizations in previous chapters of this study across ethnic/racial lines and extends the discussion that occurs in the rest of the book.

Thus the quotation with which I begin this concluding chapter references not Linda Brent's motherhood but her gentility. In this scene Brent is in the North, a fugitive slave traveling on a steamboat as nursemaid to the child of her white female middle-class employer. Brent is represented as a conventional woman in this scene, still motherly, though paid to be so as she cares for another woman's child. She is also represented as a Black woman who recognizes the potential for negative responses to her public appearance among whites. When confronted, as she had accurately feared she might be, with violating "the by-laws of the boat," she responds with unconventional female self-assertion ("'I shall not get up, unless the captain comes and takes me up'" [136]).[7] However, even her unconventional authoritative response when challenged with a breach of rules is situated somewhat genteelly.[8] That is, her response is based on prevailing race and class assumptions. The "astonishment and indignation" which prompt her self-assertion are provoked by her realization "that the speaker was a colored man." She is affronted because a man in this office is impolite to her, but particularly so because it is a Black man who behaves rudely to her. Brent's further commentary makes this plain: "If his office required him to enforce the by-laws of the boat, he might, at least, have done it politely." The scene encourages readers to recognize Brent as a conventional woman offended by speech that is rude in both language and tone, just as the impertinent assumptions of the Black speaker are rude. Brent's response and its grounding in gentility accord with Amy Richter's argument in her examination of nineteenth-century U.S. public women's travel that "many black women believed that their polite behavior could provide them with protection during travel" (46).

As with a representational strategy adopted by Sarah Kemble Knight in her *Journal,* Jacobs represents herself/Brent adhering to culturally sanctioned female codes even when, as in the scene above, her behavior transgresses those codes. Knight's correlation of speech—which she perceives as less genteel—with eating—which she views as vulgar—reappears in *Incidents* in a more complex intersection of speaking, writing, and eating. In the scene which begins this chapter, Brent anticipates that her presence at the supper table may be perceived as disruptive. She then explains to white readers in writing (not speaking) that she was barred from eating by the (c)rude speech of a Black worker, who, unlike Brent, we may infer did not know how to read or to write. Jacobs orally at the time and then later through Brent in *Incidents* responds with dignified gentility to the man's "gruff voice." In presenting this scene as she does, Jacobs indicates divisions between speaking and writing as well as speaking and eating. In Knight's *Journal* such distinctions are distinctions of class—that is, in Knight's text, the vulgar speaking of white people corresponds with their uncouth eating. Jacobs's distinctions are likewise class-inflected but are further complicated by Blackness. A Black man's crude denial of Brent's genteel attempt to dine exposes such eating, despite its trappings, as no more than coarse consumption segregated by race. Had the Black servant "done it politely"—used courteous speech that acknowledged Brent's propriety—his civil delivery would have still resulted in Brent's exile from the table, but it also would have left intact the possibility of polite dining.

This scene, however, is only one disruptive incident, as it were, though not an insignificant one, in a larger portrait of Brent's traveling. Brent's journeys differ fundamentally from the travel of white women authors discussed in this study's earlier chapters. Primarily, Brent's trips belong to a specific subset of the larger category of travel: they are not voluntary journeys so much as they are flights. Unlike white women discussed earlier, Brent travels not because she chooses to; she travels because she must. In almost every instance of her traveling, Brent is not going *to* a place so much as she is escaping *from* another place. Also, in a nineteenth-century, raced déjà-vu pattern, Brent continues to travel to places she does not wish to go.

Brent's traveling is markedly different from the white women authors' depictions of and rationales for traveling. For example, Jacobs's/Brent's presence while traveling is significantly more disruptive than Knight's unsettling presence. Knight is challenged and mistaken for a prostitute, but she is nonetheless always allowed to sit down and eat. Unlike Alcott's Tribulation Periwinkle in *Hospital Sketches,* Jacobs/Brent cannot travel alone without fearful expectations that she may be insulted, turned away, kidnapped, or raped.[9] Like that of Willis/Fern and Edmonds, Jacobs's/Brent's identity is at various times anonymous, concealed, or not fully known; but, unlike them, her life and liberty are always in danger if her identity is revealed. Indeed, on all her travels, Brent must appear in various degrees of disguise—that is, she must, at all costs, not be read as the fugitive slave she is.

In order to demonstrate these differences, I detail below a passage from *Incidents* regarding female travel. I follow this analysis by readings of similar passages from Knight's *Journal;* from Fern's "Dark Days," an early literary periodical piece; from Alcott's *Hospital Sketches;* and from Edmonds's *Nurse and Spy.* I do not wish to place undue emphasis on implications of the textual passages I have selected. However, as I discuss below, these passages offer provocative instruction regarding race and women's autobiographic uses of gentility as well as cross-dressing and travel.

To begin, toward the end of the twentieth chapter of *Incidents,* readers are presented with what initially seems to be the start of Brent's escape to the North and freedom. In this scene Brent, disguised as a Black male sailor, leaves her hiding place in the house of an unnamed white woman, a friend of her grandmother, who is married to a man who owns slaves. Brent's gentility, despite her cross-dressing, is signaled in her placid acquiescence to her complete lack of information regarding her destination. Peter, the young Black man helping her, then tells her (also informing Jacobs's readers) that her uncle is preparing a hiding place for her in the garret of her grandmother's house. To allow him time to do so, Brent is told that she and Peter will spend the night concealed in the ominously named Snaky Swamp.[10] Brent anxiously "dread[s] to enter this hiding-place" for fear of snakes, but accurately understands that she is "in no situation to choose" (90). Previously, at the beginning of the eighteenth chapter, Brent, eluding agents of Dr. Flint, had hidden "in a thicket of bushes" when

> a reptile of some kind seized my leg. In my fright, I struck a blow which loosened its hold, but I could not tell whether I had killed it; it was so dark, I could not see what it was; I only knew it was something cold and slimy. The pain I soon felt indicated that the bite was poisonous. . . . The dread of being disabled was greater than the physical pain I endured. (80)

Thus, two chapters earlier, Brent's temporarily hiding outside at night had mixed terror of capture, fear of reptiles, physical pain, and anxieties of permanent bodily impairment. Now, two chapters later, as Brent and Peter enter Snaky Swamp, the circumstances of this next concealment outside are even more difficult for Brent to endure:

> We were covered with hundreds of mosquitos. In an hour's time they had so poisoned my flesh that I was a pitiful sight to behold. As the light increased, I saw snake after snake crawling round us. I had been accustomed to the sight of snakes all my life, but these were larger than any I had ever seen. . . . [T]he number of snakes increased so much that we were continually obliged to thrash them with sticks to keep them from crawling over us. (90–91)

In this feral nighttime Eden, Brent's body is besieged by a variety of rabid life forms that desire to possess/consume Black female flesh. The mosquitoes are numerous, poisonous, and relentless. The too-phallic snakes are equally plentiful, large beyond custom, and multiplying in number throughout the night. In this situation, circumstances render Peter, Brent's male companion in hiding, effectively demasculinized; he does (can do) nothing beyond what Brent herself—not male, though disguised as a male sailor—can do in attempting to keep the snakes away. The attacking mosquitoes and snakes within the confines of Snaky Swamp substitute for the slavocracy and its predatory representatives, particularly Dr. Flint, in the larger world outside the swamp.[11] As with poisonous vermin within the swamp, poisonous human vermin outside the swamp are also driven to possess and consume the Black female body.

Traumatic as Brent's situation is as she hides in the swamp from whites who pursue her, she nonetheless crucially maintains the gentility of the middle-class woman in her text despite her male clothing, telling readers that "even those large, venomous snakes were less dreadful to my imagination than the white men in that community called civilized" (91). Brent discreetly implies the fearful reality that she would be raped by the white men should they succeed in their pursuit of her. Brent's qualifying of the term "white men" as "white men in that community called civilized" is carefully constructed for white female readers to include not all white men, but only an evil subset of Southern white men.

Brent does not want to travel to hide in the unnamed white woman's house, in the thicket of bushes, or in Snaky Swamp. She does not wish to travel to hide in the garret of her grandmother's house. But, as Jacobs knows, any Black female slave would be fortunate to have such destinations, indeed, to have any destination that would allow her to remain successfully concealed from her zealous pursuers. Brent simultaneously inhabits multiple disenfranchised personae of cross-dressed Black woman, fugitive slave, male sailor, threatened mother, and slave as she flees in terror from the close confinement and dangers of one Southern hiding place to another. If for a moment we interrupt this discussion and our reading of *Incidents* to view Brent fearfully suspended in mid-flight, we see a compelling autobiographic representation of antebellum Black female travel in the nineteenth-century U.S. South.

Readers who turned to Knight's *Journal* in 1865—or at any time after its initial 1825 publication and its reprintings throughout the nineteenth century, including 1865—would have encountered a somewhat similar scene involving a woman's unconventional nighttime travel. Knight recounts her journey with her guide John, a white man she had met and hired that day:

> When we had Ridd about an how'r, wee come into a thick swamp, wch. by Reason of a great fogg, very much startled mee, it being now very Dark. But nothing dismay'd John: Hee had encountered a thousand and a thousand such Swamps, having a Universall Knowledge in the woods; and readily Answered all my inquiries wch. were not a few. (90)

Knight's swamp, of course, differs from Jacobs's by climate and region. Also, Knight reaches this Northern swamp in conditions of early autumn while Brent hides in a Southern swamp in conditions of early summer. However, without diminishing these distinctions, Knight's New England swamp compared to Jacobs's depiction of Snaky Swamp appears plain and uninhabited. Where Brent's swamp experience was rife with multiple images of the erect phallus—long proboscises of mosquitoes, enormous snakes, thrashing sticks, and sexually violent white men—Knight's swamp experience is virtually bereft of all images "by Reason of fogg." The strongest reaction that her swamp experience evokes from Knight is that it "very much startled" her, and only then because the fog obscures the sight of the swamp as Knight and John approach it.

Unlike Brent's, Knight's agency is such that she does not have to hide or even stop in the swamp. That agency extends to Knight's selective observations of the swamp itself. While the swamp through which Knight traveled surely teemed with insects and reptiles, Knight has the privilege of disregarding them. She is on horseback and in transit. She is not the object of a hunt and indeed has voluntarily and without duress chosen to travel. Each of these aspects helps exempt Knight from concerns of insects and reptiles. Additionally, all of Knight's unknowns—everything she does notice about the swamp—are "readily answered" by her practiced white male travel guide. Her "inquiries wch. were not a few" are satisfied by John's "Universall Knowledge in the woods." Knight's satirical remarks concerning the self-important nature of John's knowledge ("Hee had encountered a thousand and a thousand such Swamps") should not obscure the representation of John as a white man with information and Knight as an inexperienced (read: genteel) white woman.[12]

In Fanny Fern's "Dark Days" (4 Dec. 1852, *Olive Branch*), recently widowed Jane Grey cannot afford the care that would save the life of Charley, her sick son. After Charley's death, on the way to "the 'poor man's lot,'" Jane Grey rides next to the sexton who drives the wagon holding Charley's coffin. The funeral is attended only by Jane Grey and the sexton. The following occurs after the burial:

> When the sexton touched her arm, and pointed to the wagon, she followed him mechanically, and made no objection, when he said "he guessed he'd drive a little faster, now that the lad was out." He looked at her once or twice, and thought it very odd that she didn't cry; but he didn't profess to understand women folks.

Like Brent's journey to Snaky Swamp, Jane Grey's nighttime travel also entails a traumatic destination, in this case her son's burial, which is the object of the trip. However, Jane Grey travels in a wagon, not, like Brent, on foot. Though she must remain outside for a time, she is not pursued, and she does not need to hide. The natural surroundings that Fern describes in "Dark Days" are as free of predators as Knight's swamp. Tragic as the representation of Jane Grey is, Fern can nonetheless accurately and without activating readers' skeptical attention portray her as having the genteel privilege of taking no notice of such matters. Indeed, in this scene Fern depicts no living things at all aside from the sexton and Jane Grey herself.

As with John, Knight's male guide, the sexton represents local self-centered masculine authority. He performs his tasks adequately—driving the wagon, burying the coffin—but does no more than that. The sexton's passing interest in Jane Grey, such as it is, registers her divergence from gendered expectations (he "thought it very odd that she didn't cry"). But that observation is immediately followed by his untroubled and unexamined dismissal of her and of women in general ("he didn't profess to understand women folks"). Linda Brent needs her male friend Peter to help plan her next concealment, accompany her to the swamp and back, and offer what protection he can in those fraught circumstances. However, Knight and Fern's Jane Grey are less dependent in such situations, requiring men only to guide or to drive them and to perform these duties correctly. In their travels Knight and Jane Grey are represented as having more autonomy and less trepidation than Linda Brent. As they travel, their lack of worry regarding male violence, for instance, is reflected in the absence of multiple images of the phallus like those employed by Jacobs. Shielded by readily perceived identity markers of white female gentility, Knight and Jane Grey do not need additional protection from men, and they do not need to cross-dress or present themselves androgynously.

This contrast may have seemed less absolute in the lives Fern and Jacobs lived outside their texts, particularly so because the two women knew each other.[13] Joyce Warren interestingly aligns Fern's and Jacobs's situations, noting that "in desperation, Fanny Fern left her husband, just as Harriet Jacobs fled rather than submit sexually to the master whom she despised" (*Fanny Fern* 303).[14] Warren extends this association to argue that

> a comparison of the two writers provides a significant comment on the position of women in nineteenth-century America: slave or free, women were dependent upon and answerable to men; without autonomy in society or in the home, their bodies and their children were not their own. (303)

I agree with Warren's argument, up to a point. Certainly an understanding of women's lives in the nineteenth-century United States must foreground oppressive cultural forms and practices of patriarchy. Further, it is likely that Willis herself would have been in agreement with Warren's analysis. Regarding the relationship between Fern and Jacobs, Warren quotes Thomas Butler Gunn, a frequent guest in the Fern/Parton household, who wrote that "Fern had told him that she felt a special obligation to Harriet Jacobs, who, she said, was one of the few people who stuck by her when others did not" (223).

However, I diverge from Warren's conclusions in what I see as her less convincing grouping of all nineteenth-century U.S. women in the broad category of "slave or free." As much as Warren is correct regarding female dependence, autonomy, and disenfranchisement, it is, I would argue, an oversimplification to speak even momentarily in terms of "slave or free." Put another way, to privilege gender over race places an undue emphasis on gender that necessarily diminishes the crucial role of race. Willis's sustained honoring of Jacobs's loyalty to her at a very vulnerable time when she had few supporters indeed speaks well of both Willis and Jacobs, and of their beliefs, practices, and values.[15] Without at all trivializing those admirable connections between Willis and Jacobs, however, I maintain that Fern's representation of Jane Grey in "Dark Days" (to cite just one example) interrogates discourses of power regarding gender while at the same time unexaminedly upholding assumptions concerning constructions of race.

Such partial scrutiny regarding gender but not race is also displayed by Alcott in *Hospital Sketches*. Alcott's unimpeachable abolitionist credentials should not be read as guaranteeing the presence of a consciousness regarding race and its constructions. In *Hospital Sketches*, Tribulation Periwinkle, on her way to nurse in the Civil War hospital, records the last stage of her journey from New England:

> Washington.—It was dark when we arrived; and, but for the presence of another friendly gentleman, I should have yielded myself a helpless prey to the first overpowering hackman, who insisted that I wanted to go just where I didn't. Putting me into the conveyance I belonged in, my escort added to the obligation by pointing out the objects of interest which we passed in our long drive. Though I'd often been told that Washington was a spacious place, its visible magnitude quite took my breath away. (17)

While Alcott constructs Trib's travel by train and steamboat as vexing, she also represents the difficulties and frustrations of a woman traveling alone as fairly easy to negotiate. Because Trib's travel is not desperate or life-threatening, Alcott can employ humor and have its usage correspond with the nature of Trib's travel experiences. When Trib arrives at her intermediate destination, she then comically exaggerates her status as a woman traveling alone, referring to herself as "helpless prey." By representing Trib to her readers as "prey," Alcott allows them to perceive Trib as a genteel white woman unable to politely contradict a domineering, working-class man. The worst thing that such an "overpowering man" could do to Trib in this scene as it is constructed is to drive her to an incorrect, but by implication still entirely safe, destination. Like Jacobs's Linda Brent, Trib also has an intermediate destination in her journey; unlike Brent, however, the most serious danger that awaits Trib when she arrives at that destination is an imagined officious white man.

With "helpless prey," Alcott employs vocabulary and definitions that culturally and experientially diverge sharply from those in Jacobs's lexicon. The "overpowering" men whom Trib fears and their potential "insist[ing] that I wanted to go just where I didn't" also derive from this linguistic/cultural location. Such language is only lightly freighted for Alcott and, by implication, for readers. If we were to transfer these exact phrases from Alcott's *Hospital Sketches* into Jacobs's *Incidents,* their meanings would be transformed from humorous to life-threatening and dire.

Trib's male companion, "another friendly gentleman," is as knowledgeable as Knight's guide John. He conducts Trib to the proper vehicle and then instructs and entertains her on their extended nighttime trip. Not only does Trib not have to hide on her journey, but the natural world that she experiences on this part of her travels is "spacious," not enclosed or rife with dangers. Indeed, it is in the language of sightseeing that Trib comments on the "visible magnitude [which] quite took my breath away." The nature she experiences is so broad as to dazzle her—it is impressive and not in the least alarming.

It is in Edmonds's *Nurse and Spy* that a white woman's nighttime travel bears more resemblance to Linda Brent's fraught journey. In the scene quoted below, Edmonds has been passing to her Union Army employers as a man, "Frank Thompson." As Frank Thompson, she plans to next adopt the disguise of "an Irish female peddler" (147) in order to infiltrate a Confederate Army camp. Like Brent in the scene above, Edmonds is a woman on foot, cross-dressing as a man in order to travel with her identity concealed.

Edmonds's intended disguise as an Irish woman invites critical speculation regarding gender and ethnicity. As David Roediger and others have discussed, mainstream nineteenth-century U.S. culture regularly conjectured about what was then commonly classified as the Catholic Irish "race," making frequent raced Black/Irish comparisons and in general "call[ing] the whiteness of the Irish into question" (133).[16] Edmonds thus portrays herself entering the swamp in a disguise in which she has been perceived as a white man, intending to emerge from the swamp the next morning in a disguise in which, if successful, she will be perceived as a non-white woman.

Edmonds sets out to "spend the night in the swamp, as the only safe retreat," planning in the morning to "ask admission [at the Confederate camp] as one of the fugitives . . . flying from the approach of the Yankees" (148). On her way to Chickahominy Swamp, Edmonds crosses the river and then "fear[s] the consequences of spending the night in wet clothing, especially in that malaria-infested region" (149). She subsequently becomes "delirious" as she endures a feverish night in the swamp:

> The remembrance of the sufferings of that night seem to be written upon my memory "as with a pen of iron." There I was, all alone, surrounded by worse, yes, infinitely worse, than wild beasts—by bloodthirsty savages—who considered death far too good for those who were in the employment of the U.S. Government. That night I was attacked by severe chills—chills beyond description, or even conception, except by those who have experienced the freezing sensation of a genuine ague chill. During the latter part of the night the other extreme presented itself, and it seemed as if I should roast alive. . . . My mind began to wander, and I became quite delirious. There seemed to be the horrors of a thousand deaths concentrated around me; I was tortured by fiends of every conceivable shape and magnitude. Oh, how it makes me shudder to recall the scenes which my imagination conjured up during those dark weary hours! Morning at last came, and I was aroused from the horrible night-mare which had paralyzed my senses through the night, by the roar of cannon and the screaming of shell through the forest. (149–50)

Recording her harrowing "remembrance of the sufferings of that night" that "seem to be written upon my memory 'as with a pen of iron'" causes Edmonds still to "shudder." Such heightened emotional language as well as her physically delicate response to her recollections underscores Edmonds's female gentility. Despite her long-term cross-dressing and autonomous, solo female journey, Edmonds represents herself as a genteel woman extensively traumatized by nighttime travel.

Edmonds's experience in this scene aligns provocatively with Brent's night in the swamp. Both women are dressed as men, in hiding, and surrounded by white male enemies. Neither sleeps or feels safe; both wake to sounds of danger. Further, both Snaky Swamp and Chickahominy Swamp are feral, natural locations rife with elements (mosquitoes, snakes, ague, and fever) that cause physical agony.

Linda Brent has a male companion with her (as do, for that matter, Sarah Kemble Knight with John, her guide; Fanny Fern's Jane Grey with the sexton; and Louisa May Alcott's Tribulation Periwinkle with the "friendly gentleman"), and Edmonds technically does not. Yet I would argue that the text provides material for a reading of "Frank Thompson"—Edmonds's male persona—as her male companion in this scene. Edmonds first inhabited the persona of Frank Thompson when, at age seventeen, she ran away from home disguised as a boy in order to avoid marriage. Later, having continued to live as Frank Thompson, she enlisted as a private in the Union Army under the name Franklin Thompson. Successfully disguised as a man, she fought in the war for two years. The access to masculine agency gained by Frank Thompson allowed him potentially to serve Edmonds as effectively as Brent's companion, Peter, was able to aid Brent. That is to say, just as Peter was of very limited help to Brent in Snaky Swamp, so Frank Thompson is equally unsuccessful in helping Edmonds in Chickahominy Swamp.

Edmonds's night in Chickahominy Swamp concludes very differently than did Brent's night in Snaky Swamp. Brent's experience was so traumatic that she and Peter left earlier than they had planned for Brent's new hiding place in her grandmother's garret. Edmonds, however, in Chickahominy Swamp the next morning, catches sight of her "Irish costume," thinks about her preparations for that disguise, and as "the perfect absurdity of my position rushed over my mind . . . it made me for the moment forget my lamentable condition, and with one uncontrollable burst of laughter I made that swamp resound in a manner which would have done credit to a person under happier circumstances, and in a better state of health" (150). Edmonds's spontaneous, ringing laughter effectively recasts what she had described as her "sufferings" of the previous night. What prompts this laughter is her recognition of the "perfect absurdity of [her] position"—that is, ostensibly that she, a white woman, had been planning to pass as Irish. Disturbing as her night in the swamp had been, Edmonds rebounds with an implicit identification with her whiteness (i.e., her non-Irishness) which leads to her quick turn to humor. Like Knight and Alcott, Edmonds successfully uses humor to mediate stated difficulties of white women's nighttime travel.

It is here that the correspondence between Brent's travel and Edmonds's travel breaks apart. In *Incidents,* Jacobs cannot use humor to mediate Brent's night in Snaky Swamp primarily because nothing about it is comical. When Brent leaves the swamp, her life is in danger: she is a fugitive female slave, cross-dressed as a man, walking disguised among people she knows, on her way to an unimaginable seven-year confinement. Where Edmonds erupts into an "uncontrollable burst of laughter," Brent will have little to laugh about indeed over the next seven years.

Yet the reasons for and implications of similarities between the female travels of Brent and Edmonds need not be dismissed. Edmonds is like and yet unlike Brent. Cross-dressed as a white man, Frank Thompson, Edmonds for years lived in constant peril. Had her female identity been exposed, Edmonds would have been in immediate danger. Edmonds's daily life of anxious vulnerability thus shares aspects of Brent's daily life. I do not wish to overstate this general correspondence. Edmonds's position—a white woman passing as a white man—was largely her own choice and of her own making. Brent's position—a Black female slave subject to arbitrary domination of Southern white men and women—was forced upon her. Yet we can nonetheless see the nature of Brent's and Edmonds's different, vexed identities mirrored in their nighttime travel experiences.

Sarah Kemble Knight, Fanny Fern's Jane Grey, and Louisa May Alcott's Tribulation Periwinkle are all genteel white women readily perceived as such by strangers they encounter in their travels. The nighttime travel experiences of each of them, as discussed above, are uncommon yet still fundamentally safe. In their nighttime travel scenes, Edmonds and Brent are, respectively, a white woman perceived as a white man and a Black woman perceived as a Black man. Unlike Knight, Jane Grey, and Tribulation Periwinkle, Brent and Edmonds travel on foot. Edmonds's nighttime travel experience is uncommon and harrowing; Brent's nighttime travel experience is uncommon and significantly traumatic. While not at all equating Edmonds with Brent, I wish to underscore that in these similar passages of women's nighttime travel, it is only when a white woman is secretly cross-dressed as a man that moments of her life are even marginally close to the dangers of a Black woman's life.

In the autobiographic representations of the self that appear in these passages from the texts under discussion, only Linda Brent and S. Emma E. Edmonds, both cross-dressed as men, must conceal themselves in the dangerous wild. Beyond that, however, only Brent is compelled by circumstances to travel to an outside location that, reflective of the nature of the dangers her experience has taught her to anticipate, is overwhelmingly phallic. And only Brent's travel leads her to further disabling concealment and danger. Taken separately and together, these passages demonstrate that a Black woman's (self-) representations borrow from, but also necessarily and fundamentally revise, white female authors' treatment of topics such as gentility, cross-dressing, and travel.

Discussing Black women's autobiographical writings, Lauren Berlant argues:

> It is always the autobiographer's task to negotiate her specificity into a spectacular interiority worthy of public notice. But the minority subject who circulates in a majoritarian public sphere occupies a specific contradiction: insofar as she is exemplary, she has distinguished herself from the collective stereotype; and, at the same time, she is also read as a kind of foreign national, an exotic representative of her alien "people" who reports to the dominant culture about collective life in the crevices of national existence. This warp in the circulation of identity is central to the public history of African American women, for whom coerced sexualization has been a constitutive relay between national experience and particular bodies. ("The Queen of America" 100)

In well-known parts of *Incidents* that are prominent in the critical record, Jacobs is correctly read as very much "negotiat[ing] her specificity into a spectacular interiority worthy of public notice." Her text's record of her extraordinary seven-year concealment along with her fairly open discussion of sex with a white man has indeed made her "an exotic representation" of nineteenth-century African American women. However, in an attempt to diminish middle-class white female readers' identification of her as non-normative, Jacobs portrays Brent's behavior once she has escaped from the Southern slavocracy as typically genteel. When Brent is in the North as a fugitive slave, she is constructed as circumstantially better able to adhere to standards of (white) middle-class female behavior because she is physically away from the slavocracy. Once out of the South and more removed from the sexual violence of slavery, Brent is depicted as genteelly normative. This is not to suggest that Jacobs aligns Brent with whiteness but that, significantly, she portrays Brent as genteel after and despite her transgressive sexual experiences in the slavocracy. As Stephen Matterson argues, "for her contemporary readers Jacobs's destabilization of the womanly virtues would be less striking than her appropriation of them, her assumption that they are ideals equally available to her and equally relevant to her" (86). In *Incidents,* slavery leads to violation of a Black woman's body and forces the woman temporarily to modify her behavior, but it cannot permanently alter her gentility.

Jacobs's text reflects the even more extensive obstacles to autobiographical writing confronted by women whose race, class, and/or sexuality mark them as multiply transgressive. I turn to Jacobs's text in my final chapter because of its status as the primary canonical text by a nineteenth-century African American woman, a work accurately described by Carby as "the most sophisticated, sustained narrative dissection of the conventions of true womanhood by a black author before emancipation" (47).[17] Indeed, *Incidents* is by all measures the object of more critical consideration than any of the other texts in this study. Placing the primary Black female autobiographical text of the U.S. nineteenth century in relation to other, lesser-known white women's autobiographical texts provides a fundamental display of what whiteness enables. As Carby valuably observes, "Jacobs used the material circumstances of her life to critique conventional standards of female behavior and to question their relevance and applicability to the experience of black women" (47).

Such a display is important to this book because it uncovers privileges accorded to and unrecognized by U.S. nineteenth-century middle-class white women. Critical whiteness studies have labeled this "white skin privilege." Birgit Bander Rasmussen et al. define the term as "the many ways in which whiteness signifies and underwrites various kinds of social, political, and economic advantages" (2–3).[18] Whiteness, of course, did not necessarily allow white middle-class women to live with any degree of autonomy given the location of whiteness "within a larger system of oppressive and normalizing structures" (Stokes 13).[19] But whiteness did make it very unlikely that, for instance, a white middle-class woman would be publicly whipped or that her children would be born into slavery. When Jacobs's text is positioned next to other texts in this study, the whiteness that was previously less visible comes strongly and swiftly into focus. With Jacobs's text at hand, whiteness emerges conspicuously as the default race in Knight's, Fern's, Alcott's, and Edmonds's texts. Indeed, it is in texts such as these that whiteness is "so ubiquitous and entrenched as to appear natural and normative" (Rasmussen et al. 10). Correspondingly, the fraught attempts by women under discussion in this study to write the self appear—suddenly and obviously—as white women's attempts.

With the privilege to be unmindful of one's race, women whose skin color allows them to be perceived as members of the dominant race identify themselves as female and their behavior and assumptions as middle-class, but they are very rarely concerned in their texts with identifying themselves as white.[20] Such women presumptively and unconsciously understand that their whiteness is the ultimate cultural identity indication. Rasmussen et al. compellingly argue that whiteness "operates as the unmarked norm against which other identities are marked and racialized, the seemingly un-raced center of a racialized world" (10). Knight, Fern, Alcott, Edmonds, Livermore, and Wittenmyer are correspondingly unaware that their middle-class whiteness at all times supplies them with cultural advantage. Instead, they are alert to what does/does not happen to them because they are perceived as female. Introducing Jacobs's *Incidents* into this group of texts illuminates privileges of whiteness because Jacobs clearly understands that whether she is in the North or South, she is always perceived first as Black. As she well knows, everything that happens to her during her lifetime occurs because she is Black.[21]

At the same moment that other texts in this study were being published (or, in the case of Knight's *Journal,* republished), Jacobs's text was struggling its way into existence. The slow progress of the writing and the delayed publication of *Incidents* resulted from obstacles linked directly to race. Given *Incidents*'s canonical presence, it is ironic that, much more so than other texts in this study, the idea of Jacobs's text and the text itself emerged slowly. At first, Jacobs planned to dictate her experiences to Harriet Beecher Stowe. She initiated contact with Stowe through Cornelia Grinnell Willis and also asked if Stowe would "permit Jacobs' daughter Louisa to accompany her [on a planned trip] to England as a 'representative southern slave'" (Yellin, "Written by Herself" 482). Jacobs "had saved enough from her wages to pay her daughter's expenses" (Yellin, *Harriet Jacobs* 120). Stowe's raced response was negative on all counts. She refused to take Louisa with her, fearing that, as Jacobs wrote to white abolitionist Amy Post, "it would be much care to her to take Louisa . . . and she was afraid that if her situation as a Slave should be known it would subject her to much petting and patronizing . . . and [Mrs. Stowe] was very much opposed to it with this class of people" (qtd. in Yellin, *Harriet Jacobs* 121). Additionally, Stowe questioned the veracity of Jacobs's experiences and then suggested that if they were true, she would use them in *The Key to Uncle Tom's Cabin,* which she was then writing. When Jacobs resisted this idea, her subsequent letters as well as Willis's to Stowe went unanswered. Jacobs "later expressed her racial outrage" in another letter to Post, criticizing Stowe's response and writing, "Well, what a pity we poor blacks can't have the firmness and stability of character that you white people have!" (Yellin, "Written by Herself" 483).

After Stowe and Jacobs failed to agree on a collaboration, Jacobs, though fearing that she would relive the painful past as she wrote, decided to write the narrative herself.[22] Once she completed the book in 1858, Jacobs "spent several years trying to find a publisher" (Foster 59) in England and in the United States. "Jacobs's account was so original and striking that they [publishers] required more than the usual endorsements by others" (59), such as "an endorsement from [her employer, Nathaniel Parker] Willis or Stowe" (Yellin, "Written by Herself" 483). Jacobs wrote to Amy Post "that Stowe's devastating rejections made her 'tremble at the thought of approaching another satellite of so great magnitude'" (Yellin, *Harriet Jacobs* 140). Lydia Maria Child's agreement to write a preface to the manuscript resulted in *Incidents*'s finally being published in the United States in 1861 and in England in 1862.[23] The last-minute bankruptcy of Jacobs's publishers, Thayer and Eldridge, so threatened the book's publication that "apparently using what was left of her savings, Jacobs paid half the price outright and bought the [previously cast stereotype] plates. Somehow—doubtless with Child's help, perhaps with the aid of Cornelia Willis's publisher friend James T. Fields—she arranged to have her book printed and bound" (143). The eight years that bridge Jacobs's decision to write her story and the publication of *Incidents* began with Stowe's raced response and ended only once a preface had been successfully solicited from a well-known white female abolitionist and once the Black female writer working as a nursemaid had emptied her life savings.

The slow progress of *Incidents*—the writing and publication of which extends a year beyond the time of Jacobs's seven-year concealment—marks the pivotal role of whiteness in the writing and publication histories of other texts in this study. For instance, though Knight's *Journal* remained unpublished in her lifetime, Knight was able to write it in a timely fashion and circulate it privately. Once economic desperation had forced Sara Willis to turn to publication, she wrote prolifically, and her writing began to be published regularly. Within the space of a year, Alcott nursed in the Civil War hospital, kept a journal, contracted typhoid, nearly died, used the journal to write *Hospital Sketches*, and successfully arranged for the book's publication. Edmonds wrote and arranged for prompt publication of *Nurse and Spy* despite having to conceal her wartime cross-dressing in the text. Though the writing and publication of all these texts involved various modifications and concealments, none of them reflect the extensive raced delays seen in Jacobs's writing and publication of *Incidents in the Life of a Slave Girl*.

I do not at all suggest that white women discussed in this study experienced an effortless entrance into the nineteenth-century U.S. print market as a result of their whiteness. As I have argued throughout this study, virtually all women encountered a range of arbitrary barriers in their attempts to write and publish their work. Such gender-specific, culturally sanctioned impediments were indeed characteristic of the nineteenth-century U.S. literary marketplace. Whiteness offered no assurance of or easy access to publication for the woman writer. However, the female author perceived as nonwhite confronted and contended with an even more formidable and heightened mix of obstacles regarding writing and publication of her work.

Jacobs's recognition of the agency located in whiteness and female middle-class gentility is signaled in her representation of the first and second Mrs. Bruce and their relationships with Brent, which enact Jacobs's desired constellation of gender, class, and race. As Carby notes, "Jacobs's position as a domestic servant contrasted with the lives of the white women who surrounded and befriended her" (48). At various points in the text, the first and second Mrs. Bruce compassionately provide Brent with clothing, respect, and sympathy. Though Brent is a Black nursemaid and they are genteel white women, the beliefs and actions of both women are repeatedly correspondent with Brent's beliefs and actions. The text's constructions of each Mrs. Bruce are representations of what Brent can be (female, kind, conventional, maternal) and what she cannot be (white, privileged, relatively ignorant of social injustices). Brent's alignment with each Mrs. Bruce allows Jacobs to repeatedly represent her self as a normative, genteel woman.

This association is significantly enacted when Brent learns that Dr. Flint has once again discovered her whereabouts and sent his agents after her. Brent "immediately informed Mrs. Bruce of my danger, and she took prompt measures for my safety" (150).[24] In an attempt to safeguard Brent from being abducted and forcibly returned to slavery, Mrs. Bruce sends Brent away from home, and "this generous, sympathizing lady proposed that I should carry her baby away" (150). According to Brent, Mrs. Bruce explains, "'It is better for you to have baby with you, Linda; for if they get on your track, they will be obliged to bring the child to me; and then, if there is a possibility of saving you, you shall be saved'" (150).

Mrs. Bruce appears to be at her most maternally sacrificing in this passage. She provides Brent with, as Caroline Levander points out, "a surrogate motherhood" (37) by giving her child to a fugitive from the law, a woman who is in very real danger of being apprehended by Dr. Flint's agents. Jacobs emphasizes the maternal nature of Mrs. Bruce's sacrifice as Brent exclaims that "few mothers would have consented to have one of their own babes become a fugitive, for the sake of the poor, hunted nurse, on whom the legislators of the country had let loose the bloodhounds!" (150). Viewing Mrs. Bruce's action through the lens of motherhood is accurate, up to a point. However, a racially contextualized reading brings this scene more clearly into focus.

When Mrs. Bruce hands her baby to Brent, she participates in a long-standing tradition of white women turning to Black women to care for their children. Additionally, it is implicitly clear that in lending her child to Brent, Mrs. Bruce is correctly confident of at least two cultural arrangements: that a Black woman is always potentially in danger while in public and that the white child of a middle-class mother will very rarely be. My intention here is not to diminish Mrs. Bruce's acts as much as it is to clarify them. In my reading of this scene, Mrs. Bruce's most significant "generosity and sympathy" (150) emerge from her (white) recognition of Brent as a hunted Black woman ("'for if they get on your track'" [150])—that is, her ability to at least partially comprehend Brent's dire raced situation despite her very limited resources for understanding that situation.

Further, the abstract cultural value given to Mrs. Bruce's white baby contrasts starkly with the crude, monetary price assigned to Brent's mixed-race children. Social and cultural arrangements that protect Mrs. Bruce's child are recognized by Brent/Jacobs and Mrs. Bruce. The raced differences between these women are harshly apparent in the irony that Brent, of course, cannot legally keep her own children, much less lend them to others. Though Brent is the mother of her children by standards (biological and otherwise) on which the culture relies, her children are nonetheless not hers to keep or give. However, by recognizing and responding to Brent as a woman in need (and so lending Brent her child and thus her motherhood status), Mrs. Bruce reinforces the alignment upon which Brent and she implicitly concur: that Brent is a normative, genteel woman who is Black.

This identity is put to the test in yet another travel scene in *Incidents*. During the same steamboat journey with Mrs. Bruce referenced earlier, Brent goes to supper in a room with other nurses ("thirty or forty nurses were there, of a great variety of nations. . . . I was the only nurse tinged with the blood of Africa") and their child charges. A seating problem regarding Brent immediately occurs:

> A young man, who had the ordering of things, took the circuit of the table two or three times, and finally pointed me to a seat at the lower end of it. As there was but one chair, I sat down and took the child in my lap. Whereupon the young man came to me and said, in the blandest manner possible, "Will you please to seat the little girl in the chair, and stand behind it and feed her? After they have done, you will be shown to the kitchen, where you will have a good supper." This was the climax! I found it hard to preserve my self-control, when I looked round, and saw women who were nurses, as I was, and only one shade lighter in complexion, eyeing me with a defiant look, as if my presence were a contamination. However, I said nothing. I quietly took the child in my arms, went to our room, and refused to go to the table again. (137)

In this scene Brent's class status is carefully aligned with that of others in this large ("thirty or forty nurses") group. They are all women, nursemaids, and employees. Brent's African blood is characterized as just one example of the "great variety of nations" represented. The rejection of these commonalities by the young man and the other women puts pressure on Brent's self-definition. Brent's self-perceived membership in this assembly of women and their individual and group rejection of her ("eyeing me with a defiant look, as if my presence were a contamination") paradoxically imply Brent's conventional female identity: she is a woman behaving according to female cultural scripts traveling among women who are not.

But more is at issue here in terms of identity. It is Brent's similarity to these other female nursemaids—separated by "only one shade lighter in complexion"—and their rejection of that similarity that threatens her self-control. That same similarity threatens the other women's self-definitions. For each woman in this scene, her perception of a coherent self rests uneasily on that one shade of color. When Brent, seeing the group's rejection of her, finds "it hard to preserve my self-control," she precariously retains her ability to claim a self. To lose self-control is to release the momentarily coherent self, that is, to lose self-coherence. That potential loss of discipline would, it is implied, take the form of unruly, unregulated speech. Rejecting such unmodified speech ("However, I said nothing") and its attendant self-disruption, Brent preserves the self by leaving the scene and refusing to go back. To return would be to yield her self-definition to others or to again risk losing self-control, devastating to her perception of her self as genteel.

Being read as other than white disrupts Jacobs and *Incidents*. The ways that Jacobs's text was written, published, and read all differ from those of the other texts under discussion in this study. Whatever the circumstance, Jacobs's/Brent's complexion and its scrutiny by others always proclaimed her as Black and complicated her self-representation. As Berlant has written, "[f]or Jacobs, writing before Emancipation, the nation as a category of experience is an archive of painful anecdotes, bitter feelings, and precise measurements of civic failure" ("The Queen of America" 107). As this study documents, Sarah Kemble Knight, Fanny Fern, Louisa May Alcott, S. Emma. E. Edmonds, Mary Livermore, and Annie Turner Wittenmyer struggled—painfully, contradictorily, compellingly—with their autobiographic identities and with gender representation. Yet of all these women and in all their texts, only Harriet Jacobs/Linda Brent—genteelly dressed and just one shade darker in complexion—must walk out of a room full of women, her lips pressed tightly together, in order to retain her self.

NOTES

INTRODUCTION

1. For *Ruth Hall*'s mixed reception, see Warren's Introduction to *Ruth Hall*.

2. For provocative discussion of the normative and its restrictive implication, and of conservative gay and lesbian politics, see Warner.

3. As Amy Kaplan writes, "The 'cult of domesticity,' the ideology of 'separate spheres,' and the 'culture of sentiment' have together provided a productive paradigm for understanding the work of white women writers in creating a middle-class American culture in the nineteenth century. Most studies of this paradigm have revealed the permeability of the border that separates the spheres, demonstrating that the private feminized space of the home both infused and bolstered the public male arena of the market, and that the sentimental values attached to maternal influence were used to sanction women's entry into the wider civic realm from which those same values theoretically excluded them. More recently, scholars have argued that the extension of female sympathy across social divides could violently reinforce the very racial and class hierarchies that sentimentality claims to dissolve" (581). Also, as Shirley Samuels writes, scholars have recently tried to arrive at "a more thoroughly situated and engaged sense of how sentimental texts produce effects and how social and cultural meanings are embodied" (8). For a retrospective on Welter's work and scholarly responses to it, see Kelley, Commentary. For a useful summary of the "Cult of True Womanhood," see Saulsbury.

4. See Gollin's *Annie Adams Fields*.

5. See Baym's "Delia Bacon: Hawthorne's Last Heroine" and "Delia Bacon, History's Odd Woman Out."

6. Examples in this section are drawn from Cornell University's indispensable site *Making of America*. See http://cdl.library.cornell.edu/moa/.

7. Lehuu provides compelling discussion of visual texts in *Godey's Lady's Book*. Also, Ballier, though concerned with conventional illustrations of women in post–Civil War periodicals, documents the diversifying of women's professional activities against continuing normative female representations in the press.

8. For discussion of illustrations that appeared following Maria Bickford's murder, see Halttunen, especially 182–83. Bickford's death was multiply and variously

trivialized. Her murderer's "fans . . . applauded at his verdict of 'not guilty' . . . and wax figures of both murderer and victim were displayed by a traveling wax museum, which advertised that the dress and jewelry adorning its model . . . had actually belonged to the victim" (Haltunnen 88).

CHAPTER 1

1. See Michaelsen's summary of the *Journal*'s publication history (33-34).
2. Margolies provides crucial information regarding dates, authenticity, and versions of the journal in the nineteenth century.
3. Balkun briefly discusses Dwight's publishing of Knight's text.
4. For criticism of the *Journal*, see Arner; Derounian; Derounian-Stodola; Margolies; Seelye 292-309; Spengemann 39-44; and Julia Stern ("To Relish"). To summarize disparate readings, Buell characterizes Knight's text as travel narrative and humor writing (283, 377); Michaelsen and Stern as a chronicle of class, etiquette, and consumption; Spengemann as related to works by John Bunyan and Aphra Behn; and Derounian-Stodola as picaresque narrative ("The New England Frontier").
5. Biographical information used here is largely drawn from Bush's Introduction. See especially 69-70.
6. See Shields's discussion of women's reading and literary interests ("Eighteenth-Century" 460-65).
7. From Sarah Kemble Knight, *The Journal of Madam Knight*, in William L. Andrews et al., eds., *Journeys in New Worlds*. All subsequent references are to this edition.
8. Dwight's musings on travel and landscape changes are echoed two years later in Sedgwick's *Hope Leslie* (1827). See especially chapters 6 and 8.
9. For discussion of authorship and publication in the nineteenth-century United States, see Charvat's foundational study. Also see Hackel and Kelly for essays responding to Charvat's work.
10. See Caesar's examination of U.S. travel abroad.
11. Imbarrato lists popular tourist guides of the time (33). She also notes that Dwight wrote three tourist guidebooks (all published after his edition of the *Journal*).
12. See Imbarrato's comprehensive bibliography, 231-45.
13. Margolies's essay, essential reading for students of Knight's text, cites these responses.
14. Felt's *Annals of Salem* (1827) was one of Hawthorne's primary sources for *The House of the Seven Gables*. See Kesselring.
15. Dwight's letter was written to Charles Deane in 1846 in response to Deane's letter concerning the authenticity of Knight's text. Thirty years later, at the December 1877 meeting of the Massachusetts Historical Society, Deane read Dwight's letter to the group; it was subsequently incorporated into their minutes, which were published annually. According to the minutes, "Mr. Dwight's prompt reply put to rest all doubts as to the genuineness of this quaint production, and some extracts from his letter were published in the 'Boston Evening Transcript,' of January 6, 1847,—that is, a few days after it was received" ("December Meeting" 388).
16. Charles Deane is not to be confused with William R. Deane, who edited an edition of Knight's text, though the two were close friends (Margolies 27).
17. As I focus on the nineteenth-century United States, I do not discuss later editions of the journal. However, Winship's Introduction to the 1920 edition reflects continued evolution of Knight ("the plump mistress . . . [with an] independent mind and energetic, withal somewhat feminist, character" [v]) and her text.

18. For further biographical information regarding Crocker, see Ruth Rosenberg. For discussion of Crocker's life and writing, see Post. For brief discussion of Crocker and excerpts from her work, see Harris; and Westbrook and Westbrook.

19. By 1825 Crocker knew of Knight's journal and provided information concerning it. See *Historical Magazine & American Notes & Queries* (341).

20. Excerpts from Knight's *Journal* in *The Museum of Foreign Literature and Science* were reprinted from those published a year earlier in the British *Blackwood's Edinburgh Magazine* (Margolies 29).

21. Of seventy-four notes to Learned's edition, fourteen are written by others (e.g., William R. Deane); twenty-seven are quoted from books Learned cites; eight translate vernacular or archaic language; and twenty-two are factual explanations. Only three are Learned's opinionated commentary.

22. Unlike Learned, Knight criticizes the blurring of racialized boundaries: "But [whites are] too Indulgent (especially the farmers) to their slaves: suffering too great familiarity from them, permitting them to sit at Table and eat with them, (as they say to save time,) and into the dish goes the black hoof as freely as the white hand" (104–5).

23. Margolies writes that the unverified story of Franklin as Knight's student originated with Crocker. See 26n8.

24. Saar describes Tyler's text: "Spanning over one hundred and fifty years, and describing the works of almost one hundred and fifty writers, *A History of American Literature* is remarkable in its thoroughness." Further, "the comprehensiveness and accuracy of Tyler's research enabled scholars to survey, for the first time, the whole of early American literature" (247).

25. See Vanderbilt on Tyler and his work.

26. Howells wrote the "Editor's Study" feature of *Harper's* from January 1886 to March 1892. For Howells's collected "Editor's Study" columns, see Simpson. (Howells's authorship of the "Editor's Study" feature is well-known. However, to my knowledge, I am the first to point to Howells's commentary on Knight.)

27. This volume was published by Charles L. Webster and Company, the publishing firm of Mark Twain. The series was well-received but failed to make enough profit, contributing to the company's bankruptcy and Twain's own financial difficulties.

28. References to Knight's journal appear regularly in nineteenth-century U.S. periodicals and books. While I do not cite every reference, I attempt to provide sufficient examples to demonstrate this appearance across the nineteenth century. Cornell's *Making of America* site (http://cdl.library.cornell.edu/moa/) is an indispensable source for such references.

29. In trial transcripts Thomas Shephard, alarmed by Hutchinson's speech, tellingly employs a travel metaphor regarding this "verye dayngerous Woman." Shephard criticizes "the Flewentness of her Tonge and her Willingness to open herselfe and to divulge her Opinions and to sowe her seed in us that are but highway side" (Hall, *Antinomian* 353). For Shephard, when Hutchinson speaks ("the Flewentness of her Tonge"), she commands the main road, crowding Puritan leaders off to the side. I thank Allison Giffen for bringing this section of the transcripts to my attention.

30. See Kamensky's historical and linguistic treatment of Hutchinson, the Salem trials, and transgressive female speech in New England, especially 71–81, 150–79. Some women accused as witches during the delusion were, like Knight, married women managing business or property while their husbands were away. Witchcraft accusations were a way of gaining property at a time when the state had lost its charter and legal authority to resolve property disputes. Familial and civic circumstances of these women led to disruptive female visibility linked to autonomy and prop-

erty. A husband's absence—while he was away on business, in the fields, fighting Indians—increased a visible woman's vulnerability, despite the limited protection her socioeconomic status might have typically provided.

31. For other early American white women's travel narratives, see *Journeys in New Worlds* (Andrews et al.); *Puritans among the Indians* (Vaughan and Clark); and *Women's Indian Captivity Narratives* (Derounian-Stodola). For a study of white women's captivity narratives extending from early America to the abduction of heiress Patty Hearst, see Castiglia.

32. For unresolved questions of early American literacy, see Davidson, 56. For readings that "track the dramatic emergence of girls and women as important participants in the production and consumption of texts" from 1500 to 1800 "and as statistically meaningful possessors of literacy," see Hackel and Kelly.

33. As Balkun observes, "Knight always gets the last word in any given situation; her days typically end with the recording of events, the translation of action and word into a self-authorizing text" (17).

34. For discussions of cultural authority of voice in printed texts in early national narratives, see both Fliegelman and Looby.

35. I follow Kerber's understanding of eighteenth-century American women's community: "Like most women in preindustrial societies eighteenth-century American women lived in what might be called woman's domain. Their daily activities took place within a feminine, domestic circle: infants were delivered by midwives, the sick were cared for by nurses, women who traveled overnight stayed at boardinghouses owned or run by females. We may think of women as forming a tradition-bound, underdeveloped nation within a larger, more politically sophisticated one" (7).

36. Julia Stern concludes that "Knight is mistaken for a prostitute" because "a woman of her social rank . . . on the road late at night in fine clothes could be understood in no other way in rural Connecticut of 1704" ("To Relish" 3).

37. For a less gendered reading of Knight's system of social classification, see Michaelsen, 38.

38. See Breitwieser's discussion of Lot's wife, 95–102.

39. For an excellent discussion of Knight's use of poetry, see Imbarrato, 159–61.

40. Bush posits this reference as "possibly a witty allusion to baptism by immersion, as practiced by the Baptists, who had settled in Rhode Island (where Madam Knight then was) in the previous century" (Introduction 92n15).

CHAPTER 2

1. In this chapter I use "Sara Willis" to identify the woman variously known as Sara Payson Willis Eldredge, Sara Payson Willis Farrington, and Sara Payson Willis Parton.

2. In her February 1854 contract, Willis agreed to perform no other literary writing while working on *Ruth Hall*. See Warren, *Fanny Fern*, 120.

3. The popularity of Fern's early periodical writing underscores the efficacy of strategies of female multiplicity. In an overt example of such success, a *Harper's* review, "Literary Notices," praised the "rapid transitions from fun to pathos" in Fern's early periodical writing as "very effective," noting that "[h]er pictures of domestic life . . . excite alternate smiles and tears" (July 1854).

4. Joyce Warren in her foundational work on Fern details the punitive conditional financial support that Charles Eldredge's disapproving parents, Hezekiah and Mary Eldredge, were willing to provide their widowed daughter-in-law and her two

daughters, the only children of their only child (of four) who had survived to adulthood. Hezekiah Eldredge, who died in 1853, stipulated in his will "that his estate was to go to his wife and two granddaughters, *provided* they were brought up by their grandmother" (*Fanny Fern* 106; emphasis in original). Mary Eldredge, who died four years later in 1857, willed the majority of her estate to charity. She left virtually all Eldredge family possessions, including her son's portrait, to non–family members. A reading of these documents today clearly conveys the Eldredges's censorious view of their daughter-in-law. See *Fanny Fern*, 106–7.

5. Both Homestead (152) and Warren (*Fanny Fern* 123) identify the anonymous editor as the *True Flag*'s William U. Moulton.

6. Much of the biographical information in this section is drawn from Warren's Introduction to *Ruth Hall*.

7. Throughout her writing Willis repeatedly criticizes hypocrisies regarding gender construction and women's limited economic choices: "As a general thing there are few people who speak approbatively of a woman who has a smart business talent or capability. No matter how isolated or destitute her condition, the majority would consider it more 'feminine' would she unobtrusively gather up her thimble, and, retiring into some out-of-the-way-place, gradually scoop out her coffin with it, than to develop that smart turn of business which would lift her at once out of her troubles; and which, in a man so situated, would be applauded as exceedingly praiseworthy. The most curious part of it is, that they who are the loudest in their abhorrence of this 'unfeminine' trait, are they who are the most intolerant of dependent female relatives. . . . 'Do something for yourself,' is their advice in general terms; but, above all, you are to do it quietly, unobtrusively; in other words, die as soon as you like on sixpence a day, but don't trouble *us!*"("A Bit of Injustice," 8 June 1861, *New York Ledger*).

8. Various contemporary sources characterize Willis as permanently damaged by her experiences. However, it is difficult to determine the accuracy of such remarks. For instance, James Parton, Willis's husband, wrote in "Memoir of Fanny Fern" that after Charles Eldredge's death "his widow and her two little children found themselves suddenly reduced from a condition resembling affluence, to a situation inexpressibly forlorn and miserable—dependence in a third-rate boarding house. I shall not dwell upon the next seven years. They were years of wretchedness, which left deep traces upon her nature, never wholly obliterated" (49). In her unpublished biography of Willis, Ethel Parton, Willis's granddaughter wrote, "So many repeated blows of fate, the bitter anxiety, the long strain, had told upon her severely, leaving her nerves in an over-sensitive condition to be assuaged, but never wholly repaired, by happier fortunes" (138).

9. Characterizations of Fern as masculine continued throughout Willis's life. In "One Sort of Woman" (written nearly two decades after her identity had been revealed), Fern writes that a plumber she has called tells her, "'Why, ma'am, I judged from your writings that you were three-quarters a man yourself, and wouldn't need one of us to tell you what to do!'"

10. Mary Kelley valuably examines nineteenth-century U.S. population growth and rising literacy rates (*Private Woman* 10–11). For discussion of changes in mid-nineteenth-century U.S. "print technology [that] resulted in a whole new kind of literature for the masses," see Reynolds, especially 81–97.

11. For fascinating discussion of changing mid-nineteenth-century U.S. periodical publication and its intersection with copyright laws, see Homestead, especially chapter 4.

12. Discussing growth of the U.S. publishing industry, Kelley writes that "a new publishing empire emerged in the United States, grew with the nation, and provided

for women in the United States an opportunity such as they had never confronted before" (*Private Woman* 7).

13. For discussion of Bonner's hiring celebrity authors to write exclusively for his paper, see Warren, *Fanny Fern,* 144–49.

14. For details on Bonner's editorial policies regarding his carefully selected writers, see Warren, "Uncommon Discourse," especially 61 and 64.

15. For discussion of nineteenth-century U.S. advertising strategies, see Reynolds, 344–47.

16. Once Willis turned to the novel, she began to satirize readers' letters. Williams reads this as "a sign . . . of the growing sense that celebrity authors needed to distance themselves from their readers." In *Ruth Hall* Willis "devoted several chapters to fictionalized fan mail . . . showing how many liberties readers took with authors as they demanded everything from literary advice to money to marriage" (106).

17. Bonner's "final tribute to Fern was to purchase the huge marble tombstone for her grave" (Warren, "Uncommon Discourse" 57). The elaborate tombstone, shaped as a cross, is draped and entwined with granite fern leaves. "Fanny Fern" is engraved at its base. See Warren, *Fanny Fern,* photograph facing page 155.

18. For details and analysis of Willis's 1856 lawsuit to establish exclusive legal claim to the name Fanny Fern, see Tonkovich, 47–49.

CHAPTER 3

1. "'I even think of trying the *Atlantic,*' she noted in her journal in the autumn of 1859. 'There's ambition for you!' The ambition was shared, as William Dean Howells observed, by every young writer hoping to join his name to the august list of Boston authors associated with that magazine" (Jones, Introduction ix). After having a story accepted by the *Atlantic,* Alcott wrote, "'People seem to think it a great thing to get into the *Atlantic,* but I've not been pegging away all these years in vain, and may yet have books and publishers and a fortune of my own'" (qtd. in Jones ix).

2. Apologetic forewords, introductions, and letters by nineteenth-century U.S. women writing in a range of genres are familiar to readers in this period. In recent years, much interesting criticism has been devoted to this subject. See especially Kelley's groundbreaking *Private Woman, Public Stage* and Brodhead's classic "Veiled Ladies."

3. Readings of sexual identity and gender construction in Alcott's life and writing appear in, among others, Bedell; Elbert; Saxton; and Showalter, *Sister's Choice.*

4. We owe our knowledge of particulars of Alcott's delirium to a 20 February 1863 letter written by Sophia Peabody Hawthorne to Annie Adams Field. The sixteen-page letter has never been published in its entirety. To quote partially from it: "On Monday I saw her for a few moments. . . . She was so changed, I think I should not have known her. After that, no one saw her but the physician, for she was delirious almost uninterruptedly, and often very furious, and Mrs. Alcott told me she was haunted by hospital scenes and men. . . . Sometimes she would say 'If you will only take that man away, I can bear the rest.' One day she sprang out of bed, when they left her for a moment, and beneath they heard a sudden step . . . , and then a heavy fall. Horror stricken—they rushed up, and Louisa was stretched upon the floor. . . . Abby dragged up Louisa and laid her on the bed, when she exclaimed 'How could you leave me alone when the room was full of men!'" (qtd. in Julie E. Hall, "Crisis" 69).

5. For discussion of nineteenth-century sexology and Krafft-Ebing theories of

homosexuality popularized late in Alcott's life, see Smith-Rosenberg's landmark *Disorderly Conduct,* especially 268–73.

6. For detailed discussion of women's train travel and its behavioral strictures in the nineteenth-century United States, see Richter.

7. Comprehensive listings of Civil War nursing accounts published after *Hospital Sketches* appear in Schultz, "Embattled Care," 115, and Jones, Introduction, xlii–xliii. Walt Whitman's reading of *Hospital Sketches* resulted in his planning to write his *Memoranda during the War* (1876) (Schultz, *Women at the Front* 228). For the number and types of Civil War narratives—published and archival—see Schultz's excellent "The Inhospitable Hospital," 364. For examples of representative Civil War nursing narratives, see *Notes of Hospital Life from November, 1861, to August, 1863;* George Barton, *Angels of the Battlefield;* Fannie A. Beers, *Memories;* Jane (Mrs. A. H.) Hoge, *The Boys in Blue;* Mrs. A. M. Holstein (Ellis), *Three Years in Field Hospitals;* Henriette Stratton Jaquette, ed., *South after Gettysburg;* Mary A. Livermore, *My Story of the War;* Charlotte E. McKay, *Stories of Hospital and Camp;* Adelaide W. Smith, *Reminiscences of an Army Nurse;* Susie King Taylor, *A Black Woman's Civil War Memoirs;* Annie Turner Wittenmyer, *Under the Guns;* Jane Stuart Woolsey, *Hospital Days;* and Katharine Prescott Wormeley, *The Other Side of War.*

8. For Nightingale's influence on U.S. female nursing, particularly in the post–Civil War period, see Schultz, "The Inhospitable Hospital," 364 and 390; and Vicinus, 85–120.

9. For further discussion of Nightingale, see Fish's reading of Mary Seacole, "a freeborn woman of color from Kingston, Jamaica" (64), who worked as a healer in the Crimean War. Fish reads "Seacole's text as a counternarrative to the white, Western myth of Florence Nightingale" (2).

10. Alcott's supervisor in the Union Hotel Hospital, Hannah Ropes (who also contracted typhoid and unlike Alcott died from it soon after), was also influenced by Nightingale's *Notes on Nursing.* See Schultz, *Women at the Front,* 47.

11. Louisa May Alcott, *Hospital Sketches,* reprinted in *Alternative Alcott,* 51 and 55; hereafter cited parenthetically in the text.

12. For discussion of gradual public acceptance of female nursing, see Schultz, *Women at the Front,* especially 54–55.

13. Edmonds's plagiarizing of sections from *Hospital Sketches* is plain in a comparison of the two texts. This borrowing of Alcott's passages may not have been recognized or uncovered at the time (I have been unable to locate references to the borrowing).

14. For a history of the professionalization and desexualization of women nurses, see Reverby, 20, 43.

15. The Battle at Fredericksburg resulted in grim defeat for the Union Army and "nearly 13,000 Union casualties, compared to around 5,000 for the Confederates" (Fahs 20).

16. Unlike her letters home—from which *Hospital Sketches* was composed—Alcott's Washington journal survives in manuscript and was used by both Cheney and Myerson. Though letters Alcott wrote home have not been recovered (Madeleine Stern, Introduction xxiv), Cheney describes sections of *Hospital Sketches* as "almost a literal reproduction of her letters to her family" (139). It is unclear whether Cheney had access to the original letters.

17. While some of Alcott's work saw increased critical attention in the late 1970s and early 1980s with the rise in interest in popular U.S. nineteenth-century women writers (Baym, *American Women Writers;* Tompkins), *Hospital Sketches* received little notice until its reprinting in *Alternative Alcott.* For recent discussions of *Hospital Sketches,* see Showalter, Introduction, ix–xliii; Schultz, "Embattled Care";

Cappello; and Young, *Disarming the Nation*. For a recent edition of *Hospital Sketches*, see Fahs.

18. "In the North, 'nurse' was the most prestigious tag.... 'Matron' was ... sometimes used to refer to the regimental women who nursed, cooked, and did laundry, and sometimes to designate the woman in charge of ward nurses in a hospital"; also, "Confederates used 'matron' in lieu of 'nurse,' the latter term bearing generic and the former, titular, weight" (Schultz, "The Inhospitable Hospital" 369–70). Here, Alcott uses "matron" in the sense of marital status while also implying its wartime institutional sense.

19. Alcott's characterization of John, as well as her naming and descriptions of other wounded soldiers, aligns with the tendency of Civil War nurses "to individualize [the] suffering" (380) of their patients, as opposed to the tendency of Civil War surgeons to refer to the same patients "in the abstract or to refer to the clinical details of a particular treatment without mentioning the soldier's name at all" (Schultz, "The Inhospitable Hospital" 378–79).

20. Schultz goes further, arguing, "Only in John's death does Trib step out of the maternal role and meet him as a sexual equal. As his life ebbs away, John holds Trib's hand so tightly that she has difficulty extricating it when he is dead. She notices that the mark of his grasp still makes an imprint on her hand after her circulation has returned. One of the orderlies cautions Trib that it is 'unsafe for dead and living flesh to lie so long together,' but she 'could not but be glad that, through its touch, the presence of human sympathy ... had lightened that hard hour.'" Schultz sees Trib "finally acknowledg[ing] her own sexual power as the symbolic beloved of the most virile and gentle soldier of all" ("Embattled Care" 113).

21. I quote here from the insightful report of one of my anonymous readers. I am unable to improve on this felicitous phrasing and meaning.

22. For Alcott's reaction to her father's arrival, see endnote 25, below.

23. Alcott accurately assigns to Trib what she herself was paid for war nursing. See Schultz, *Women at the Front*, 41.

24. Alcott's establishing an opposition between "experiment" and convention suggests scientific discourse. Her choice of "experiment" gestures toward the distancing that occurs in Civil War surgeons' accounts of war service. See endnote 19, above.

25. When Alcott was hospitalized, Bronson Alcott was sent for without her permission or knowledge. Recognizing this affront to her independence, Alcott was "amazed" at her father's arrival and "was very angry at first" (Myerson et al., *Journals* 116). (Her journal entry shows that she initially wrote "mad" and then crossed it out and substituted "angry" [122].)

26. Trib's loss of hair due to illness is close to circumstances of Alcott's own hair loss. Alcott lost her 1½ yards of long hair (Myerson et al., *Journals* 117) when the doctor ordered her head shaved. She subsequently wore a wig for many months (Myerson et al., *Letters* 84, 95). Alcott reads Trib's hair loss as a wartime sacrifice intended to help save the nation. Alcott's own wartime sacrifice was significant: not only did she lose her hair, but mercury she ingested as treatment for typhoid fever damaged her health and eventually killed her. For discussion of Alcott's hair loss in *Little Women*, see Young, *Disarming the Nation*, especially 86–87.

27. Despite her poem on Trib's death, Alcott continued to use the Tribulation Periwinkle name, if perhaps not the full persona. In addition to signing "A Postscript" chapter with Trib's name, Alcott, in correspondence with *Hospital Sketches* publisher James Redpath, signed a letter "T.P." and told him that the American consul at Venice had "sent his compliments to 'Nurse P'" (Madeline B. Stern, "Louisa Alcott's Self-Criticism" 360, 361). As late as 1869—six years after *Hospital Sketches* was

published—Alcott used the Tribulation Periwinkle persona when writing a letter to the *Springfield Republican* (Myerson et al., *Letters* 126–28).

28. The series in which the book *Hospital Sketches* appeared was published by ardent abolitionist James Redpath, whose interviews and articles had brought John Brown his earliest national attention and who subsequently wrote the first biography of Brown. Redpath's involvement with Concord abolitionists led him to Alcott and helped begin her career. Redpath, who donated a percentage of the (very successful) Brown biography profits to the Brown family, sold *Hospital Sketches* at a reduced price to improve morale. He also included an advertisement in the book in which he resolved "to devote at least five cents for every copy sold to the support of orphans made fatherless or homeless by the war. . . . Should the sale of the little book be large, the orphans' percentage will be doubled." See Madeleine B. Stern, Introduction, xxiv–xxv. I thank Albert von Frank for alerting me to Redpath's publications and marketing strategies.

29. In *Hospital Sketches* Alcott's uses of the war narrative to explore gender considerations are limited to concerns of one white, Northern, middle-class U.S. woman. Black women, working-class women, men and women who are not hospital patients—male surgeons and male and female relatives of the dead and wounded—receive only glancing notice. That they appear at all points to Alcott's awareness of those outside her race, class, sex, and situation, while suggesting that for her the dominant and nearly exclusive focus of her nursing experience is her intimate contact with wounded men. Schultz's reminder that Alcott, once hospitalized, was nursed by a Black woman, Matilda Cleaver, furthers the white focus of the text (*Women at the Front* 118).

CHAPTER 4

1. S. Emma E. Edmonds, *Nurse and Spy in the Union Army* (Hartford, CT: W. S. Williams and Co., 1865); Mary Livermore, *My Story of the War* (Hartford, CT: A. D. Worthington, 1889); and Annie Turner Wittenmyer, *Under the Guns: A Woman's Reminiscences of the Civil War* (Boston: E. B. Stillings, 1895). Subsequent references are from these editions and will be given in parentheses.

2. For documentation of women's war participation, see Moore (whose work contains over forty chapters on individual women and women's war work); and Brockett and Vaughan (nearly eight hundred pages of small print on administrators, aid society organizers, and volunteers in non-nursing capacities).

3. For contemporary Civil War narratives that mention cross-dressing, see Young, "Confederate Counterfeit." For Civil War histories that mention cross-dressing and appeared well after the war, see Larson.

4. See Hall, *Patriots,* 205–12.

5. This is not to say that Schultz disregards the (in)authenticity of Edmonds's narrated experience: "*Nurse and Spy*'s authenticity as a historical narrative is dubious at best. In the course of the narrative, Edmonds' performances become increasingly outlandish, inviting readers to suspend their disbelief and interpret *Nurse and Spy* as fiction. While the text is based on historically documented evidence of Edmonds' soldiering, its embellishments consign it to a more speculative mode" ("Performing Genres" 75).

6. Bristow's discussion of the development of sexology in the 1860s and 1870s is particularly useful; see 12–61.

7. Notions of non-normative sexual appearances and behaviors were provisionally linked in discussion of the time: "In their effort to understand homosexuality

and to identify what could be done to correct it, physicians and sexologists employed the term 'psychical hermaphroditism'" (Matta 79). See Matta's discussion of homosexuality and hermaphroditism in the nineteenth century.

8. For valuable background, see Reis.

9. Schultz provides crucial publication and sales data. *Nurse and Spy* was "published in 1865 by W. S. Williams in Hartford (in 1864 DeWolfe, Fiske in Boston had brought it out as *The Female Spy of the Union Army* and the Philadelphia Publishing Company as *Unsexed; or, The Female Soldier*)" (*Women at the Front* 227). "By 1900, three more editions had been published, including one in German" ("Performing Genres" 73n4). And "*Nurse and Spy* and its alternately titled editions sold over 175,000 copies" ("Performing Genres" 78), "more than any other nursing narrative" (*Women at the Front* 227).

10. Biographical information on Edmonds is largely derived from Edmonds's *Nurse and Spy*, as well as Fladeland.

11. As David T. Mitchell and Sharon L. Snyder write regarding Melville's *The Confidence-Man:* "Jacksonian America provided an important venue for practices that were founded on empirical observation: craniometry, phrenology, palmistry, psychology, and physiognomy. All these sciences of the surface named external body features as reliable signs by which the identity of a person could be fixed and known" (35). While Edmonds's phrenological examination ostensibly revealed qualities of an able soldier, it missed signs of female identity.

12. Fladeland (451) and Richard Hall (68) speculate briefly on this scene's authenticity. Both Edmonds's recording of the scene and readings of it as imaginative mark the intersection of cross-dressing, authenticity, and fiction.

13. Edmonds wrote in an 1883 letter that, ill with malarial fever and fearing disclosure of her sex, she had left the hospital ("to remain and become a helpless patient in a hospital was sure discovery, which to me was far worse than death" [Fladeland 455]). Frank Thompson's desertion was another compelling reason for Edmonds to keep that impersonation out of *Nurse and Spy*.

14. Schultz writes that "[t]he illustrations . . . [to *Nurse and Spy*] were a series of wood engravings done by R. O'Brien. The single exception is the portrait of Edmonds with which the narrative begins—a steel engraving done by George E. Perine" ("Performing Genres" 82n29).

15. For background regarding Livermore's and Wittenmyer's writing long after the war, see Schultz, *Women at the Front,* 231.

16. Between 1870 and 1895, "during her twenty-five year Lyceum lecture career," Livermore delivered more than 150 speeches "in small towns across the nation" and traveled over 25,000 miles (Gayle and Griffin 55, 57). Biographical information on Livermore is largely derived from *My Story of the War.* For further details regarding Livermore, see Schultz, *Women at the Front,* 166–67; Gayle and Griffin; and Venet.

17. The alignment of Livermore's text with convention as opposed to Edmonds's less conventional material helps explain why Edmonds's text "sold 175,000 copies, more than any other nursing narrative and roughly three times as many as Mary Livermore's, the next most successful" (Schultz, *Women at the Front* 227).

18. Venet argues that while the war altered Livermore's antebellum rejection of political activism, nonetheless "in her writings and speeches as a woman suffragist, Livermore upheld and even glorified women's traditional role within the household" (144, 164).

19. This biographical information on Wittenmyer is largely derived from *Under the Guns*. For further biographical details regarding Wittenmyer, see Schultz, *Women at the Front,* 168–69 and 196–98; and Leonard, *Yankee Women.*

CONCLUSION

1. From Harriet Jacobs, *Incidents in the Life of a Slave Girl*. Subsequent references will be from this edition and will be noted parenthetically in the text.

2. Lydia Maria Childs's Introduction to *Incidents* specifies the audience as "conscientious and reflecting women at the North" (6). The Preface by "Linda Brent" expresses her "desire to arouse the women of the North to a realizing sense of the condition of two millions of women at the South, still in bondage, suffering what I suffered, and most of them far worse" (5). I am in agreement with McKay and Foster who argue, "This is not to suggest that African Americans, especially women, did not buy and read books like Jacobs's for their own instruction, only that in her text, Jacobs appealed directly to a group of other women from whom she hoped for a compassionate hearing and for an understanding of the far-reaching effects of slavery, especially how it linked together the sexual defilement of slave women and the violation of the natural laws of mother/child relationships" (x).

3. Two different women are named "Mrs. Bruce" in *Incidents*. The first Mrs. Bruce is Mary Stace Willis (c. 1816–45); the second, Cornelia Grinnell Willis (1825–1904). Mary Stace Willis is the Mrs. Bruce who, "true to her English upbringing, insisted that she [Jacobs] receive equal treatment" on board the *Knickerbocker* (Yellin, *Harriet Jacobs* 73).

4. See Julia Stern's valuable essay "Live Burial and Its Discontents," 76.

5. In his 1845 *Narrative*, Frederick Douglass provides a foundational example of what W. E. B. Du Bois, as noted in the text, later described as "double-consciousness." Douglass writes of listening to the singing of "slaves selected to go to the Great House Farm" (23), explaining that he "did not, when a slave, understand the deep meaning of those rude and apparently incoherent songs. I was myself within the circle; so that I neither saw nor heard as those without might see and hear" (24).

6. See, for instance, the excellent discussions conducted by Taves; Valerie Smith; and Burnham. Since its landmark 1973 recovery and subsequent 1981 authentication, *Incidents* has received significant critical study. Works essential to Jacobs scholarship include the meticulous authentication work of Jean Fagan Yellin as well as Yellin's biography *Harriet Jacobs*; and Carby's fundamental readings of Jacobs's *Incidents*, and the ideology of true womanhood. More recent scholarship on *Incidents* considers roles of legal discourses (Accomando) and the capitalistic, free-labor economy of the North (Cope). For a selected bibliography of criticism on *Incidents*, see McKay and Foster, 389–90.

7. In her study of nineteenth-century U.S. women's train travel, Amy Richter notes that "in important ways the steamboat captured the same urban qualities of railroad travel" (171n14).

8. Two decades later another Black woman, Ida B. Wells, would respond in a more heightened fashion to an attempt to evict her from travel spaces perceived as raced. When asked "to leave a first-class car on the Chesapeake, Ohio & Southwestern Railroad in May of 1884," Wells refused. "When the conductor tried to remove her physically, Wells struggled, bit the conductor, and was dragged out of the car by three white men" as white passengers applauded (Richter 54). Richter terms the white male response of "physical force [as] the ultimate denial of a black woman's status as a lady" (100).

9. After her escape North in 1842 and until her freedom was purchased in 1852 by Cornelia Grinnell Willis (the second Mrs. Bruce), Jacobs was relentlessly pursued by her former owners and their representatives. Passage of the 1851 Fugitive Slave Law (see note 22, below) exacerbated this fear for Jacobs, for other escaped slaves, and for many free Blacks.

10. "Snaky Swamp" was Jacobs's fictive name for Cabarrus Pocosin ("pocosin," derived from the Eastern Algonquian language, was used to signify a type of swamp). It "lay near the Great Dismal Swamp, for two centuries the largest hideout for fugitive slaves in North Carolina and Virginia" (Yellin, *Harriet Jacobs* 47). For a description of Cabarrus Pocosin in Jacobs's day, see Yellin, *Harriet Jacobs,* 47–48 and 280n47. For a far-ranging discussion of swamps and their resonances, see Miller's *Dark Eden.*

11. This comparison is explicit later in *Incidents* when Jacobs, now a fugitive slave in New York, fears recognition by vacationing Southerners. She "dreaded the approach of summer, when snakes and slaveholders make their appearance" (150).

12. Spengemann reads this scene more narrowly as Knight's being forced to "admit her dependence on the very backwoodsmen she has scoffed at earlier" (42), arguing that it reflects "Knight's becoming someone new as she travels" (44). See 38–44.

13. Warren argues that Jacobs "probably knew Fern during the times that she (Jacobs) was living in Boston between 1844 and 1849 and perhaps during her flights to New England in 1851 and 1852. Jacobs was working as a seamstress in Boston at the time of Fern's first husband's death (October 1846), and she returned to New England after Fern had left her second husband (January 1851) and was shunned by her family and friends" (*Fanny Fern* 223).

Willis's sense of obligation and loyalty to Jacobs can be seen in the fact that Jacobs's daughter lived with Willis for an extended period. Warren writes, "from July 1856 to April 1858, when she was in her early twenties, Jacobs's daughter Louisa Matilda Jacobs lived with Fern" (*Fanny Fern* 222), serving as governess to Willis's daughter Ellen. Thomas Butler Gunn, who had once been a regular visitor to the Willis household but later disparaged Willis, wrote in his diary that Willis was sexually jealous of Louisa which, he claimed, led to Louisa's dismissal. See Yellin, *Harriet Jacobs,* 133.

14. Lauren Berlant also compares Willis and Jacobs, as well as *Incidents* and *Ruth Hall,* through their connections with Nathaniel Parker Willis, Willis's brother and Jacobs's Northern employer. Berlant makes an especially effective comparison between the endings of *Ruth Hall* and *Incidents.* Where Ruth Hall receives a substantial banknote that signals her economic success, Brent is given her bill of sale: "Both women have struggled to procure these papers, but while the one denotes the minimal unit of freedom experienced by an American citizen, the other denotes a successful negotiation of the national-capitalist public sphere, a profitable commodification of female pain and heroism in an emerging industry of female cultural workers" ("The Female Woman" 448).

15. But see endnote 13, above, regarding reports of Louisa Jacobs's experience in the Parton household.

16. See Roediger, especially chapter 7, "Irish-American Workers and White Racial Formation in the Antebellum United States."

17. Jacobs's papers, "the only papers of a woman held in American slavery known to have survived" (Yellin, *Harriet Jacobs* 262), consist of over six hundred documents by and about Jacobs, many from her life and writing after *Incidents.* Completion of the Harriet Jacobs Papers Project promises to further enrich understanding of Jacobs and her work. See Yellin, *Harriet Jacobs,* 262 and 268nxx.

18. I borrow the term "critical whiteness studies" (as opposed to "whiteness studies") and the rational for this choice from Rasmussen et al., 17n1.

19. Mason Stokes's epilogue (178–92) to his fascinating book, *The Color of Sex,* discusses critical whiteness studies and the complexities of such treatments, as does the Introduction to Rasmussen et al. (1–24).

20. See chapter 4's discussion of Edmonds's passing as Black.

21. The accuracy of Jacobs's perception that Blackness determined every aspect of her life is borne out by Roediger's noting that in 1860, 89% of African Americans were slaves (56).

22. Also, as Accomando notes, Jacobs wrote "after Congress had further federalized slavery by passing the Fugitive Slave Act" (231).

23. Information in this section on Jacobs's writing and publication of *Incidents* is largely drawn from McKay and Foster, xii–xiii. For further details of last-minute obstacles to the publication of *Incidents,* see Yellin, *Harriet Jacobs,* 142–43.

24. The Mrs. Bruce referred to in this scene is the second Mrs. Bruce (i.e., the woman who married Nathaniel Parker Willis after the death of his first wife), Cornelia Grinnell Willis.

WORKS CITED

Accomando, Christina. "'The laws were laid down to me anew': Harriet Jacobs and the Reframing of Legal Fictions." *African American Review* 32, no. 2 (1998): 229–45.

Adams, Rachel. "'A Mixture of Delicious and Freak': The Queer Fiction of Carson McCullers." *American Literature* 71, no. 3 (1999): 551–83.

Alcott, Louisa May. *Alternative Alcott*. Ed. Elaine Showalter. New Brunswick: Rutgers University Press, 1988.

———. *Hospital Sketches and Camp and Fireside Stories*. Boston: Roberts Brothers, 1894.

"American Institutions: The Monroe Doctrine." *DeBow's Review* 15 (6 Dec. 1853): 584–95. *Making of America*. Cornell University, 25 Apr. 2007. http://cdl.library.cornell.edu/moa/.

Andrews, William L., Sargent Bush, Jr., Annette Kolodny, Amy Schrager Lang, and Daniel B. Shea, eds. *Journeys in New Worlds*. Madison: University of Wisconsin Press, 1990.

Arner, Robert D. "Sarah Kemble Knight." In *American Writers before 1800*, ed. James A. Levernier and Douglas R. Wilmes. Westport, CT.: Greenwood Press, 1983. 857–59.

Ashbridge, Elizabeth. *The Life of Elizabeth Ashbridge. Journeys in New Worlds*. Ed. William L. Andrews. 147–71.

Balkun, Mary McAleer. "Sarah Kemble Knight and the Construction of the American Self." *Women's Studies* 28 (1998): 7–27.

Balliet, Barbara J. "'Let Them Study as Men and Work as Women': Georgina Davis, New Women, and Illustrated Papers." *Common-Place* 7, no. 3 (Apr. 2007). www.common-place.org.

Barr, Reverend J. T. "A Chapter on Epitaphs." *The Ladies Repository* 14 (6 June 1854): 258–61. *Making of America*. Cornell University, 25 Apr. 2007. http://cdl.library.cornell.edu/moa/.

Barton, George. *Angels of the Battlefield: A History of the Labors of the Catholic Sisterhoods in the Late Civil War*. Philadelphia: The Catholic Art Publishing Co., 1897.

Baym, Nina. *American Women Writers and the Work of History, 1790–1860*. New Brunswick: Rutgers University Press, 1995.

———. "Delia Bacon: Hawthorne's Last Heroine." *Nathaniel Hawthorne Review*. 20.2 (Fall 1994): 1–10.

———. "Delia Bacon, History's Odd Woman Out." *New England Quarterly* 69 (1996): 223–49.

Bedell, Madelon. *The Alcotts*. New York: Potter, 1980.
Beers, Fannie A. *Memories*. Philadelphia: J. B. Lippincott, 1891.
Bell, Michael Davitt. "Conditions of Literary Vocation." *The Cambridge History of American Literature: Volume 2, 1820–1865*. New York: Cambridge University Press, 1995. 9–123.
Benstock, Shari. "Authorizing the Autobiographical." In *The Private Self*, ed. Shari Benstock. Chapel Hill: University of North Carolina Press, 1988. 10–33.
Berlant, Lauren. "The Female Woman: Fanny Fern and the Form of Sentiment." *American Literary History* (Fall 1991): 429–54.
———. "The Queen of America Goes to Washington City: Harriet Jacobs, Frances Harper, Anita Hill." In *American Literary Studies*, ed. Michael A. Elliott and Claudia Stokes. New York: New York University Press, 2003. 95–123.
Blake, John Lauris. *The Farm and the Fireside*. Auburn, NY: Alden, Beardsley, and Co., 1852. *Making of America*. Cornell University, 25 Apr. 2007. http://cdl.library.cornell.edu/moa/.
Blodgett, Harriet. *Centuries of Female Days*. New Brunswick: Rutgers University Press, 1991.
Breitwieser, Mitchell Robert. *American Puritanism and the Defense of Mourning*. Madison: University of Wisconsin Press, 1990.
Bristow, Joseph. *Sexuality*. New York: Routledge, 1997.
"British Philanthropy and American Slavery." *DeBow's Review* 14 (3 March 1853): 258–80. *Making of America*. Cornell University, 25 Apr. 2007. http://cdl.library.cornell.edu/moa/.
Brockett, Linus P., M.D. and Mary C. Vaughan. *Women's Work in the Civil War*. Philadelphia: Zeigler, McCurdy, 1867.
Brodhead, Richard H. *Cultures of Letters*. Chicago: University of Chicago Press, 1993.
———. "Veiled Ladies: Toward a History of Antebellum Entertainment." *American Literary History* (Summer 1989): 273–94.
Buckingham, Joseph T. *Specimens of Newspaper Literature*. Boston: Ayer Company Publishers, 1852. *Making of America*. Cornell University, 25 Apr. 2007. http://cdl.library.cornell.edu/moa/.
Buell, Lawrence. *New England Literary Culture*. New York: Cambridge University Press, 1986.
Burnham, Michelle. "Loopholes of Resistance: Harriet Jacobs' Slave Narrative and the Critique of Agency in Foucault." *Arizona Quarterly* (Summer 1993): 53–73.
Bush, Sargent, Jr. Introduction to Sarah Kemble Knight's *Journal*. In *Journeys in New Worlds*, ed. William L. Andrews. 69–83.
———. "Sarah Kemble Knight (1666–1727)." *Legacy* 12, no. 2 (1995): 112–20.
Caesar, Terry. *Forgiving the Boundaries*. Athens: University of Georgia Press, 1995.
Cappello, Mary. "'Looking about Me with All My Eyes': Censored Viewing, Carnival, and Louisa May Alcott's *Hospital Sketches*." *Arizona Quarterly* 50, no. 3 (1994): 59–88.
Carby, Hazel V. *Reconstructing Womanhood*. New York: Oxford University Press, 1987.
Castiglia, Christopher. *Bound and Determined*. Chicago: University of Chicago Press, 1996.
Charvat, William. *The Profession of Authorship in America 1800–1870*. Ed. Matthew J. Bruccoli. New York: Columbia University Press, 1992.
Cheney, Ednah. *Louisa May Alcott*. Boston: Roberts Brothers, 1889.
Childs, Lydia Maria. Introduction to Harriet Jacobs's *Incidents in the Life of a Slave Girl*. Ed. Nellie Y. McKay and Frances Smith Foster. New York: Norton, 2001.
Cope, Virginia. "'I Verily Believed Myself to Be a Free Woman': Harriet Jacobs's Journey into Capitalism." *African American Review* 38, no. 1 (Spring 2004): 5–21.

Crocker, Hannah Mather. *Observations on the Real Rights of Women*. Boston: Printed for the Author, 1818.

Dannett, Sylvia G. L. *She Rode with the Generals*. New York: Thomas Nelson and Sons, 1960.

Davidson, Cathy N. *Revolution and the Word*. New York: Oxford University Press, 1986.

Deane, William R. "Journal of Madam Knight." *The Living Age* 736, no. 26 (26 June 1858): 963–67. *Making of America*. Cornell University, 25 Apr. 2007. http://cdl.library.cornell.edu/moa/.

"December Meeting, 1877." *Proceedings of the Massachusetts Historical Society 1876–1877*. Boston: Published by the Society, 1878. 386–88.

Derounian, Kathryn Zabelle. "Genre, Voice, and Character in the Literature of Six Early American Writers, 1650–1812." PhD diss., Pennsylvania State University, 1980.

Derounian-Stodola, Kathryn Zabelle. "The New England Frontier and the Picaresque in Sarah Kemble Knight's *Journal*." In *Early American Literature and Culture: Essays Honoring Harrison T. Meserole*. Newark: University of Delaware Press, 1992. 122–31.

———, ed. *Women's Indian Captivity Narratives*. New York: Penguin, 1998.

Douglas, Ann. Introduction. *Little Women*. By Louisa May Alcott. New York: Penguin, 1983. vii–xxvii.

Douglass, Frederick. *Narrative of the Life of Frederick Douglass. Autobiographies*. Ed. Henry Louis Gates, Jr. New York: Library of America, 1996.

DuBois, W. E. B. *The Souls of Black Folk*. Ed. Henry Louis Gates, Jr. and Terri Hume Oliver. New York: W. W. Norton, 1999.

Durivage, Francis. *Life Scenes*. Boston: S. W. Rouse, 1853. *Making of America*. Cornell University, 25 Apr. 2007. http://cdl.library.cornell.edu/moa/.

Dwight, Theodore. Introduction to *The Journal of Madam Knight*, ed. Sargent Bush, Jr. In *Journeys in New Worlds*, ed. William L. Andrews. 85–86.

Easton, Alison M. J. "My Banker and I Can Afford to Laugh! Class and Gender in Fanny Fern and Nathaniel Hawthorne." In *Soft Canons*, ed. Karen L. Kilcup. Iowa City: University of Iowa Press, 1999. 219–36.

"Editorial." *Musical World and Times*. 28 May 1853.

"Editorial." *New York Ledger*. 9 Nov. 1872.

"Editorial." *Olive Branch*. 5 March 1853.

Edmonds, S. Emma E. *Nurse and Spy in the Union Army*. Hartford, CT: W. S. Williams and Co., 1865.

Elbert, Sarah. *A Hunger for Home*. New Brunswick: Rutgers University Press, 1987.

Epstein, Julia and Kristina Straub. "The Guarded Body." In *Body Guards: The Cultural Politics of Gender Ambiguity*, ed. Julia Epstein and Kristina Straub. New York: Routledge, 1991. 1–28.

Fahs, Alice, ed. Introduction. *Hospital Sketches*. By Louisa May Alcott. New York: Bedford/St. Martin's Press, 2004. 1–49.

Felt, Joseph Barlow. *An Historical Account of Massachusetts Currency*. Boston: Perkins and Marvin, 1839.

Fern, Fanny. "A Bit of Injustice." *New York Ledger*. 8 June 1861.

———. "All's Well." *Musical World and Times*. 6 Nov. 1852.

———. "Dark Days." *Olive Branch*. 4 Dec. 1852.

———. "Everybody's Vacation Except Editors." *Olive Branch*. 14 Aug. 1852.

———. *Fresh Leaves*. New York: Mason Brothers, 1857.

———. "Hints to Young Wives." *Olive Branch*. 14 Feb. 1852.

———. "How Woman Loves." *Fern Leaves from Fanny's Portfolio*. Auburn: Derby and Miller, 1853. 28.

———. "Independence." *New York Ledger*. 30 July 1859.

———. "The Invalid Wife." *Olive Branch.* 16 Oct. 1852.
———. "The Model Stepmother." *Olive Branch.* 7 Aug. 1852.
———. "The Model Widow." *Olive Branch.* 26 June 1851.
———. "The Model Widower." *Olive Branch.* 26 June 1851.
———. "One Sort of Woman." *New York Ledger.* 19 Nov. 1870.
———. "A Rainy Day." *Olive Branch.* 14 Feb. 1852.
———. "Self-Conquest." *Olive Branch.* 28 Feb. 1851.
———. "The Stray Lamb." *Fern Leaves from Fanny's Portfolio.* Auburn: Derby and Miller, 1853. 27.
———. "Summer Friends, or 'Will Is Might.'" *True Flag.* 28 Aug. 1852.
———. "The Tear of a Wife." *Olive Branch.* 28 Aug. 1852.
———. "Thanksgiving Story." *Musical World and Times.* 20 Nov. 1852.
———. "What Mrs. Smith Said." *True Flag.* 20 November 1852.
———. "A Whisper to Romantic Young Ladies." *True Flag.* 12 June 1852.
Fish, Cheryl J. *Black and White Women's Travel Narratives.* Gainesville: University Press of Florida, 2004.
Fladeland, Betty. "Alias Franklin Thompson." *Michigan History* 42 (1958): 435–62.
Fleischner, Jennifer. *Mrs. Lincoln and Mrs. Keckly.* New York: Random House, 2003.
Fliegelman, Jay. *Declaring Independence.* Stanford: Stanford University Press, 1993.
Foster, Frances Smith. "Resisting *Incidents.*" In *Harriet Jacobs and* Incidents in the Life of a Slave Girl: *New Critical Essays,* ed. Deborah M. Garfield and Rafia Zafar. New York: Cambridge University Press, 1996. 57–75.
Foucault, Michel. *The History of Sexuality.* New York: Vintage, 1980.
Fradenburg, Louise and Carla Freccero, eds. *Premodern Sexualities.* New York: Routledge, 1996.
Gayle, Barbara Mae and Cindy L. Griffin. "Mary Ashton Rice Livermore's Relational Feminist Discourse: A Rhetorically Successful Feminist Model." *Women's Studies in Communication* 21, no. 1 (1998): 55–77.
Gilmore, Leigh. *Autobiographics.* Ithaca: Cornell University Press, 1994.
Gollin, Rita. *Annie Adams Fields.* Boston: University of Massachusetts Press, 2002.
Gregg, Edith E. W., ed. *The Letters of Ellen Tucker Emerson.* Kent, OH: Kent State University Press, 1982.
Hackel, Heidi Brayman and Catherine E. Kelly. *Reading Women: Literacy, Authorship, and Culture in the Atlantic World, 1500–1800.* Philadelphia: University of Pennsylvania Press, 2008.
Hall, David D., ed. *The Antinomian Controversy 1636–1638.* Durham: Duke University Press, 1990.
Hall, Julie E. "At the Crisis of Our Fate: Sophia Peabody Hawthorne's Civil War Correspondence." In *Reinventing the Peabody Sisters,* ed. Monika M. Elbert, Julie E. Hall, and Katharine Rodier. Iowa City: University of Iowa Press, 2006. 61–76.
Hall, Richard. *Patriots in Disguise.* New York: Paragon House, 1993.
Haltunnen, Karen. *Murder Most Foul.* Cambridge: Harvard University Press, 1998.
Hamilton, Kristie. "The Politics of Survival: Sara Parton's *Ruth Hall* and the Literature of Labor." In *Redefining the Political Novel,* ed. Sharon M. Harris. Knoxville: University of Tennessee Press, 1995. 86–108.
Harris, Sharon M., ed. *Women's Early American Historical Narratives.* New York: Penguin, 2003. 229–49.
Hawkins, Joellen Watson. "Louisa May Alcott." In *Dictionary of American Nursing Biography,* ed. Martin Kaufman. New York: Greenwood Press, 1988. 4–6.
Higonnet, Margaret R. "Civil Wars and Sexual Territories." In *Arms and the Woman,* ed. Helen M. Cooper, Adrienne Auslander Munich, and Susan Merrill Squier. Chapel Hill: University of North Carolina Press, 1989. 80–96.

Hill, Amelia Leavitt. "Travel in Early New England." *The New England Magazine* 23 (1 Sept. 1897): 82–88. *Making of America*. Cornell University, 25 Apr. 2007. http://cdl.library.cornell.edu/moa/.

Historical Magazine & American Notes & Queries. New York: Charles B. Richardson, 1859. *Making of America*. Cornell University, 25 Apr. 2007. http://cdl.library.cornell.edu/moa/.

History of Rye, West Chester County New York 1660–1870 by Charles W. Baird. Review. *North American Review* 113, no. 232 (July 1871): 223. *Making of America*. Cornell University, 25 Apr. 2007. http://cdl.library.cornell.edu/moa/.

Hoge, Jane (Mrs. A. H.). *The Boys in Blue*. New York: E. B. Treat, 1867.

"Holidays." *United States Democratic Review* 34 (1 July 1854): 56–67. *Making of America*. Cornell University, 25 Apr. 2007. http://cdl.library.cornell.edu/moa/.

Holstein, Mrs. A. M. (Ellis). *Three Years in Field Hospitals of the Army of the Potomac*. Philadelphia: J. B. Lippincott, 1867.

Homestead, Melissa. *American Women Authors and Literary Property, 1822–1869*. New York: Cambridge University Press, 2005.

Hosmer, James Kendall. *The Life of Thomas Hutchinson*. Boston: Houghton, Mifflin, 1896.

Howells, William Dean. "Editor's Study." *Harper's New Monthly Magazine* 77, no. 459 (Aug. 1888): 476–80. *Making of America*. Cornell University, 25 Apr. 2007. http://cdl.library.cornell.edu/moa/

Imbarrato, Susan Clair. *Traveling Women: Narrative Visions of Early America*. Athens, OH: Ohio University Press, 2006.

Jacobs, Harriet. *Incidents in the Life of a Slave Girl*. Ed. Nellie Y. McKay and Frances Smith Foster. New York: Norton, 2001.

Jameson, Frederick. *The Political Unconscious*. Ithaca: Cornell University Press, 1981.

Jaquette, Henriette Stratton, ed. *South after Gettysburg: Letters of Cornelia Hancock 1863–1868 from the Army of the Potomac*. New York: Crowell, 1937.

Jewett, Susan. "How I Came to Be Spontaneous." *The Ladies Repository* 18 (5 May 1858): 266–72. *Making of America*. Cornell University, 25 Apr. 2007. http://cdl.library.cornell.edu/moa/.

Jones, Bessie Z. Introduction. *Hospital Sketches*. By Louisa May Alcott. Cambridge: Harvard University Press, 1960. vii–xliv.

Kamensky, Jane. *Governing the Tongue*. New York: Oxford University Press, 1997.

Kaplan, Amy. "Manifest Domesticity." *American Literature* 70, no. 3 (Sept. 1998): 581–606.

Kelley, Mary. Commentary. *Locating American Studies*. Ed. Lucy Maddox. Baltimore: Johns Hopkins University Press, 1999. 67–70.

———. *Learning to Stand and Speak*. Chapel Hill: University of North Carolina Press, 2006.

———. *Private Woman, Public Stage*. New York: Oxford University Press, 1984.

———. "'Vindicating the Equality of Female Intellect': Women and Authority in the Early Republic." *Prospects* 17 (1992): 1–27.

Kerber, Linda K. *Women of the Republic*. Chapel Hill: University of North Carolina Press, 1980.

Kesselring, Marion. *Hawthorne's Reading: 1828–1850*. New York: New York Public Library, 1949.

Knight, Sarah Kemble. *The Journal of Madam Knight*. *Journeys in New Worlds*. Ed. William L. Andrews. 85–116.

Kolodny, Annette. *The Land before Her*. Chapel Hill: University of North Carolina Press, 1984.

Lang, Amy Schrager. *The Syntax of Class*. Princeton: Princeton University Press, 2003.

Larson, C. Kay. "Bonny Yank and Ginny Reb." *Minerva* 8 (1990): 33–48.
Learned, William Law. Preface. *The Private Journal of a Journey from Boston to New York in the Year 1704.* By Madam Knight. Albany: Frank H. Little and Co., 1865. iii–xii.
Lehuu, Isabelle. "Sentimental Figures: Reading *Godey's Lady's Book* in Antebellum America." In *The Culture of Sentiment,* ed. Shirley Samuels. New York: Oxford University Press, 1992. 73–91.
Leonard, Elizabeth D. *Yankee Women.* New York: Norton, 1994.
Levander, Caroline. "'Following the Condition of the Mother': Subversions of Domesticity in Harriet Jacobs's *Incidents in the Life of a Slave Girl.*" In *Southern Mothers,* ed. Warren Nagueyalti and Sally Wolff. Baton Rouge: Louisiana State University Press, 1999. 28–38.
"Literary Notices." *Harper's Magazine* 9, no. 50 (July 1854): 277. *Making of America.* Cornell University, 25 Apr. 2007. http://cdl.library.cornell.edu/moa/.
Livermore, Mary. *My Story of the War.* Hartford, CT: A. D. Worthington, 1889.
The Living Age 58, no. 739 (24 July 1858): 242. *Making of America.* Cornell University, 25 Apr. 2007. http://cdl.library.cornell.edu/moa/.
Looby, Christopher. *Voicing America.* Chicago: University of Chicago Press, 1996.
Margolies, Alan. "The Editing and Publication of 'The Journal of Madam Knight.'" *PBSA* 58 (1964): 25–32.
Matta, Christina. "Ambiguous Bodies and Deviant Sexualities: Hermaphrodites, Homosexuality, and Surgery in the United States, 1850–1904." *Perspectives in Biology and Medicine* 48, no. 1 (Winter 2005): 74–83.
Matterson, Stephen. "Shaped by Readers: The Slave Narratives of Frederick Douglass and Harriet Jacobs." In *Soft Canons,* ed. Karen L. Kilcup. Iowa City: University of Iowa Press, 1999. 82–96.
McGinnis, Patricia I. "Fanny Fern, American Novelist." *Biblion. The Journal of the New York Public Library.* SUNY at Albany (1969): 2–37.
McKay, Charlotte E. *Stories of Hospital and Camp.* Philadelphia: Claxton, Remsen, and Haffelfinger, and Co., 1876; repr. Freeport, NY: Books for Libraries Press, 1971.
McKay, Nellie Y. and Frances Smith Foster, eds. Introduction. *Incidents in the Life of a Slave Girl.* By Harriet Jacobs. New York: Norton, 2001. ix–xxiii.
Michaelsen, Scott. "Narrative and Class in a Culture of Consumption: The Significance of Stories in Sarah Kemble Knight's *Journal.*" *College Literature* 21 (1994): 33–46.
Miller, David C. *Dark Eden: The Swamp in Nineteenth-Century American Culture.* New York: Cambridge University Press, 1989.
Miller, Nancy K. "Women's Autobiography in France: For a Dialectics of Identification." In *Women and Language in Literature and Society,* ed. Sally McConnell-Ginet, Ruth Borker, and Nelly Furman. New York: Praeger 1980. 258–73.
Mills, Sara. *Discourses of Difference.* London: Routledge, 1991.
Mitchell, David T. and Sharon L. Snyder. "Masquerades of Impairment: Charity as a Confidence Game." *Leviathan* 8, no. 1 (March 2006): 35–60.
Moore, Frank. *Women of the War.* Hartford, CT: S. S. Scranton, 1866.
Moulton, Louise Chandler. "Louisa May Alcott." In *Our Famous Women,* ed. Elizabeth Stuart Phelps. 1883; repr. Freeport, NY: Books for Libraries Press, 1975. 48–54.
Myerson, Joel, Daniel Shealy, and Madeleine B. Stern, eds. *Journals of Louisa May Alcott.* Boston: Little, Brown, 1989.
———. *Selected Letters of Louisa May Alcott.* Boston: Little, Brown, 1987.
Neal, Mrs. Joseph C. "The Nest at Home." *Godey's Lady's Book* 40 (Feb. 1850): 88. *Making of America.* Cornell University, 25 Apr. 2007. http://cdl.library.cornell.edu/moa/.
Nightingale, Florence. *Notes on Nursing: What It Is, and What It Is Not.* Philadelphia: J. B Lippincott, 1992.
Notes of Hospital Life from November, 1861, to August, 1863. Philadelphia: J. B. Lippincott, 1864.

Notes & Queries 146 (16 Oct. 1858): 310. *Making of America*. Cornell University, 25 Apr. 2007. http://cdl.library.cornell.edu/moa/.

Nussbaum, Felicity A. "Eighteenth-Century Autobiographical Commonplaces." In *The Private Self*, ed. Shari Benstock. Chapel Hill: University North Carolina Press, 1988. 147–71.

Parton, Ethel. "Fanny Fern, An Informal Biography." Unpublished Ms. Sophia Smith Collection, Smith College, n.d.

Parton, James. "Memoir of Fanny Fern." In *Fanny Fern, A Memorial Volume*, ed. James Parton. New York: GW Carlton, 1873. 15–84.

Post, Constance J. "Hannah Mather Crocker." In *American Women Prose Writers to 1820*, ed. Carla Mulford, Angela Vietto, and Amy E. Winan. Detroit: Gale Research, 1999. 85–93.

Rasmussen, Birgit Bander, Eric Klinenberg, Irene J. Nexcia, and Matt Wray, eds. *The Making and Unmaking of Whiteness*. Durham: Duke University Press, 2001.

Reis, Elizabeth. "Impossible Hermaphrodites: Intersex in America, 1620–1960." *The Journal of American History* 92, no. 2 (2005): 80 pars. http://www.historycooperative.org/journals/jah/92.2/reis.html. 3 Aug. 2006.

Reverby, Susan M. *Ordered to Care*. New York: Cambridge University Press, 1987.

"Review." *A Journey in the Back-Country* by Frederick Law Olmsted. *Atlantic Monthly* 6, no. 37 (Nov. 1860): 635–37. *Making of America*. Cornell University, 25 Apr. 2007. http://cdl.library.cornell.edu/moa/.

"Review." *Harper's*. July 1854. *Making of America*. Cornell University, 25 Apr. 2007. http://cdl.library.cornell.edu/moa/.

Reynolds, David S. *Walt Whitman's America*. New York: Vintage, 1996.

Richter, Amy G. *Home on the Rails*. Chapel Hill: University of North Carolina Press, 2005.

Roediger, David R. *The Wages of Whiteness*. New York: Verso, 1999.

Rosenberg, Charles E., ed. Introduction. *Florence Nightingale on Hospital Reform*. New York: Garland Publishing, 1989.

Rosenberg, Ruth. "Hannah Mather Crocker." In *A Dictionary of British and American Women Writers, 1660–1880*, ed. Janet Todd. New York: Rowman and Allanheld, 1985. 95–96.

Ross, Christine. "Logic, Rhetoric, and Discourse in the Literary Texts of Nineteenth-Century Women." *Rhetorical Society Quarterly* 32, no. 2 (2002): 85–109.

Saar, Doreen Alvarez. "Moses Coit Tyler." In *American Literary Critics and Scholars, 1850–1880*, ed. John W. Rathburn and Monica M. Grecu. Detroit: Gale Research Co., 1988. 242–50.

Samuels, Shirley. *The Culture of Sentiment*. New York: Oxford University Press, 1992.

Saulsbury, Rebecca. "Cult of True Womanhood, 1820–1900." *The Literary Encyclopedia* (27 Apr. 2008). http://www.LitEncyc.com.

Saxton, Martha. *Louisa May*. Boston: Houghton Mifflin, 1977.

Schriber, Mary Suzanne. *Writing Home: American Women Abroad, 1830–1920*. Charlottesville: University Press of Virginia, 1997.

Schultz, Jane E. "Embattled Care: Narrative Authority in Louisa May Alcott's *Hospital Sketches*." *Legacy* 9 2 (1992): 104–18.

———. "The Inhospitable Hospital: Gender and Professionalism in Civil War Medicine." *Signs* (Winter 1992): 363–92.

———. "Performing Genres: Sarah Edmonds' *Nurse and Spy* and the Case of the Cross-Dressed Text." In *Dressing Up for War: Transformations of Gender and Genre in the Discourse and Literature of War*, ed. Aránzazu Usandizaga and Andrew Monnickendam. Amsterdam, Netherlands: Rodopi, 2001. 73–91.

———. *Women at the Front: Hospital Workers in Civil War America*. Chapel Hill: University of North Carolina Press, 2004.

Seelye, John. *Prophetic Waters*. New York: Oxford, 1977.
Shields, David S. *Civil Tongues & Polite Letters in British America*. Chapel Hill: University of North Carolina Press, 1997.
———. "Eighteenth-Century Literary Culture." In *The Colonial Book in the Atlantic World*, ed. Hugh Amory and David D. Hall. New York: Cambridge University Press, 2000. Vol. 1 of *A History of the Book in America*. 5 vols. 434–76.
Showalter, Elaine, ed. Introduction. *Alternative Alcott*. By Louisa May Alcott. New Brunswick: Rutgers University Press, 1988. ix–xliii.
———. *Sister's Choice*. New York: Oxford University Press, 1991.
Sigaud, Louis A. *Belle Boyd, Confederate Spy*. Richmond, VA: Dietz Press, 1944.
Simpson, James W. *Editor's Study by William Dean Howells*. Troy, NY: Whitston Press, 1983.
Smith, Adelaide W. *Reminiscences of an Army Nurse during the Civil War*. New York: Greaves, 1911.
Smith, Sidonie. *A Poetics of Women's Autobiography*. Bloomington: Indiana University Press, 1987.
———. "Resisting the Gaze of Embodiment: Woman's Autobiography in the Nineteenth Century." In *American Women's Autobiography*, ed. Margo Culley. Madison: University of Wisconsin Press, 1992. 75–110.
Smith, Sidonie and Julia Watson. Introduction. *Interfaces: Women/Autobiography/Image/Performance*. Ann Arbor: University of Michigan Press, 2001. 1–46.
———. Introduction. *Women, Autobiography, Theory*. Madison: University of Wisconsin Press, 1998. 3–52.
Smith, Valerie. *Self-Discovery and Authority in Afro-American Narrative*. Cambridge: Harvard University Press, 1987.
Smith-Rosenberg, Carroll. *Disorderly Conduct*. New York: Oxford University Press, 1985.
Southworth, E.D.E.N. *The Hidden Hand, or Capitola the Madcap*. 1859. Ed. Joanne Dobson. New Brunswick: Rutgers University Press, 1996.
Spengemann, William C. *The Adventurous Muse*. New Haven: Yale University Press, 1977.
Stern, Julia. "Live Burial and Its Discontents: Mourning Becomes Melancholia in Harriet Jacobs's *Incidents*." In *Symbolic Loss*, ed. Peter Homans. Charlottesville: University Press of Virginia, 2000. 62–82.
———. "To Relish and To Spew: Disgust as Cultural Critique in *The Journal of Madam Knight*." *Legacy* 14 (1997): 1–12.
Stern, Madeleine B. *Critical Essays on Louisa May Alcott*. Boston: G. K. Hall, 1984.
———. Introduction. In *Selected Letters of Louisa May Alcott*, ed. Joel Myerson, Daniel Shealy, and Madeleine B. Stern. Boston: Little, Brown, 1987. xvii–xlii.
———. "Louisa Alcott's Self-Criticism." In *Studies in the American Renaissance*, ed. Joel Myerson. Charlottesville: University Press of Virginia, 1985. 333–82.
Stokes, Mason. *The Color of Sex*. Durham: Duke University Press, 2001.
Taves, Anne. "Spiritual Purity and Sexual Shame: Religious Themes in the Writings of Harriet Jacobs." *Church History* (March 1987): 59–72.
Taylor, Susie King. *A Black Woman's Civil War Memoirs*. Ed. Patricia Romero. New York: Markus Wiener, 1988.
Temple, Gale. "A Purchase on Goodness: Fanny Fern, *Ruth Hall*, and Fraught Individualism." *Studies in American Fiction* 31, no. 2 (2003):131–63.
Thompson, John D. "Notes on Nursing: Stirring the Spirit of Reform." In *Notes on Nursing* by Florence Nightingale. Philadelphia: J. B. Lippincott Company, 1992.
Titus, Anson. "Madam Sarah Knight: Her Diary and Her Times, 1666–1726." *Bostonian Society* IX (1912): 101–26.

Tompkins, Jane. *Sensational Designs*. New York: Oxford University Press, 1985.
Tonkovich, Nicole. *Domesticity with a Difference*. Jackson: University Press of Mississippi, 1997.
"Travelling in America." *The Museum of Foreign Literature and Science* VIII (1826): 30–38. *Making of America*. Cornell University, 25 Apr. 2007. http://cdl.library.cornell.edu/moa/.
Tyler, Moses Coit. *A History of American Literature*. New York: G. P. Putnam, 1878.
Ulrich, Laurel Thatcher. *Good Wives*. New York: Knopf, 1982.
Vaiden, Thomas. *Rational Religion and Morals*. New York: 1852. n.p. *Making of America*. Cornell University, 25 Apr. 2007. http://cdl.library.cornell.edu/moa/.
Vanderbilt, Kermit. "The Literary Histories of Moses Coit Tyler." In *American Literature, Culture, and Ideology*, ed. Beverly R. Voloshin. New York: Peter Lang, 1990. 299–330.
Vaughan, Alden T. and Edward W. Clark, eds. *Puritans among the Indians*. Cambridge: Harvard University Press, 1981.
Venet, Wendy Hamand. "The Emergence of a Suffragist: Mary Livermore, Civil War Activism, and the Moral Power of Women." *Civil War History* XLVIII, no. 2 (2002). 143–64.
Vicinus, Martha. *Independent Women*. Chicago: University of Chicago Press, 1985.
Waldron, William Watson. *Huguenots of Westchester and Parish of Fordham*. New York: W. H. Kelley & Brother, 1864. *Making of America*. Cornell University, 25 Apr. 2007. http://cdl.library.cornell.edu/moa/.
Warner, Michael. *The Trouble with Normal*. Cambridge: Harvard University Press: 2000.
Warren, Joyce W. *Fanny Fern*. New Brunswick: Rutgers University Press, 1992.
———. Introduction. *Ruth Hall and Other Writings*. New Brunswick: Rutgers University Press, 1986. ix–xxxix.
———, ed. *Ruth Hall and Other Writings*. New Brunswick: Rutgers University Press, 1986.
———. "Uncommon Discourse: Fanny Fern and the *New York Ledger*." In *Periodical Literature in Nineteenth-Century America*, ed. Kenneth M. Price and Susan Belasco Smith. Charlottesville: University Press of Virginia, 1995. 51–68.
Welter, Barbara. "The Cult of True Womanhood: 1820–1860." *American Quarterly* 18, no. 2 (Summer 1966): 151–74.
Westbrook, Arlen and Perry D. Westbrook, eds. *The Writing Women of New England, 1630–1900*. Metuchen, NJ: Scarecrow Press, 1982. 62–72.
"Which: The Right, or the Left?" New York: Garrett & Co., 1855. *Making of America*. Cornell University, 25 Apr. 2007. http://cdl.library.cornell.edu/moa/.
Williams, Susan S. "Authors and Literary Authorship." In *A History of the Book in America: The Industrial Book 1840–1880*, ed. Scott E. Casper, Jeffrey D. Groves, Stephen W. Nissenbaum, and Michael Winship. Chapel Hill: University of North Carolina Press, 2007. 90–116.
Winship, George Parker. Introductory Note. *The Private Journal Kept by Madam Knight, On a Journey From Boston to New-York, In the Year 1704*. By Sarah Kemble Knight. Boston: Small, Maynard & Co., 1920.
Wittenmyer, Annie Turner. *Under the Guns*. Boston: E. B. Stillings, 1895.
Woolsey, Jane Stuart. *Hospital Days*. New York: D. Van Nostrand, 1870.
Wormeley, Katharine Prescott. *The Other Side of War*. Boston: Ticknor, 1889.
———. *The U.S. Sanitary Commission*. Boston: Little, Brown, 1863.
Wright, Elizabethada A. "'Joking Isn't Safe': Fanny Fern, Irony, and Signifyin(g)." *Rhetoric Society Quarterly* 31, no. 2 (2001): 91–111.
Yellin, Jean Fagan. *Harriet Jacobs: A Life*. New York: Basic Civitas Books, 2004.

———. "Written by Herself: Harriet Jacobs' Slave Narrative." *American Literature* 3, no. 53 (1981): 379–486.

Young, Elizabeth. "Confederate Counterfeit: The Case of the Cross-Dressed Civil War Soldier." In *Passing and the Fictions of Identity,* ed. Elaine K. Ginsberg. Durham: Duke University Press, 1996. 181–217.

———. *Disarming the Nation.* Chicago: University of Chicago Press, 1999.

INDEX

A

Academy of Arts and Sciences, 6
Adams, Rachel, 6
Alcott, Bronson, 100, 164n25
Alcott, Louisa May: autonomy in, 86, 99–100, 102, 144–45; background, 2; comparison to other writers, 80, 83–86, 88–89, 98, 106, 118, 139, 144–45, 147, 148, 150, 151; documents of, 89, 163n16; fears of, 82, 92, 99–100, 162n4; on female communities, 44, 85–86; genres of, 79–82, 102–3; influences on, 87–88; nursing experiences, 82, 87–89, 95, 99–105; public perception of, 10, 12; relationship with father, 100; self-representation, 5, 14, 16, 19, 74, 79–83, 102, 108, 109, 164n27; and sex-gender identity, 19, 79–83, 87–105, 165n29; unconventional female position of, 115; writing and publication of, 152; writing process of, 89–90
Alternative Alcott (Showalter), 90
American Association for the Advancement of Women, 6
American Surgeon General, 110
Anthony, Susan B., 101
asexuality, 98–100, 103, 104, 108
Ashbridge, Elizabeth, 30, 40, 45
Ashford, Mary, 9
Atlantic Monthly, 34, 36, 79, 162n1

"autobiographics," 14
autobiography: anonymity in, 11–12, 80, 81, 104; autonomy in, 16; elasticity of self in, 64–74, 80–81, 109; and periodical writing, 55–58, 76; practices of, 13–21, 41; and race/ethnicity, 133, 137, 150–53; sex-gender identity in, 14–16; study of women's, 3–5

B

Bacon, Delia, 6
Baird, Charles W., 36
Balkun, Mary McAleer, 24, 28, 30, 31
Barnard, A. M., 80
Barr, Rev. J. T., 9
Battle at Fredericksburg, 89, 163n15
Baym, Nina, 84
Bell, Michael Davitt, 29
Benstock, Shari, 39
Berlant, Lauren, 60, 62, 70, 77, 149, 156
Bickford, Maria, 7–10, 157n8
Biographical Memoir of Daniel Boone (Flint), 30
Blake, John Lauris, 8–9
Blake, Rev. Mortimer, 34
The Blithedale Romance (Hawthorne), 7
Blodgett, Harriet, 96
Bonner, Robert, 4, 60, 63, 64, 77–78, 162n17
Boone, Rebecca, 30
Boston *Commonwealth,* 12, 79, 90, 102

181

Boston *Olive Branch*, 54, 55, 62, 63, 69, 70, 72, 79
Boyd, Belle, 131
Brent, Linda: fears, 139–42, 147; and female gentility, 134–38, 143, 149–50, 153, 155–56; identity, 13, 135, 139; sexual transgressions, 135–36. *See also* Jacobs, Harriet
Bristow, Joseph, 83, 109
Brockett, Linus P., 89
Brodhead, Richard H., 81–82
Brown, John, 165n28
Bruce, Mrs., 135, 153–54, 167n3, 169n24
Buckingham, Joseph T., 9
Buell, Lawrence, 41
Bush, Sargent, Jr., 24, 25, 26

C

Cabarrus Pocosin, 168n10
Carby, Hazel, 136, 150, 153, 167n6
Catharine Beecher's Female Seminary, 58
Cheney, Ednah, 163n16
Child, Lydia Maria, 13, 28–29, 135, 152, 167n2
Civil War: attitudes toward women during, 128–29; as cultural moment, 15–16, 35, 78, 106–8, 122, 130, 132; Livermore's work during, 123; nursing during, 87–89, 93–105, 163n7, 164n19, 164n24; and sex-gender identity, 97–101, 109–12, 114; stage performances on, 131–32; Wittenmyer's work during, 127; women's writing on, 2–5, 19–20, 80–81, 83, 106–8
Cleaver, Matilda, 165n29
courage, 48–49, 72
Crimean War, 87
Crocker, Hannah Mather, 24, 33, 38
cross-gender impersonation: motivations for, 123–28, 139, 143, 145–48; public perception of, 12–13, 19–20, 110, 112–14, 122, 123, 129–32, 165n7; in war narratives, 106–7, 117–19; women's writing on, 83
cultural scripts: and Alcott, 97–105; during Civil War, 97–101, 106–10, 122, 132; and Edmonds, 119; and Fern, 54, 56, 58, 60–61, 64, 67, 69, 70, 72–74, 75; and Knight, 17, 38–47, 51, 160n35; in periodical publishing, 62–64; and race/ethnicity, 154–55; and travel, 38–41, 137–38, 154–55, 167nn7–8; and womanhood, 6–10, 129, 130, 134–38, 157n3; and women's autobiography, 3–5
Cushman, Pauline, 131

D

"Dark Days" (Fern), 65, 139, 142–44
Deane, Charles, 32, 158n15
Deane, William R., 31–32, 34, 35, 158n16
death, 96–98, 101–2, 164n20
DeBow's Review, 7
divorce, 35–36
"double-consciousness," 135, 167n5
double-voicedness, 81
Douglass, Frederick, 167n5
Du Bois, W. E. B., 135, 167n5
Durivage, Francis, 8
Dustan, Hannah, 40
Dwight, Theodore, Jr., 4, 24, 26–35, 52, 158n15
Dyer, Mary, 39, 43

E

Easton, Alison, 59, 66
economics, 34, 59–61, 65–67, 121–22, 131–32, 160n4, 161n7
Edmonds, S. Emma E.: autonomy in, 119, 146; background, 2–4, 111; comparison to other writers, 83, 88–89, 98, 106, 108, 130, 139, 145–51, 163n13; on female communities, 44; phrenological examination of, 113, 166n11; point of view, 80–81; public perception of, 10, 12–13, 166n11; on race and social class, 115–16; as rebel boy, 119–21; self-representation, 5, 14, 16, 19–20, 91, 109, 116–21; and sex-gender identity, 116–22, 131; as soldier, 113–19, 121–22, 166n13; on women in war, 87; writing and publication of, 152
Eight Cousins (Alcott), 81
Eldredge, Charles "Handsome Charlie" Harrington, 58, 59, 160n4

Eldredge, Ellen, 58, 168n13
Eldredge, Grace, 58
Eldredge, Hezekiah, 59, 160n4
Eldredge, Mary (daughter), 58, 59
Eldredge, Mary (mother-in-law), 59, 160n4
Emerson, Ellen Tucker, 88
Emerson, Ralph Waldo, 88
Epstein, Julia, 110
"Everybody's Vacation Except Editors" (Fern), 67, 69

F

The Farm and the Fireside (Blake), 8–9
Felt, Joseph Barlow, 31
female moon, 48
Fern, Fanny: advertisements for, 72–73; autonomy in, 1–2, 143–44; comparison to other writers, 53, 80, 139, 142–44, 147, 148, 150, 151; death, 77–78, 162n17; development of persona, 59–61; model essays, 69; public perception of, 10–12; revelation of identity, 54, 77–78, 121; self-representation in novels, 75–77, 162n16; self-representation in periodicals, 5, 14, 16, 55–58, 63–75, 77–78, 108, 109; and sex-gender identity, 11–12, 56–58, 61, 64, 76, 108, 109, 161n9; style of, 62–64, 65–69; unconventional female position of, 115; women's speech in, 58, 64, 65. *See also* Willis, Sara Payson
Fern Leaves from Fanny's Portfolio (Fern), 59, 71
fiction, 7, 41, 74–77, 80–82, 107, 162n16
Field, Annie Adams, 162n4
Fields, Annie, 6
Fields, James T., 6, 152
Fladeland, Betty, 106–7
Flint, Timothy, 30
Flower Fables (Alcott), 79, 88
Foucault, Michel, 77
Franklin, Benjamin, 25, 36
Fugitive Slave Law (1851), 167n9

G

Gilmore, Leigh, 14
Godey's Lady's Book, 7

Grant, Ulysses S., 88
Gunn, Thomas Butler, 144, 168n13

H

hair, 100–101, 113, 164n26
Hale, Sarah Josepha, 29
Hall, Richard, 107
Hamilton, Kristie, 75, 76
Harper's, 37, 160n3; *Harper's Weekly*, 73
Harriet Jacobs (Yellin), 167n6
Hawthorne, Nathaniel, 7
Hawthorne, Sophia Peabody, 162n4
heterosexuality, 137
Hill, Amelia Leavitt, 37–38
"Hints to Young Wives" (Fern), 66–69
A History of American Literature, 1607–1765 (Tyler), 36–37, 159n24
History of Rye, West Chester County New York 1660–1870 (Baird), 36
Hobomok (Child), 28–29
Homestead, Melissa, 55–58, 62–63, 75, 76
homosexuality, 109–10, 118, 165n7
Hope Leslie (Sedgwick), 29
Hosmer, James Kendall, 37
Hospital Sketches (Alcott): description of, 2, 12, 79–80; plagiarism of, 88–89, 163n13; publication of, 16, 90, 102–3, 152, 163n17, 165n28; structure, 89–90; as travel narrative, 83–86
Hospital Sketches and Camp and Fireside Stories (Alcott), 90, 102
Howells, William Dean, 4, 24, 37, 162n1
"How I Came to Be Spontaneous" (Jewett), 7
Huguenots of Westchester and Parish of Fordham (Waldron), 36
humor, 147–48
Hutchinson, Anne, 39, 43, 159nn29–30
Hutchinson, Ellen Mackay, 37
Hutchinson, Thomas, 33

I

Imbarrato, Susan Clair, 26, 30, 52
Incidents in the Life of a Slave Girl (Jacobs): description of, 3, 4, 13, 134–35, 167n2; publication of, 16, 151–53; scholarship on, 135, 167n6

"Independence" (Fern), 1
"The Invalid Wife" (Fern), 65

J

Jackson, Rachel Donelson, 34
Jacobs, Harriet: background, 3, 4; on Blackness, 151, 169n21; comparison to other writers, 139–49; as fugitive, 139, 167n9, 168n11; point of view, 133, 135; public perception of, 10, 13; scholarship on, 150, 168n17; self-representation, 14, 16, 20–21, 134–35, 137, 138, 155–56; and Sara Willis, 143, 144, 168nn13–14; on women's speech, 138, 155. *See also* Brent, Linda
Jacobs, Louisa Matilda, 151, 168n13
Jameson, Frederick, 102
Jemison, Mary, 30
Jewett, Sarah Orne, 6
Jewett, Susan, 7
journal (genre), 38–39, 44
Journal of a Tour from Boston to New-York (Knight): authenticity of, 31–32, 158n15; description of, 2, 4, 16–18, 24–25; publication of, 16, 23–35, 38, 52–53, 152; public reaction to, 31–33; references to, 36–38, 159n28; sales of, 29–31; structure, 40, 41, 44; value of, 26–28, 30–31; Winship's introduction to, 158n17
A Journal of a Tour in Italy (Dwight), 30
A Journey in the Back-Country (Olmsted), 36

K

Kelley, Mary, 31, 61, 161n10
Kemble, Thomas, 25
The Key to Uncle Tom's Cabin (Stowe), 152
Knight, Elizabeth, 25, 33
Knight, Richard, 25
Knight, Sarah Kemble: autonomy of, 10, 17, 41–44, 47, 52, 86, 108, 143; background, 2, 4, 16–18, 25; comparison to other writers, 80, 84–86, 138, 139, 141–43, 147, 148, 150, 151; criticism of women, 44, 46–48, 50–51, 85–86, 108; William Deane on, 34; public perception of, 10; self-representation, 5, 14, 16, 17, 31, 38, 74, 91, 108, 109, 138; style of, 28, 33, 35, 40; unconventional female position of, 115; on women's speech, 44–48, 50–52, 138; writing and publication of, 152
Kolodny, Annette, 30
Krafft-Ebing biological model, 83, 109

L

The Ladies' Repository, 9
Lang, Amy Schrager, 46, 95
Larson, C. Kay, 107
Learned, William Law, 35–36, 159n21
Levander, Caroline, 153
Library of American Literature (Stedman), 37
The Life of Thomas Hutchinson (Hosmer), 37
Life Scenes (Durivage), 8
Lincoln, Abraham, 88, 98
Lincoln, Mary (Todd), 9
literacy rates, 61, 161n10
Littell, Eliakim, 34
"The Little Sunbeam" (Fern), 54
Little Women (Alcott), 12, 81, 90
Livermore, Daniel, 123
Livermore, Mary: background, 3, 123–27, 166n16; comparison to other writers, 83, 98, 106, 108, 122; and sex-gender identity, 19, 20, 91, 123–27; and whiteness, 151; on women in war, 87, 88, 125–26, 166n18
The Living Age, 36
Lot's wife, 48, 50
Lowell, James Russell, 36

M

MacVicar, Anne Grant, 30
Margolies, Alan, 24, 29, 31
marriage, 35–36, 65–68, 97
Massachusetts Historical Society, 31–32, 158n15
Mather, Cotton, 33
Mather, Hannah Hutchinson, 33
Mather, Increase, 33
Mather, Richard, 33
Mather, Samuel, 33

"matron," 90, 164n18
Matta, Christina, 110
Matterson, Stephen, 149–50
Memoirs of an American Lady (MacVicar), 30
Memoranda during the War (Whitman), 163n7
Michaelsen, Scott, 46
Miller, Nancy K., 70
Mitchell, Maria, 6
Moore, Frank, 89
motherhood, 13, 65–66, 71, 135–37, 153–54
Moulton, Louise Chandler, 82
multiple selves, 58, 70–76, 81–82, 91, 108, 109, 160n3
The Museum of Foreign Literature and Science, 34
Musical World & Times, 55, 63, 71, 72
Myerson, Joel, 163n16
My Story of the War (Livermore): description of, 3, 83, 106, 122–27; popularity of, 131, 166n17

N

Narrative of the Life of Mrs. Mary Jemison (Seaver), 29, 30
Neal, Mrs. Joseph C., 7
"The Nest at Home" (Neal), 7
The New England Magazine, 37–38
Newport, RI, 88
New York Ledger, 1, 16, 60, 63, 64, 77
Nightingale, Florence, 87–88
North American Review, 36
Northwood (Hale), 29
Norton, Charles Eliot, 36
Notes & Queries, 36
Notes on Hospitals (Nightingale), 87, 163n10
Notes on Nursing (Nightingale), 87
"nurse," 90, 164n18
Nurse and Spy in the Union Army (Edmonds): Alcott's influence on, 88–89; authenticity of, 165n5, 166n12; description of, 2–3, 12–13, 83, 106, 111–23; illustrations, 121, 166n14; popularity of, 131, 166n9, 166n17; publication of, 16, 111–12, 152
nursing, 82, 87–89, 93–105, 163n7, 164n19, 164n24
Nussbaum, Felicity, 15, 51, 107–8

O

Observations on the Real Rights of Women (Crocker), 24, 33
Olmsted, Frederick Law, 36
"One Sort of Woman" (Fern), 161n9

P

Parton, Ethel, 161n8
Parton, James, 60, 161n8
patriotism, 112–14, 118, 131–32
Patriots in Disguise (Hall), 107
periodicals, 55–58, 61–62, 73–78
Periwinkle, Tribulation: characteristics of, 86; "death," 101–2; development of character, 89, 90, 108; end of nursing career, 99; identity of, 83, 102, 164n27; references to, 88–89; self-representation, 19, 90–94, 96–98, 101; travel of, 144–45
Portsmouth Grove Army Hospital, 88
Post, Amy, 151, 152
postcaptivity narratives, 40
Post, Constance, 33–34
Protestant Telegraph, 34
publishing industry, 61, 161n10, 161n12
Puritans, 39, 40, 159n29

Q

Quakers, 44, 45, 50

R

race: in Alcott, 165n29; in Edmonds, 115–16, 145–46; and publication of Jacobs, 150–53; and self-representation, 20–21, 134–39; and womanhood, 149–55; and women's autobiography, 3, 133
Ranney's bookstore, 73
Rasmussen, Birgit Bander, 150, 151
Rational Religion and Morals (Vaiden), 7
The Rebels (Child), 29
Reconstruction period, 127
The Recorder, 58
Redpath, James, 164n27, 165n28
religion, 42, 44, 45, 48, 50–52, 97, 160n40
Reynolds, David, 61
Richter, Amy, 138, 167nn7–8

Roediger, David, 145–46
Ropes, Hannah, 163n10
Rose in Bloom (Alcott), 81
Ross, Christine, 57
Rowlandson, Mary, 40
Ruth Hall (Fern), 2, 55, 59, 75–77, 160n2, 162n16, 168n14

S

Saar, Doreen Alvarez, 36–37, 159n24
satire, 58, 65–69
Saxton, Martha, 82
Schriber, Mary Suzanne, 31, 39, 40, 84, 86
Schultz, Jane E., 86, 87, 107, 108, 113, 114, 118, 120, 165n5
Seacole, Mary, 163n9
Seaver, James E., 29, 30
Sedgwick, Catharine Maria, 29
"Self-Conquest" (Fern), 65
sentimentality, 58, 65–66, 97, 157n3
sexology, 109–10, 113
sexual acts, 135, 149–50
sexual inversion, 109–10
Shakespeare, William, 6
Shephard, Thomas, 159n29
Shields, David S., 26, 41, 47
Showalter, Elaine, 81, 90
slavery, 35, 136, 140–43, 149–50, 159n22, 167n9
Smith-Rosenberg, Carroll, 87
Smith, Sidonie, 3, 14, 21, 58, 64, 76, 135
Snaky Swamp, 139–43, 147, 168n10
social class: Alcott on, 95–97, 165n29; Edmonds on, 115–16; in Jacobs, 137, 154–55, 167n8; and travel, 40, 46, 84–85, 160n36; of widowed women, 59–61; Wittenmyer on, 129; and women's autobiography, 3; and women's speech, 46–48
Some Account of the Fore Part of the Life of Elizabeth Ashbridge (Ashbridge), 30
Specimens of Newspaper Literature (Buckingham), 9
Stedman, Edmund Clarence, 37
Stern, Julia, 42–45, 50
Stern, Madeleine B., 80
Stowe, Harriet Beecher, 9, 151–52
Straub, Kristina, 110
Swarton, Hannah, 40

T

"The Tear of a Wife" (Fern), 67–68, 69
Temple, Gale, 62
"Thanksgiving Story" (Fern), 65–66
Thayer and Eldridge publishers, 152
Thompson, Frank: assumption of identity, 83, 109, 112–13, 147, 148; and revelation of identity, 111, 121–22, 131, 166n13; travel of, 145
Ticknor and Fields, 6
Titus, Anson, 42–43
Tonkovich, Nicole, 63
travel: in Alcott, 83–86, 90, 102, 144–45; comparison of women's experiences, 138–49; and cultural scripts, 38–41, 137–38, 154–55, 167nn7–8; popularity of literature about, 30–31; and sex-gender identity, 40; and war experiences, 106
"Travel in Early New England" (Hill), 37–38
Trist, Elizabeth House, 40
Trowbridge, Caleb, 25
True Flag, 55, 62, 63, 71
Tyler, Moses Coit, 36–37, 159n24

U

Ulrich, Laurel Thatcher, 43
Uncle Tom's Cabin (Stowe), 9
Under the Guns: A Woman's Reminiscences of the Civil War (Wittenmyer), 3, 83, 106, 122–23, 127–31
Union Hotel Hospital, 89, 99, 163n10
United States Democratic Review, 36
Unsexed (Edmonds), 114
U.S. Sanitary Commission, 123

V

Vaiden, Thomas, 7
Vaughan, Mary C., 89

W

Waldron, William Watson, 36
Warren, Joyce, 143–44, 168n13
Warren, Mercy Otis, 34
Washington, Martha Dandridge, 34
Watson, Julia, 3, 14
Wells, Ida B., 167n8
Welter, Barbara, 6

"A Whisper to Romantic Young Ladies" (Fern), 68, 69
whiteness, 150–53. *See also* race
Whitman, Walt, 98, 163n7
widowhood, 59–61, 65, 160n4, 161n8
Willis, Cornelia Grinnell, 135, 151, 152, 167n3, 167n9, 169n24
Willis, Hannah Parker, 58, 59
Willis, Mary Stace, 167n3
Willis, Nathaniel, 58, 59
Willis, Nathaniel Parker, 4, 59, 135, 152, 168n14
Willis, Richard Storrs, 72
Willis, Sara Payson: background, 2, 58–59, 160n4, 161n8; earnings, 62–63; and Jacobs, 143, 144, 168nn13–14; sex-gender identity, 108, 109; writing career, 55, 59–61, 152. *See also* Fern, Fanny
Winship, George Parker, 158n17
witchcraft, 39, 42, 159n30
Wittenmyer, Annie Turner: autonomy in, 128; background, 3, 127; comparison to other writers, 83, 98, 106, 108, 122, 130; and female communities, 129–30; point of view, 81; and sex-gender identity, 19, 20, 91–92, 128–31; and whiteness, 151; on women in war, 87
Wittenmyer, William, 127
womanhood: in Alcott, 96, 97, 100–101; and cross-dressing, 113–14, 129, 130; cultural scripts on, 6–10, 129, 130, 134–38, 157n3; domestic sphere of, 31, 157n3; and gentility, 134–38, 143, 146, 149–50, 153, 155–56; and race/ethnicity, 149–55
Woman's Work in the Civil War (Vaughan), 89
Women of the War (Moore), 89
Women's Christian Temperance Union (WCTU), 127
women's rights, 33–34
women's writing: and female communities, 44, 66–67, 85–86; in periodicals, 61–62, 73–78; public reception of, 28, 37, 38; subjects of, 38–40, 64, 103–5
Wright, Elizabethada, 69

Y

Yellin, Jean Fagan, 167n6
Young, Elizabeth, 107, 110, 114, 117–18

www.ingramcontent.com/pod-product-compliance
Lightning Source LLC
Chambersburg PA
CBHW031628160426
43196CB00006B/324